OCR

GCSE Modern World History

Revision Guide

Second Edition

Wayne Birks and **Ben Walsh**

HODDER
EDUCATION
AN HACHETTE UK COMPANY

Acknowledgements

The Publishers would like to thank the following for permission to reproduce copyright material:

Photo credits
p.39 © Solo Syndication/Associated Newspapers Ltd; **p.60** Cartoon by Abu Abraham published in Observer, 24 May 1964 © Ayisha Abraham, image from British Cartoon Archive, University of Kent, www.cartoons.ac.uk; **p.107** *l* © Weidenfeld & Nicolson Archives, a division of Orion Publishing Group, *r* © The Granger Collection, NYC / TopFoto; **p.146** © The Women's Library/Mary Evans Picture Library'; **p.148** © 2003 Topham Picturepoint/TopFoto; **p.151** *tl* © Amoret Tanner / Alamy, *tr* © The Print Collector/HIP/TopFoto, *b* © Punch Ltd; **p.158** © 2002 Topham Picturepoint/TopFoto.

Every effort has been made to contact copyright holders, and the publishers apologise for any omissions which they will be pleased to rectify at the earliest opportunity.

Although every effort has been made to ensure that website addresses are correct at time of going to press, Hodder Education cannot be held responsible for the content of any website mentioned in this book. It is sometimes possible to find a relocated web page by typing in the address of the home page for a website in the URL window of your browser.

Hachette UK's policy is to use papers that are natural, renewable and recyclable products and made from wood grown in sustainable forests. The logging and manufacturing processes are expected to conform to the environmental regulations of the country of origin.

Orders: please contact Bookpoint Ltd, 130 Milton Park, Abingdon, Oxon OX14 4SB. Telephone: (44) 01235 827720. Fax: (44) 01235 400454. Lin[e] 9.00–5.00, Monday to Saturday, with a 24-hour message-answering [service.] our website at www.hoddereducation.co.uk.

© Wayne Birks and Ben Walsh.
This edition published in 2014.

First published in 2011 by Hodder Education,
An Hachette UK company,
338 Euston Road,
London NW1 3BH

Impression number	5	4	3	2	1
Year	2018	2017	2016	2015	2014

Cover photo: Fallen statue of Stalin © David Turnley/CORBIS
Illustrations by Barking Dog Art, Peter Lubach and Phoenix Photosetting
Typeset in 11.5pt Garamond by Integra Software Services Pvt. Ltd., Pondicherry, India
Printed in Spain

A catalogue record for this title is available from the British Library

ISBN: 978 1471 829 727

Contents

Unit 1: Core content: Aspects of International Relations, 1919–2005

Unit 2: Studies in Depth

Unit 3: British Depth Studies

How to use this book

Focus points (beginning of chapter)

The focus points are what the examiners will have in mind when they are setting questions. The examiners would never ask you to 'write everything you know about X or Y', they always have an angle. These focus points are 'the angle'. The reason for learning the rest of the facts is so that you can answer questions about these focus points. The content of this book follows exactly what the OCR specification says about those focus points.

Comment

These boxes provide extra information to accompany the main text, placing certain events in context and bringing to light extra issues that you should be aware of.

Key terms

These boxes help you to learn the essential vocabulary by providing you with new or difficult words and giving a definition of their meaning. These are specialist terms that might be used in an exam without any explanation so you need to be able to understand them and use them confidently in your own writing. You could make your own glossary in your notebook.

Revision task

Use these tasks to make sure you have understood every topic and to help you record key information. These tasks help you to think about the content and encourage you to apply your knowledge.

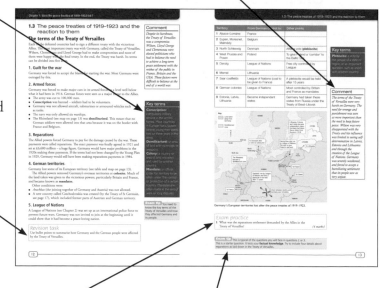

Exam practice

These boxes provide sample exam questions for each topic. You can check your answers against sample answers online at www.hodderplus.co.uk/modernworldhistory to help to improve your grades.

Exam tip

These tips accompany the exam practice questions. They give you extra tips on how to answer the questions successfully in order to get the best grades possible.

Source Evaluation

The interpretation and evaluation of sources is a key feature of OCR's GCSE examination. Chapter 7 onwards, therefore, provides you with an example of how to interpret and evaluate sources from specific evidence relevant to the topic being studied.

Summary/revision plan (end of chapter)

This is a revision checklist. Be sure you know about each term or phrase in this summary. You can also check your knowledge of each topic with our free 'quick quizzes' which you can find online at www.hodderplus.co.uk/modernworldhistory.

Introduction

You will soon be taking your GCSE in Modern World History. Your aim is to get the best grade you can. Our aim in this book is to help you get that grade.

To improve your grade you need to:
- get organised – this book will help you make a revision plan and stick to it
- know the content – this book will help you learn the core content for your course
- apply your knowledge – this book will help you apply what you know to actual examination questions.

How to revise

There is no single way to revise, but there are some good ideas to use.

1 *Know the objectives of your course*
   Ask your teacher for full details of the course you are taking or look on the OCR website, www.ocr.org.uk. This book is geared to the OCR Modern World History Syllabus.

2 *Make a revision plan and stick to it*
   Start your revision early – the earlier the better. Revise regularly – regular, short spells are better than panicky six-hour slogs until 2a.m.

3 *Revise actively*
   Be a scribbler; make notes as you learn. You will need an exercise book for most of the revision tasks but you can also write in this book.

The rest of this introduction is about how to apply these rules to your revision and make sure that you get the grade you are aiming for.

1. Know the objectives of your course

Assessment objectives in GCSE History

1 *Recall, select and communicate knowledge and understanding of history.*
   You have to know things, and be able to explain what you know in a way that shows you understand what you are writing. This means:
- using your knowledge of a topic to support what you say in your answer
- organising this knowledge to answer the question set.

2 *Demonstrate understanding of the past through explanation and analysis of:*
- *key concepts: causation, consequence, continuity, change and significance within a historical context*
- *key features and characteristics of the periods studied and the relationship between them.*
   This means organising your answer in order to:
- show the ability to analyse when this is asked for, rather than to describe what happened
- show understanding of why things happened and how and when change occurred.

3 *Understand, analyse and evaluate:*
   (a) a range of source material as part of an historical enquiry
   This means using any kind of material, including photographs, diaries, books, recorded interviews and films from the period you are studying.

   You are expected to:
- be able to select important information from the source
- interpret what is being said and draw appropriate conclusions about what is being said in the source
- decide how useful or reliable the source is to a historian.

(b)   how aspects of the past have been interpreted and represented in different ways as part of a historical enquiry (this is examined under the controlled assessment part of your course)

This means showing that you understand why an event has been seen differently by different people (e.g. more or less important) and explaining whether you agree.

You are expected to:

- decide how fair or accurate an interpretation is
- compare different interpretations of an event.

In all this, remember that the examiner is interested in seeing how much you can think for yourself and apply your knowledge and understanding to the question set.

Spelling, punctuation and grammar

Your work will also be assessed for the quality of your written communication. This means you must ensure:

- the examiner can read your work clearly
- words are spelled correctly and capital letters and full stops are used where necessary.

2. Know your own target

Most of you will have your own individual GCSE target grade for each subject.

There are several target-setting methods used, but you may be familiar with one of the following:

- Target grade based on your Key Stage 2 (Primary School) grade
- FFT (Fischer Family Trust) target grade
- Estimated Grade (what your history teacher thinks you will achieve)
- Target grade based on a minimum of three or four levels of progress since Key Stage 2 (primary school).

You should also have a current grade. This is the grade your teacher will expect you to achieve if you took the exam now. You are likely to find your current grade and target grade on your last school report or progress check. You may even have been asked to put these grades into your exercise book. Hopefully, your current grade is the same or better than your target grade. If it is not, you are in danger of underachieving in history and you should use this book and ask your teacher's advice to get back on target. You may wish to make a table to show how you are progressing in relation to your target grade.

Subject	FFT target grade	Grade Sept	Grade Dec	Mock GCSE grade	Grade March	Controlled Assessment grade
History	A	C	B	B	A	A
English	A	B	B	A	A	A*

3. Know what a good answer looks like and how the mark schemes work

This book and the online materials that accompany it will help you write high quality answers to each question.

It is also important, however, that you use the guidance from the examination board OCR to help you with your answers. On their website – www.ocr.org.uk – you will find sample examination questions and answers together with mark schemes.

For example, look at this question below from OCR Paper 1, core content.

Explain why the Soviet Union blockaded West Berlin in 1948.   *(8 marks)*

The examiner has given the above question 8 marks spread over four levels: level 0: 0 marks; level 1: 1–2 marks; level 2: 3–4 marks; level 3: 5–8 marks.

Obviously, you will want to produce a high level answer, but to do this you need to be clear what a high level answer looks like. For example:

- A level 0 answer would have no evidence or simply no answer to the question.
- A level 1 answer would show limited knowledge of the reasons for the blockade.
- A level 2 answer would identify a single reason for the blockade and show some understanding of events.
- A level 3 answer would give one (5–6 marks), two or more (6–8 marks) explained reasons for the blockade showing a good knowledge of events.

Therefore, in this way, you can begin to see what the examiners want in a good answer and use this book to produce it.

4. Make a revision plan

You not only need to plan your revision for history, but you need to fit it in with your revision for all your other GCSE subjects. You could use the following table to plan your overall revision.

Dates		Revision targets and deadlines			
Month	Week	History	English	French	Others
Jan	4	Key points summary card for Germany			
Feb	2		Test on set book		
Mar				Mock oral	

You could then construct a table like the one below to plan your history revision. In your plan, aim to come back to each topic several times so that you revise in stages.

Stage 1: Put the date normal school-based work on a topic will be/was completed.

Stage 2: Put the target date for finishing your own summary of the key points for each topic.

Stage 3: Decide when you will give yourself memory tests.

Stage 4: Schedule time for fine-tuning your revision (for example, final memorising and/or practice examination questions).

History topics	Date	Key points summary	Memory test	Fine tuning
1 Treaty of Versailles		March	April	Specimen Paper
2 League of Nations				

5. Revise actively

When faced with revising for GCSE history, most students say:

The ideas in this book are aimed at helping you to remember the core content.

Use the revision tasks in this book

The best way to remember information is to use it – to revise actively. To take an everyday example: to start with it is difficult to remember a new telephone number, but the more you use it the easier it is to remember it.

  Throughout this book, you will find revision tasks. Don't miss them out. If you use the information you will remember it better. The more you use the information the better you will remember it.

Use the 'key terms' method

Think of your brain as a computer. To read a file on a computer, you need to know the name of the file. The file name is the key, and if you do not have this key you cannot get to the file, even though the computer has the file in its memory.

Your brain works in a similar way. When you read something it goes in, but to get the information out again you need the key to unlock your memory. So one way to jog your memory is to use a 'key terms' method. This is how it works.

1 As you read through each paragraph, highlight one or two key terms. For example, when answering the question:
   'What were the main political and economic features of the USA during the 1920s?'
● It had a *democratic system of government*. The President and Congress of the USA were chosen in free democratic elections.
● It had a *capitalist economy*. Business and property were privately owned. Individuals could make profits in business or move jobs if they wished. However, they might also go bankrupt or lose their jobs.
● The USA was the world's wealthiest country, but under capitalism there were always *great contrasts* – some people were very rich, others were very poor.
2 You can then use cue cards, or the revision plan at the end of each chapter, to summarise your key terms for each subheading. In this way, you can summarise a whole topic on one sheet.
3 Later on, return to your revision plan and recall or rewrite important paragraphs using just the key terms to jog your memory.

Other revision ideas

Different people revise in different ways and you may have your own ideas on how to work. Here are some other techniques that students have used:
● summarising events in diagrams or pictures
● making a recording of the text and playing it back
● using acronyms, mnemonics or mind maps
● working with friends:
   – testing each other
   – comparing your answers to practice questions
   – use Hodder online resources.

How to answer exam questions

OCR GCSE History B (Modern World)

Paper 1 – 2 hour written paper, 45% of total mark

Paper 2 – 1 hour 30 minute written paper, 30% of total mark

Controlled Assessment (Historical Enquiry), 25% of total mark (Controlled Assessment to be written in class over 8 hours).

Paper 1 of the examination

Paper 1 has two parts.

- Part 1: Core content – sections A, B and C.
- Part 2: Studies in Depth.

Chapters 1–6 cover the core content of Paper 1 of the examination, **Aspects of International Relations, 1919–2005**.

Part 1: core content

- Section A: Inter-War Years, 1919–1939
- Section B: The Cold War, 1945–1975
- Section C: A New World? 1948–2005 (not covered in this book)

Candidates must answer questions on ONE of these sections depending on the section studied. Make sure you only revise the chapters that apply to you.

Section A: The Inter-War Years, 1919–1939

1 Were the peace treaties of 1919–1923 fair? (pages 9–19)

2 To what extent was the League of Nations a success? (pages 20–29)

3 Why had international peace collapsed by 1939? (pages 30–39)

Section B: The Cold War, 1945–1975

4 Who was to blame for the Cold War? (pages 40–50)

5 Who won the Cuban missile crisis? (pages 51–57)

6 Why did the USA fail in Vietnam? (pages 58–66)

The other topics in Section C of the core content on Paper 1 are not covered in this book.

When you have selected a section, you must answer Question 1 and either Question 2 or 3 from that section.

Question 1

Question 1 is a compulsory question worth 10 or 12 marks and usually looks like this:

(a) A question that needs you to use your knowledge of the topic to interpret the source. The question may begin *'What is the message of …?'*

What is required?

- Summarise the message of the source quickly and efficiently. Keep to the point.
- Describe three or four features of the source that help convey the message.
- Use your knowledge and information in the caption to interpret the source.

Do not:

- describe the source in detail
- speculate or guess about things you cannot support from your own knowledge.

(b) A question that asks you to explain some aspect of the topic. It is worth 8 marks, and usually begins with *'Explain why…'*

What is required?

- Write in paragraphs, approximately eight lines per paragraph.
- Keep to the question – for example, 'The first reason was…'
- Remember this question needs you to EXPLAIN events – for example, why they happened.

Do not:

- simply describe events
- answer briefly.

Question 2 or 3

After answering the compulsory question, you will have a choice of two questions on different topics. Both questions have a similar pattern and OCR advise you to spend 35 minutes on each question.

Question 2a or 3a will be worth 4 marks and probably begin with 'Describe …'

What is required?

- Keep it simple. Write down three or four facts to answer the question.

Question 2b or 3b will be worth 6 marks and probably begin with 'Explain why …'

What is required?

- This is similar to question 1b and marked in a similar way.
- You need to EXPLAIN the reasons in relation to the topic and NOT just describe them.
- To get maximum marks, you need to explain at least two reasons in some detail.
- Try to show how the reasons you have chosen fit into the bigger picture.

Question 2c or 3c is the most important question so far. It is worth 10 marks and will probably begin 'Evaluate …' or 'How far …?' or 'Which was more important …?' Although you will face a single question, it is often spread over two aspects of the topic and you will need to look at both. There may be a statement to examine and you will need to consider the case for and against each argument.

What is required?

- Make sure you look at both aspects of the argument. Don't ignore one aspect of the argument just because you don't agree with it.
- EXPLAIN, not just describe, the case for and against the argument.
- It is not essential to write an introduction and conclusion but it may help you give your answer a better structure.
- You could also add other arguments that you feel are relevant to strengthen your answer, but you will not be penalised if you don't.
- A really good answer will show the links between the factors you have described.

Part 2: Studies in Depth

Chapters 7–11 cover the Studies in Depth element of Paper 1 of the examination.

7 Germany, 1918–1945 (pages 67–82)
8 Russia, 1905–1941 (pages 83–97)
9 The USA, 1919–1941 (pages 98–109)
10 The causes and events of the First World War, 1890–1918 (pages 110–127)
11 The USA, 1945–1975: land of freedom? (pages 128–140)

There are other topics in the Studies in Depth section which are not covered in this guide. They are:
- Mao's China, *c.*1930–1976
- End of Empire, *c.*1919–1969.

Whichever Study in Depth you have chosen, the format will be similar. There will be a compulsory question (usually three sources) followed by a choice between questions 5 and 6.

The aims of the Depth Study questions are very specific.

- You will need to show that you understand the context in which the sources were created and how historians use sources to reach judgements.
- You will also need to show that you know the topic well by answering questions on small areas of the unit.

Question 4

Compulsory question 4 will have three parts: a, b and c. For each part, you MUST:
- read/look at the source carefully
- refer to the source in your answer
- use details from the source to support your answer
- use contextual knowledge to help you interpret the source and answer the question.

Two of the three questions will be source analysis questions, for example:
- What is the message of this source?
- Why was the source published?
- Why would XX want to publish this source?

One question will ask you to read a source on a particular issue and then explain how far you agree with a particular interpretation, for example: '"The New Deal was successful in solving America's problems in the 1930s." How far do you agree with this interpretation?' The second part of each question will always ask you to use the source and your own knowledge to explain your answer.

Questions 5 and 6

For the final question in the Depth Study, you will have a choice of two questions from which to choose. Each question will be structured in the same way and will require you to:

a) describe   *b) explain*   *c) evaluate*

Question a) needs you to DESCRIBE what is being asked. You could do this as a list, but you will only score high marks if you also mention other important factors that are relevant.

Question b) needs you to EXPLAIN an issue or say why something happened. Make sure you say why some reasons are more important than others.

Question c) is the most important question here and is worth 10 marks. You are likely to be given a statement and asked 'How far do you agree with this statement?' This is an EVALUATION question, which needs you to:
- explain and not just describe events
- write an introduction (although this is not essential)
- explain why you agree or disagree with the statement (but remember to show that you understand both sides of the argument by including other relevant factors)
- add a paragraph that shows how the relevant factors are connected.

Paper 2 of the examination

Chapters 12–13 cover what is included in Paper 2 of the examination. The British Depth Study will be either:
- How was British society changed, 1890–1918? or
- How far did British society change, 1939–1975?

The questions will be very similar whichever period you are studying.
- There will be up to eight sources of various kinds.
- Some of the sources will present different views and disagree with each other.
- The questions will take you through the sources step by step and in the final question ask you to evaluate all the sources.

Types of question on Paper 2

1. Analysis questions

For example:
- What is the message of the source?
- Why was Source X published in year Y? Use details of the source and your own knowledge to explain your answer.

What is required?
- Give some specific information about the source – for example, 'The message of the cartoon is…'
- Comment on the impression that the author/artist is trying to make.
- Make sure you have explained the message, not just the content of the source.

2. Utility questions

These are questions where you are asked to consider the usefulness of a source. For example:
- How useful is Source X to a historian studying Y?
- Is Source X more useful than Source Y to a historian studying Z?

What is required?
- The key question to ask is 'Useful for what?'
- Start with how it contains useful information.
- Then consider whether that information presents a typical, representative view of the issue or whether it is distorting the historian's view.
- Finally, ask what it reveals about the values, ideas, concerns, attitudes etc. of the author or society which produced it.

3. Reliability questions

These are questions that compare the reliability of sources. For example:
- How reliable is Source X about Y?
- Do you trust Source X more than Source Y about …?
- Which source gives a more accurate view of …?

What is required?
- Reliability questions are really asking how much you TRUST a source.
- Sources are rarely completely reliable or totally unreliable. Think of where the source would be on the line below:

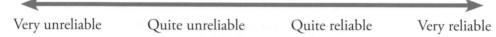

Very unreliable   Quite unreliable   Quite reliable   Very reliable

- Ask four questions of each source: the four Ws. This will assess reliability.
    - What is the source? A cartoon, a poem, a picture, a poster, etc. It will usually be for or against something.
    - Who wrote/produced/drew the source? Can you trust this person about the issue being written about?
    - When was it written/produced/drawn? Is it primary or secondary evidence?
    - Why was it written/produced/drawn? This will give you an idea about motive.
- Comment on the content of the source. Does the language appear exaggerated?
- Cross-reference with other sources.
- Don't be afraid to suggest that the source is both reliable and unreliable at the same time, providing you have reasons to support your answer. For example, an anti-suffrage cartoon is unreliable about women but it is a reliable source about some men at the time.

4. Comparison of sources questions (similarity and difference)

These are questions where you are asked to compare sources and make judgements about them using your own knowledge. For example, 'How similar are these two sources?'

What is required?
- Read each source and decide: who produced it, when it was produced and, most importantly, why it was produced (this will tell you the motive of the author).
- Explain how the sources are similar and how they are different.
- Use your knowledge to show your understanding of the time period in which they were produced.

5. Overview essay question

This will ask you to use your knowledge and the sources to argue for or against an interpretation. The interpretation will describe some issue that spans the whole period 1890-1918 or 1939-45. For example 'In the period 1890-1918 women in Britain were respected'. How far do you agree?' Your answer will be largely based on your knowledge but you should use the sources to support your argument. The important thing is to be balanced and to weigh up the arguments on both sides before reaching a conclusion.

Online resources

Example answers to exam practice questions and quick quizzes are available online at:
www.hodderplus.co.uk/modernworldhistory

Unit 1: Aspects of International Relations, 1919–2005

The Inter-War Years, 1919–1939

Chapter 1: Were the peace treaties of 1919–1923 fair?

At the end of the First World War, the leaders of the victorious powers met in Paris to decide how to deal with their defeated enemies. Their aim was to draw up peace treaties to end the war officially. The victorious leaders, however, found it very hard to agree what to do. In this chapter, you will look at the aims of each leader, the terms and conditions of the peace treaties, and public reaction to the treaties.

Focus points

Each key question in the OCR course is divided into focus points. To do well in the examination, you will need a good understanding of each focus point.

- What were the motives and aims of the Big Three at Versailles?
- Why did the victors not get everything they wanted?
- What were the immediate reactions to the peace settlement?
- Could the treaties be justified at the time?

Key content

In order to fully understand the focus points, you will need to have a good working knowledge of:

- the end of the First World War; background to the Treaty of Versailles
- the motives, aims and roles of the different leaders at the Paris Peace Conference
- the features of the peace treaties 1919–1923 (Versailles, St Germain, Trianon, Sèvres, Lausanne)
- immediate reactions to, and opinions about, the treaties, especially in Britain, France, Germany and the USA.

1.1 The end of the First World War; background to the Treaty of Versailles

The effects of the First World War

- Many parts of Europe had been devastated by the fighting and shelling of four years of war. Large areas of northern France and Belgium were in ruins.
- Millions of soldiers on both sides had been killed or injured.

- The Governments of Germany and Austria–Hungary had collapsed. These countries were defeated and exhausted.
- The victorious powers were also exhausted. Britain and France were almost bankrupt. Only the USA was in a strong financial position.

The mood in 1919

- Many people in Britain and France felt that Germany was responsible for starting the war and should be severely punished and made to pay **reparations**.
- Although there had been no fighting on British soil, most families had lost a close relative during the war. Therefore, public opinion put pressure on politicians to treat Germany harshly in the peace settlement.
- The Germans had treated the Russians harshly in the Treaty of Brest-Litovsk in March 1918. Where it became public, opinion in Britain and France hardened against Germany.
- The Germans did not believe they were solely responsible for starting the war, but they were not invited to the Peace Conference and were forced to accept the Treaty.

The Paris Peace Conference

- The conference took place in the Palace of Versailles on the outskirts of Paris. It lasted for twelve months from 1919 to 1920.
- Thirty-two nations should have been represented, but none of the defeated countries were invited.
- The Treaty of Versailles was the most important of the five treaties.
- All the important decisions were made by President Wilson (USA), Prime Minister Lloyd George (Great Britain) and Prime Minister Clemenceau (France).
- The leaders did not get on well and relations worsened over time.
- Woodrow Wilson was very ill during the conference.

1.2 The motives, aims and roles of the different leaders at the Paris Peace Conference

The most important and influential countries at the negotiations were France, Britain and the USA. Their leaders were known as the (victorious) Allies. Even at the time, it was clear that the different leaders had conflicting views about what a peace treaty should do. They could not all get what they wanted, so whose views would carry the most weight?

Georges Clemenceau: Prime Minister of France

During the First World War, France had suffered enormous damage. Large areas of northern France had been devastated and much of its industry had been destroyed. Four million French soldiers were either killed or injured during the war and Clemenceau was under pressure from the French public to make Germany suffer.

Clemenceau was also anxious about the future. He did not want Germany to recover its strength so that it could attack France again. So his aims were clear. He wanted a harsh treaty that would punish Germany severely and cripple it so that it would never be able to threaten France again.

Woodrow Wilson: President of the USA

The USA had only been in the war since 1917. War damage was slight and casualties were low compared to Britain and France who had been fighting Germany since August 1914.

Wilson believed that Germany was to blame for starting the war, but he believed that the treaty with Germany should not be too harsh because this would cause the Germans to seek revenge later. Clemenceau was very suspicious of Wilson and the two strongly disagreed at the conference.

The two most important ideas Wilson put forward at the peace conference were:

- **self-determination**
- **international co-operation**.

Wilson's views on how to achieve these aims had been published in his 'Fourteen Points' in January 1918.

The Fourteen Points

1 No secret treaties between countries.
2 Freedom of navigation upon the seas, both in times of peace and war.
3 Free trade between countries.
4 All countries to reduce their armed forces to the lowest level consistent with domestic safety.
5 Overseas colonies owned by European powers to have a say in their own future.
6 All foreign troops to leave Russia. The Russian people to be allowed to decide their own future without interference.
7 Independence for Belgium.
8 France to regain Alsace–Lorraine.
9 Italy's frontiers to be adjusted to take account of the nationalities of the people living in the border areas.
10 Self-determination for the people of Austria–Hungary.
11 International guarantees for the independence of the Balkan states. Serbia to have access to the sea.
12 Self-determination for the non-Turkish peoples in the Turkish Empire.
13 Poland to become an independent state with access to the sea.
14 A League of Nations to be set up to settle disputes between countries by peaceful means.

David Lloyd George: Prime Minister of Britain

Many people in Britain wanted a harsh peace treaty that punished Germany severely. Lloyd George understood the feelings of the British people but wanted Germany to be 'justly' punished since he believed that a harsh treaty would encourage Germany to seek revenge later. He was also concerned about the possible spread of Communism from Russia. In addition, Lloyd George wanted Britain to begin trading with Germany again in order to help Britain recover from the war.

At Versailles, Lloyd George often found himself in the middle ground between Clemenceau and Wilson. He did not agree with all of Wilson's 'Fourteen Points' – for example, he did not agree with the idea of freedom of navigation on the seas. On the other hand, he thought Clemenceau's demands would destroy Germany completely and have repercussions later.

Key terms

Self-determination: the right of nations to rule themselves.
International co-operation: countries working together to settle disputes, usually by peaceful means.

Comment

Self-determination was a good idea, but in certain areas of Europe it was very difficult to achieve. For example, the former Austro-Hungarian Empire had many different nationalities scattered across its territories. It was inevitable that people of one ethnic group would find themselves ruled by people from another.

Revision task

What were the aims of the 'Big Three' at the Paris Peace Conference? Copy and complete a table like the one below. Come back to this task later and see if you can do this again from memory.

Leader	Country	Attitude to Germany	Public opinion	Key aims

Exam tip For each leader, make sure you are able to explain what they hoped to achieve at the peace conference.

1.3 The peace treaties of 1919–1923 and the reaction to them

The terms of the Treaty of Versailles

Each of the defeated countries had to sign a different treaty with the victorious Allies. The most important treaty was with Germany, called the Treaty of Versailles. Wilson, Clemenceau and Lloyd George had to make compromises and none of them were happy with the final treaty. In the end, the Treaty was harsh. Its terms can be divided into five areas.

1. Guilt for the war

Germany was forced to accept the blame for starting the war. Most Germans were outraged by this.

2. Armed forces

Germany was forced to make major cuts in its armed forces to a level well below what it had been in 1914. German forces were seen as a major threat to the Allies.

- The army was cut to 100,000 men.
- **Conscription** was banned – soldiers had to be volunteers.
- Germany was not allowed aircraft, submarines or armoured vehicles such as tanks.
- The navy was only allowed six warships.
- The Rhineland (see map on page 13) was **demilitarised**. This meant that no German soldiers were allowed into that area because it was on the border with France and Belgium.

3. Reparations

The Allied powers forced Germany to pay for the damage caused by the war. These payments were called reparations. The exact payment was finally agreed in 1921 and set at £6,600 million – a huge figure. Germany would have major problems in the 1920s making these payments. If the terms had not been changed by the Young Plan in 1929, Germany would still have been making reparations payments in 1984.

4. German territories

Germany lost some of its European territory (see table and map on page 13).

The Allied powers removed Germany's overseas territories or **colonies**. Much of the land taken was given to the victorious powers, particularly Britain and France, and became known as **mandates**.

Other conditions were:
- *Anschluss* (the joining together of Germany and Austria) was not allowed.
- A new country called Czechoslovakia was created (by the Treaty of St Germain, see page 17), which included former parts of Austrian and German territory.

5. League of Nations

A League of Nations (see Chapter 2) was set up as an international police force to prevent future wars. Germany was not invited to join at the beginning until it could show that it had become a peace-loving nation.

Comment

Despite its harshness, the Treaty of Versailles was a compromise. Wilson, Lloyd George and Clemenceau were elected politicians who had to balance the need to achieve a long-term peace settlement with the wishes of the public in France, Britain and the USA. These factors were difficult to balance at the end of a world war.

Key terms

Conscription: compulsory military service in the armed forces. Most countries in Europe had a system where young men spent two or three years in the army.

Demilitarised: an area of land with no troops or weapons.

Colony: a country or area of land occupied and ruled by another country.

Mandate: an official order for territory to be taken under the control or protection of a certain country. Mandates are often made at the end of wars or long disputes.

Exam tip You need to know the key terms of the Treaty of Versailles and how they affected Germany and its people.

Revision task

Use bullet points to summarise how Germany and the German people were affected by the Treaty of Versailles.

Territory	From German control to:	Other points
1 Alsace–Lorraine	France	
2 Eupen, Moresnet, Malmédy	Belgium	
3 North Schleswig	Denmark	After a vote (**plebiscite**)
4 West Prussia and Posen	Poland	To give Poland a 'corridor' to the Baltic Sea
5 Danzig	League of Nations	Free city controlled by League
6 Memel	Lithuania	
7 Saar coalfields	League of Nations (coal to be given to France)	A plebiscite would be held after 15 years
8 German colonies	League of Nations	Most controlled by Britain and France as mandates
9 Estonia, Latvia, Lithuania	Became independent states	Germany had taken these states from Russia under the Treaty of Brest-Litovsk

Key terms

Plebiscite: a vote by the people of a state or region on an important question, such as union with another country.

Comment

The terms of the Treaty of Versailles were very harsh on Germany. The need for revenge and punishment was seen as more important than the need to keep future peace. Wilson was very disappointed with the Treaty and his influence was limited to seeing self-determination in Latvia, Estonia and Lithuania and through the creation of the League of Nations. Germany was severely weakened, and forced to accept a humiliating settlement that its people saw as very unjust.

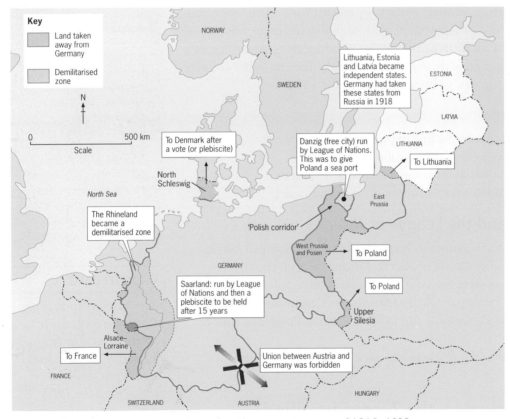

Germany's European territories lost after the peace treaties of 1919–1923.

Exam practice

1 What was the reparations settlement demanded by the Allies in the Treaty of Versailles? *(4 marks)*

Exam tip This is typical of the questions you will face in questions 2 or 3.
This is a starter question. It tests your **factual knowledge**. Try to include four details about reparations as laid down in the Treaty of Versailles.

German reaction to the Treaty of Versailles

The German people and Government, led by Friedrich Ebert, were horrified by the terms of the Treaty of Versailles. The Government even considered going back to war but eventually signed the Treaty in June 1919.

There was a real feeling of injustice in Germany:

- *Germans did not feel they had caused the war* yet they were forced to sign the war guilt clause.
- *They did not feel they had lost the war.* In 1918, many Germans did not know they had surrendered but had simply stopped fighting to make peace. Now they were being treated as the defeated enemy.
- *They felt that they should have been invited to the peace negotiations.* This did not happen. The German Government had no influence over the terms of the Treaty and had to accept the decisions of the victorious powers without question.

War guilt and reparations

Germany not only had to accept the blame for starting the war (the war guilt clause) but also had to pay for the damage caused (reparations). Germans hated this. Their country was bankrupt, in ruins, and many people were starving.

Disarmament

Germans resented losing so much of their army, navy and air force. This was a real loss of pride and became a point of resentment. Although disarmament was one of Wilson's 'Fourteen Points', the victorious Allies did not reduce their armed forces in the same way. German anger grew throughout the 1920s since no other country disarmed. Hitler was able to use this to his advantage in the 1930s.

German territories

The loss of German territory involved a loss of pride for most Germans.
- Some Germans would now be living under foreign rulers.
- The Saar, an important industrial area, was taken over by France.
- German colonies were handed over to Britain, France and Japan.

The 'Fourteen Points' and the League of Nations

Many Germans felt that Wilson's 'Fourteen Points' had not been applied fairly. For example, whilst the people of Latvia in eastern Europe were given self-determination, many Germans were forced to live under foreign rulers – for example, in the Sudetenland (now part of the new state of Czechoslovakia), in North Schleswig (now part of Denmark), and in West Prussia, Posen and Upper Silesia (now in Poland).

Germany was further insulted by not being allowed to join the League of Nations.

Was German reaction to the Treaty justified?

The German reaction to the Treaty was only partly justified. For example:
- It was widely felt that the Germans were operating double standards. The Germans had been much harsher in the terms of the Treaty of Brest-Litovsk with Russia than the Allied powers were with Germany in the Treaty of Versailles.
- Germans had no enthusiasm for Wilson's 'Fourteen Points' but complained when self-determination was not applied to them.

Exam practice

1 Explain why the Allies punished Germany harshly in the Treaty of Versailles. *(6 marks)*

Exam tip This tests your knowledge *and* **understanding**.
- A low level answer (worth 1–3 marks) will simply describe one or several reasons the Allied leaders punished Germany in the Treaty.
- A better answer (worth 4–6 marks) will need to describe AND explain the different motives of the Allied leaders, the pressures on them and the fact that the whole Treaty was a compromise.

Comment

The bitter reaction of the German people to the terms of the Treaty of Versailles would cause significant problems throughout the 1920s and 1930s. Hitler not only used this hatred of the Treaty of Versailles to win support, but later also used it to justify rearming and expanding German territory and influence.

- The reparations sum was large, but was still only two per cent of Germany's annual production.
- Clemenceau wanted Germany to be broken up at the end of the First World War, but this was not supported by the other Allied powers.

The impact of the Treaty of Versailles on Germany

Very quickly, the Treaty began to cause major problems in Germany (see page 31).

The Weimar Republic

A new elected German government was set up at the end of the war. The new republic, under its leader Ebert, was very fragile and was forced to sign the hated Treaty of Versailles. This made the Weimar Government even more unpopular.

The Kapp Putsch, March 1920

Ex-German soldiers called the Freikorps, led by Dr Wolfgang Kapp, led a **putsch** against Ebert's democratically elected government. Ebert survived the rebellion because workers in Berlin went on strike and refused to co-operate with Kapp. The rebellion failed and Kapp fled, but Germany still seemed in chaos.

Reparations

The new German Government made its first reparations payment in 1922, but it failed to make the payment date in 1923.

The French invasion of the Ruhr, January 1923

As Germany had fallen behind with its reparations payments, the French and Belgian Governments sent troops to occupy the German industrial area called the Ruhr. German workers in the Ruhr went on strike in protest at the invasion.

Hyperinflation, 1922–23

The strike in the Ruhr meant that no German goods were being produced so the German Government solved the problem by printing money. This had the disastrous effect of creating **hyperinflation**. The German economy collapsed and millions of Germans suffered as prices and wages rose out of control, and money and savings became worthless overnight.

Reaction to the Treaty of Versailles in Britain, France and the USA

In Britain, whilst the public seemed satisfied that Germany had been punished, Lloyd George thought that the harshness of the Treaty could cause another war later. He was, of course, correct.

In France, Clemenceau thought the Treaty was not harsh enough. He had wanted Germany broken up into its pre-1870 regions and the Rhineland handed over to France rather than merely demilitarised.

In the USA, Wilson was unable to get **Congress** to support the Treaty he had negotiated. Members of Congress refused to vote for it and therefore the USA did not join the League of Nations. Many Americans thought the USA should never have become involved in the First World War and did not want to be responsible for keeping the peace between the old European countries.

Comment

The years 1919–23 were years of misery for most German people. This was partly caused by the Treaty of Versailles, but partly by the effects of the First World War. Even so, most Germans blamed the Treaty and this hatred stayed with them for years.

Key terms

Putsch: a revolt, rebellion or uprising aimed at overthrowing the current government.

Hyperinflation: rapidly rising prices so that money becomes worthless.

Congress: the American representative assemblies (the equivalent of Parliament in Britain). There are two houses, the Senate and the House of Representatives.

Exam tip You need to know several reasons why each leader was satisfied or dissatisfied with the Treaty of Versailles and why the German people thought it was very harsh.

Revision task

Complete your own copy of this diagram. Show how Germany reacted to the Treaty of Versailles by putting in statements which German people might have made. We have given you one example. You can add more boxes if you need them.

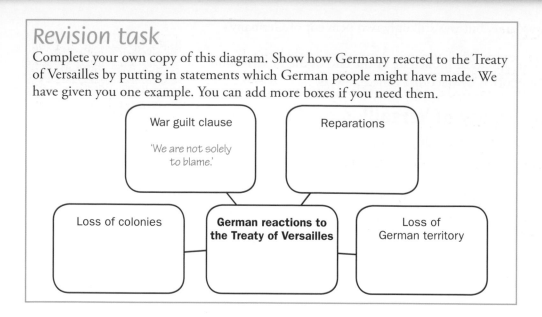

Was the Treaty of Versailles fair?

The Treaty was criticised by many people at the time and, later, by historians.

Views expressed at the time

The Treaty was criticised for different reasons.
- Some people said it was too harsh on Germany and they predicted that the Germans would seek revenge later.
- Some argued it was not harsh enough and did not punish Germany sufficiently for a war it had started, which had cost so many lives.
- Some believed the USSR should have been involved in the negotiations.

Views of historians

With hindsight we know that the treaty failed to prevent another war, and indeed some argue it helped cause the Second World War. Historians generally agree that the Treaty of Versailles had great weaknesses. In particular they say to humiliate Germany was short-sighted, however it is probably fair to say that whilst the Treaty of Versailles was harsh, the peacemakers had a very difficult task balancing the demands of people in their own countries against the need to make a secure peace. Most historians would agree that the Treaty was as fair as could have been expected at the time and circumstances in which it was created.

Revision task

Make four copies of the table below. Complete them to show the fairness and unfairness of the Treaty of Versailles according to the following leaders:
- Woodrow Wilson, President of the USA
- Georges Clemenceau, French Prime Minister
- David Lloyd George, British Prime Minister
- Friedrich Ebert, German Chancellor.

Versailles: fair	Versailles: unfair

Exam practice

1 How far were the German people dissatisfied with the terms of the Treaty of Versailles? *(10 marks)*

Exam tip This question tests your knowledge and understanding but it goes further. A question that starts 'How far …' is also inviting you to **evaluate**. In your exam, question 2c) or 3c) will usually include an element of evaluation like this.

You know that the Germans hated the Treaty of Versailles but this question is asking you to judge which aspects of it they most resented and why. Different groups in German society resented certain aspects more than others, e.g. the loss of territory, or reduction in armed forces.

Other peace treaties

The Treaty of Versailles dealt only with Germany. Once it was settled, the 'Big Three' left the conference and their assistants worked out the rest of the treaties dealing with Germany's allies. They used the Treaty of Versailles as a model.

Treaty of St Germain, 1919: Austria

- This treaty separated Austria from Hungary.
- It forbade any future *Anschluss* between Austria and Germany.
- It forced Austria to disarm.
- It also took territory from Austria as shown below:

Territory	From Austria to:	Comments
Bohemia and Moravia	New state of Czechoslovakia	
Bosnia and Herzegovina	New state of Yugoslavia	Also included the former kingdom of Serbia

- Austria also lost Galicia to Poland, South Tyrol, Istria and Trieste to Italy and Bukovina to Romania.
- After this treaty, Austria was no longer a leading power in Europe.

The old Austrian empire had already collapsed by 1918. The Treaty of St Germain was really about sorting out a chaotic jumble of territories into new states rather than punishing Austria.

Italy was not happy with this treaty. It felt it should have received more land from Austria. On the other hand, many millions in eastern Europe were given self-determination and freedom to rule themselves.

Austria suffered severe economic problems after the war, since much of its industry had gone to Czechoslovakia.

Treaty of Trianon, 1920: Hungary

This treaty was not signed until 1920 but, unlike the Treaty of St Germain, the main terms involved the transfer of territories:

Territory	From Hungary to:
Ruthenia, Slovakia	Czechoslovakia
Slovenia, Croatia	Yugoslavia

Hungary was reduced in a similar way to Austria. It lost a lot of territory and population. Its industry suffered because it lost territories from which it drew raw materials. Like Austria, Hungary had to disarm.

Treaty of Neuilly, 1919: Bulgaria

Bulgaria lost territory to Greece, Romania and Yugoslavia and also lost its access to the sea. Like the other defeated countries, Bulgaria had to disarm.

Bulgaria had played a relatively small part in the war and was treated less harshly than its allies. Nevertheless, many Bulgarians were governed by foreign powers by 1920.

Key terms

Anschluss: German union with Austria to form a single country.

Treaty of Sèvres, 1920: Turkey

Turkey was important because of its strategic position and the size of its empire. Its territorial losses are shown here:

Territory	From Turkey to:
Smyrna	Greece
Palestine, Iraq, Transjordan	League mandates under British control
Syria	League mandates under French control

Turkey also effectively lost control of the straits to the Black Sea. It also had to accept formally that many of its former lands (for example, Egypt, Tunisia, Morocco) were now independent or under British or French mandates (control). In practice, this was already true, but under this treaty, Turkey had to accept the arrangement.

This treaty outraged the Turks. Turkish nationalists, led by Mustafa Kemal, challenged its terms by driving Greeks out of Smyrna. The result was the Treaty of Lausanne (1923), which returned Smyrna to Turkey.

Sèvres was not a successful treaty. The Turks successfully resisted part of it. The motives of Britain and France in taking control of former Turkish colonies were questionable. The Arabs, who had helped the British in the war, gained little. Palestine was also a controversial area and remains a troubled region to the present day.

Judgements on the other treaties

The other peace treaties have often been criticised in a similar way to the Treaty of Versailles.
- Many of the new countries were unstable and not used to democratic elections.
- There were so many nationalities in Europe that it was not possible to apply self-determination to all of the new states created.
- In general, Versailles and the other treaties created an unstable Europe.

Revision task

Create a table like the one below and use the information on pages 17–18 to complete it.

Country	Treaty	Terms	What were the peacemakers trying to achieve and how far was each country punished?
Bulgaria			
Turkey			
Hungary			
Austria			

Summary/revision plan

You need to have a good working knowledge of the following areas. **Tick off each item** once you are confident in your knowledge.

- ❑ **1 The end of the First World War; background to the Treaty of Versailles**
  - The effects of the First World War
  - The mood in 1919
  - The Paris Peace Conference
- ❑ **2 The motives, aims and roles of the different leaders at the Paris Peace Conference**
  - Georges Clemenceau, Prime Minister of France
  - Woodrow Wilson, President of the USA
  - David Lloyd George, Prime Minister of Britain
- ❑ **3 The peace treaties of 1919–1923 and the reaction to them**
  The terms of the Treaty of Versailles
  - Guilt for the war
  - Armed forces
  - Reparations
  - German territories
  - League of Nations

  German reaction to the Treaty of Versailles
  - War guilt and reparations
  - Disarmament
  - Loss of German territories
  - The 'Fourteen Points' and the League of Nations

  Was German reaction to the Treaty justified?

  The impact of the Treaty of Versailles on Germany
  - The Weimar Republic
  - The Kapp Putsch
  - Reparations
  - The French invasion of the Ruhr
  - Hyperinflation

  Reaction to the Treaty of Versailles in Britain, France and the USA

  Was the Treaty of Versailles fair?

  Other peace treaties
  - Treaty of St Germain, 1919: Austria
  - Treaty of Trianon, 1920: Hungary
  - Treaty of Neuilly, 1919: Bulgaria
  - Treaty of Sèvres, 1920: Turkey.

Check your knowledge online with our Quick quizzes at www.hodderplus.co.uk/modernworldhistory.

Chapter 2: To what extent was the League of Nations a success?

The First World War claimed the lives of millions and devastated many parts of Europe. In 1919, a new organisation, the League of Nations, was created to encourage countries to work together to maintain peace and settle disputes by negotiation rather than force. In this chapter, you will look at how the League of Nations worked and its successes and failures in the 1920s and 1930s.

Focus points

Each key question in the OCR course is divided into focus points. To do well in the examination, you will need a good understanding of each focus point.

- What were the aims of the League?
- How successful was the League in the 1920s?
- How far did weaknesses in the League's organisation make failure inevitable?
- How far did the Depression make the work of the League more difficult?
- Why did the League fail over Manchuria and Abyssinia?

Key content

In order to fully understand the focus points, you will need to have a good working knowledge of:

- the aims of the League; its strengths and weaknesses in structure and organisation
- successes and failures in peacekeeping during the 1920s
- disarmament
- the achievements of the League's agencies and commissions
- the impact of the World Depression on the work of the League after 1929
- the failures of the League in Manchuria and Abyssinia.

2.1 The aims of the League; its strengths and weaknesses

The League of Nations had a **covenant**. It was made up of 26 articles explaining how the League was supposed to work and its aims, which were to:

- prevent aggression by any nation
- encourage co-operation between nations
- work towards international disarmament
- improve the living and working conditions of all peoples.

Comment

The most important aim of the League of Nations was to prevent war. This was a very ambitious aim. No international organisation had ever been set up to do this before. The League was also set up to encourage disarmament. The League aimed to keep peace by encouraging countries to work together and this became known as **collective security**.

Key terms

Collective security: a way of protecting world peace and security through joint actions by all nations.
Covenant: a set of rules.

Exam tip Examiners often ask candidates to assess the success and failures of the League. To answer a question such as this, it is important to know the aims of the League and the extent to which the League's actions met those aims.

The structure and organisation of the League

The Assembly

This was the debating chamber of the League and was located at the League's headquarters in Geneva, Switzerland. When the League began it had a total membership of 42 countries. Each country had a single vote in the Assembly that met once a year. It had the powers to:
- admit new members
- elect permanent members to the Council
- vote on the budget
- suggest revisions to existing peace treaties.

The Permanent Court of International Justice

The Court was based at the Hague in the Netherlands and consisted of judges who were chosen to represent the different legal systems of member countries. If requested, the Court would give a decision on a dispute between two countries. It also gave legal advice to the Assembly or Council and provided explanations about the meanings of treaties and other agreements. However, whatever ruling it made, the Court had no way of ensuring its decision was implemented.

The Council

- The Council met up to three times a year and in times of emergency.
- Membership of the Council was made up of both permanent and temporary members (who were elected for three years only).
- The five permanent members were Britain, France, Germany, Italy and Japan.
- Between 1920 and 1936, the number of countries represented on the Council varied from four to ten.

Peacekeeping role

The main duty of the Council was to solve any disputes that might occur between states. It was hoped that this would be done by negotiation. If any country was considered to have started a war through an act of aggression, then such a war became the concern of all the countries in the League who would take action against the aggressor. This action was in three stages:
- **moral condemnation**, which meant that all countries would put pressure on the aggressor in order to make them feel guilty and shame them into stopping the war and accepting the League's decision
- **economic sanctions**, which meant that all countries in the League would stop trading with the aggressor
- **military force**, in which countries in the League would contribute to an armed force that would act against the aggressor.

The International Labour Organisation (ILO)

- The ILO consisted of employers, government and workers' representatives who met once a year to work to improve the conditions of working people.
- The ILO also collected statistics and information about working conditions and attempted to persuade member countries to adopt its suggestions and ideas.
- Issues that the ILO tended to discuss were wage rates, hours of work, safety, health at work, unemployment, and the employment of women and children.

The Secretariat

The Secretariat was an international civil service that carried out the work and administration of the League. It kept records of League meetings and prepared reports for the different agencies of the League. The Secretariat was also divided into many different sections – for example, health, armaments, economic and financial.

Commissions

In addition to dealing with disputes between its members, the League also attempted to tackle major problems through the creation of commissions.
- The Mandates Commission was set up to ensure that the country in charge of a **mandated** territory acted in the interests of the people of that territory.
- The World Health Organisation (WHO) attempted to deal with the problem of dangerous diseases.
- The Refugee Organisation worked to help return people to their original homes at the end of the First World War.
- The League made recommendations on the marking of shipping waters.
- A slavery commission was set up to work for the abolition of slavery.
- The League investigated signalling for railways and produced an international highway code for road users.

Key terms

Economic sanctions: restrictions on trade with another country.
Mandate: an official order for territory to be taken under the control or protection of another country. Mandates were often made at the end of wars or long disputes.

The strengths and weaknesses of the League

The League's power in theory

Article 16 of the League's Covenant spelt out the powers of the League. If any of the League's members committed acts of aggression against any other member, the League could:

- say that it disapproved of the action of the aggressor country
- impose economic and financial sanctions and encourage its members to stop trading with the aggressor country
- use military force (military sanctions) against an aggressor – for example, go to war.

The League's power in practice

The League's actual powers were not as effective as they appeared. The League was weakened by the following.

- *It had no armed forces of its own.* The League had to rely on the co-operation of its members to carry out its decisions. Without the USA as a member, the League relied on its two strongest members, Britain and France, to act. If Britain and France did not act, the League was virtually powerless.
- *Military force would always be the last resort.* In the 1920s, both Britain and France were still recovering from the huge human and economic cost of the First World War. Both governments were not likely to go to war again in the near future.
- *Economic sanctions were difficult to enforce.* Member countries were always very unwilling to stop trading with an aggressor because it damaged their own trade as well as the aggressor's. Economic sanctions were used against Italy in 1935– 36, but were not very effective.

Membership of the League

When the League of Nations was created in 1920, there were 42 original member countries. By 1930, membership had risen to nearly 60. Unfortunately, at any one time in its history, several vital countries were not members of the League.

The USA

The USA never joined the League of Nations despite the wishes of President Woodrow Wilson in 1919. He was one of the original planners of the League of Nations and wanted his country to take a leading role in maintaining world peace. Many Americans, however, were **isolationist** and wanted to keep the USA out of European affairs. The US Senate refused to accept the Treaty of Versailles, or membership of the League of Nations, by a mere seven votes.

Russia

During 1917, a Communist government took power in Russia and made a separate peace treaty with the Germans. The new Soviet Government was very suspicious of countries in the West and saw the League of Nations as a club dominated by rich capitalist countries. The Soviets were also encouraging revolution in other countries, and in the early 1920s struggling to survive an attack by anti-Communists supported by western countries. In these circumstances, the Soviet Union was not about to join the League of Nations. The Soviet Union finally joined the League in 1934.

Comment

It had been intended by the creators of the League that the major powers would dominate the Council. Unfortunately, the refusal of the USA to join meant the number of non-permanent members matched the number of permanent members. By the 1930s the number of non-permanent members had risen to nine. Important decisions made by the Council also had to be unanimous, and it could only recommend action, not carry it out, which weakened its power. In addition, the way that the Assembly and Council were set up meant that making a decision was a slow and complicated process.

Key terms

Isolationism: withdrawing from international politics and policies.

Comment

In theory, the League had considerable power. In reality, however, it was relatively weak and relied upon the co-operation of its members to carry out its actions. The League never used military sanctions since its members were not prepared to go to war to keep world peace, and would not support the League if doing so conflicted with their own interests.

Germany

As the defeated enemy in 1918, Germany was forced to accept the Treaty of Versailles as drawn up by the victorious powers. The bitterness against Germany at the end of the First World War was such that it was not allowed to join the League of Nations. Only after seven years of steadily improving relations and the signing of the Locarno agreements in 1925 (see pages 24–25) was German membership of the League considered, and finally approved in 1926.

The membership of the League was crucial to its success or failure. With the absence of so many major powers at any one time, everything depended on the British and French Governments to supply the necessary leadership to enable the League to operate effectively. At no time before 1939 were the British and French Governments prepared to use force (military sanctions) to support the League. In fact, it has been suggested that if the British Government had known in advance that the USA would not join the League of Nations then Britain would also have refused to join.

Exam tip It is important to understand why membership of the League contributed to its success or failure. Make sure you look at who the League members were and the significance of members joining, leaving or not ever being a member.

Revision task

In what ways did the organisation and membership of the League make its failure inevitable? Copy and complete the table below.

In what ways did the organisation of the League make it strong/weak?	Strong	Weak
In what ways did the membership of the League make it strong/weak?	Strong	Weak
Did the organisation, membership and power of the League make success likely or unlikely?	League likely to succeed	League unlikely to succeed

2.2 Successes and failures in peacekeeping during the 1920s

Although war began in Europe again in 1939, the League of Nations had some important successes. However, while the League's successes tended to be unimpressive, its failures were spectacular.

The success of the League of Nations depended on its membership and ability to act against aggression. The greatest successes for the League tended to be in its work as an agency, helping refugees and fighting the spread of drug addiction, disease and slavery. It also made pioneering contributions to the rights of working people and international agreements for road, rail and shipping. There were even some successes in its major work of solving disputes between smaller countries. However, when these are analysed more closely, the League's successes are almost totally confined to the 1920s and involved small nations rather than great powers.

Exam practice

1 What were the main aims of the League of Nations? *(4 marks)*

2 Explain why the League of Nations was able to achieve some successes in the 1920s. *(6 marks)*

Exam tip

These are typical of the questions you will face in questions 2 or 3. Question 1 is a starter question. It tests your **factual knowledge**. The League had four aims – make sure you include them all.

Question 2 tests your knowledge *and* **understanding**.
- A low level answer (worth 1–3 marks) will simply describe some of the successes.
- A better answer (worth 4–6 marks) will both describe these successes AND explain the factors that helped achieve them. For example the improving economic climate in the 1920s.

Solving international disputes

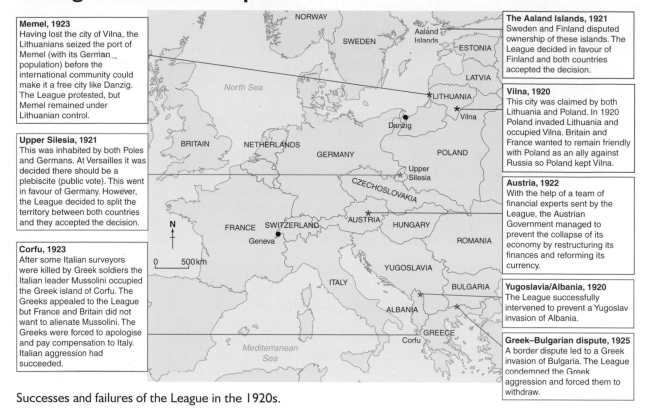

Memel, 1923
Having lost the city of Vilna, the Lithuanians seized the port of Memel (with its German population) before the international community could make it a free city like Danzig. The League protested, but Memel remained under Lithuanian control.

Upper Silesia, 1921
This was inhabited by both Poles and Germans. At Versailles it was decided there should be a plebiscite (public vote). This went in favour of Germany. However, the League decided to split the territory between both countries and they accepted the decision.

Corfu, 1923
After some Italian surveyors were killed by Greek soldiers the Italian leader Mussolini occupied the Greek island of Corfu. The Greeks appealed to the League but France and Britain did not want to alienate Mussolini. The Greeks were forced to apologise and pay compensation to Italy. Italian aggression had succeeded.

The Aaland Islands, 1921
Sweden and Finland disputed ownership of these islands. The League decided in favour of Finland and both countries accepted the decision.

Vilna, 1920
This city was claimed by both Lithuania and Poland. In 1920 Poland invaded Lithuania and occupied Vilna. Britain and France wanted to remain friendly with Poland as an ally against Russia so Poland kept Vilna.

Austria, 1922
With the help of a team of financial experts sent by the League, the Austrian Government managed to prevent the collapse of its economy by restructuring its finances and reforming its currency.

Yugoslavia/Albania, 1920
The League successfully intervened to prevent a Yugoslav invasion of Albania.

Greek–Bulgarian dispute, 1925
A border dispute led to a Greek invasion of Bulgaria. The League condemned the Greek aggression and forced them to withdraw.

Successes and failures of the League in the 1920s.

Other League involvement

Mosul, 1923–24

Mosul had been Turkish for centuries, but had been given to Iraq (controlled by Britain) in the Treaty of Sèvres (1923). The Turks refused to accept this part of the treaty and a commission was set up by the League to solve the dispute. The League awarded Mosul to Iraq, but agreed to change the terms of the British mandate so that Mosul would be given its independence before the end of 25 years.

Colombia/Peru, 1932

A regional war in South America was avoided when the League successfully intervened in a dispute when a small group of Peruvians seized a Colombian border post at Leticia. The League sent a commission to the area that supervised a ceasefire and arranged for the withdrawal of the Peruvians.

2.3 Disarmament

By the mid 1920s, it was widely believed that a build-up of arms by all sides had helped to cause the First World War. In 1925, the League set up a commission to plan a disarmament conference, but Britain and France would not co-operate and the conference never took place.

The Locarno Treaties, 1925

In October 1925, representatives of Germany, Britain, France, Italy, Belgium, Czechoslovakia and Poland met at the Swiss lakeside resort of Locarno. Here, a series of agreements was signed that became known as the Locarno Treaties.

The main features of the agreements were:

- A Rhineland pact – Belgium, France and Germany agreed their borders were fixed as laid down in the Treaty of Versailles. These borders would be guaranteed by Britain and Italy.

- The Rhineland was to remain **demilitarised**.
- France guaranteed to help Poland and Czechoslovakia if attacked by Germany.
- Germany agreed not to use force to settle disputes with its neighbours.

The Locarno agreements were seen as an important development easing international relations in the 1920s. In particular, Germany was treated as an equal partner and, by 1926, had also become a member of the League of Nations.

Although the Locarno Treaties seemed to suggest that Europe was entering a new phase of 'peace and security', in reality they accomplished very little. While Britain and Italy guaranteed Germany's western frontiers, no such guarantee was given about its eastern frontiers. This gave the impression that the Polish and Czech borders with Germany were not permanent and, in the future, Germany might be able to change them.

It has even been suggested that this part of the Locarno agreement undermined the Treaty of Versailles because Germany's eastern frontiers did not seem as permanent as her western frontiers. At the time, however, the treaties signed at Locarno began a short, but welcome, phase of **international co-operation** between the major European powers.

The Kellogg–Briand Pact (Pact of Paris), 1928

In 1928, the foreign ministers of France (Briand) and the USA (Kellogg) drew up an agreement that was signed by 65 other nations. The Kellogg–Briand Pact, or Pact of Paris, was greeted enthusiastically by people throughout the world.

The countries that signed the Pact agreed to condemn war as a way of solving international disputes. They also agreed not to go to war for five years, except in self-defence.

Attempts at disarmament in the 1930s

In 1932, another attempt was made to call countries together at a disarmament conference. The attempt failed and leaders such as Hitler looked to increase the size of their forces. Hitler withdrew from the League of Nations in 1933 and set about rearming Germany, despite the terms of the Treaty of Versailles. In 1935, Britain further undermined the League's power by signing a separate naval agreement with Germany in order to keep the German navy to within 35 per cent of the size of the British navy.

2.4 The achievements of the League's agencies and commissions

The League also tried to solve some other deep seated world problems such as child slavery, illegal sale of weapons, or post war refugees. It did this through its agencies or commissions.

League of Nations special commissions

- The League's commissions worked to eliminate the illegal sale of weapons and the use of children as slaves.
- The Minorities Commission helped to provide a restraint upon governments unsympathetic to the problems of minority groups.
- The Drugs Commission and World Health Organisation enjoyed some success in reducing the sale of dangerous drugs and helping countries to control outbreaks of life-threatening diseases.
- The League was particularly successful with its refugee organisation, which helped to repatriate approximately 400,000 First World War prisoners under the leadership of the Norwegian Fridtjof Nansen.

Key terms

Demilitarised: no armed forces or weapons.
International co-operation: countries working together to settle disputes, usually by peaceful means.

Comment

The signing of the Kellogg–Briand Pact could be seen as the high point of friendly international relations during the 1920s.

The agreement, however, had its weaknesses. Nothing was said about how the terms of the Pact would be enforced if one country broke the rules. This meant the agreement would only work if members kept their word. The Kellogg–Briand Pact was not able to prevent the Japanese invasion of Manchuria in 1931.

The International Labour Organisation

The International Labour Organisation (ILO) made several important contributions to the improvement of working conditions for people throughout the world. It:

- agreed to a target working day of eight hours and a working week of 48 hours
- accepted that all workers should have the right to join a trade union and have annual paid holidays
- agreed that no one should be in full-time work under fifteen years of age
- regularly published its findings and recommendations in order to increase pressure on governments throughout the world.

The work of the ILO was continued by the United Nations in 1946.

Revision task

How successful was the League in the 1920s?

To answer this question, look at the statements below. Use evidence to show which statement is the most accurate description of the League in 1929.

- The League was a major force for world peace.
- The events of the 1920s showed just how weak the League really was.
- The League had some successes, but usually in dealing with small-scale problems.

2.5 The impact of the Depression on the work of the League after 1929

The effects of the Wall Street Crash

In the 1920s and 1930s, the USA was the world's richest country, so problems there could seriously affect the whole of the world's trade.

This is exactly what happened. In 1929, the US economy crashed. Americans stopped buying goods from other countries. American banks asked foreign businesses to pay back loans they had been given earlier in the 1920s. Trade collapsed and before long there was a worldwide economic depression.

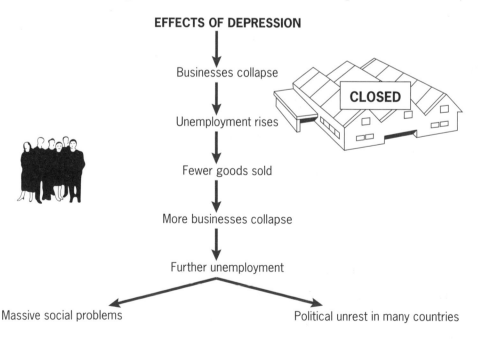

EFFECTS OF DEPRESSION

Businesses collapse

Unemployment rises

Fewer goods sold

More businesses collapse

Further unemployment

Massive social problems   Political unrest in many countries

The effects of the Depression

The USA was a market for many companies in Europe. As the USA stopped buying, companies that exported to the USA began to suffer. Industrial production in Europe fell by a third. Britain, Germany and the rest of Europe began to suffer unemployment and depression as well.

The USA also stopped lending money to other countries. This made matters worse. The Depression was an economic problem but it caused political problems too.

As trade declined, many countries tried **protectionism**. They charged tariffs and duties on goods imported from foreign countries. The aim was that these duties made foreign goods more expensive and so made home-produced goods more attractive. The idea was to protect home industries and jobs from foreign competition.

Although protectionism worked in some cases, protectionist policies simply reduced the amount of world trade. In the long term, it made the effects of the Depression worse and slowed down recovery.

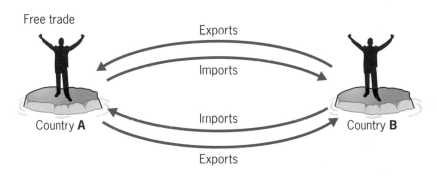

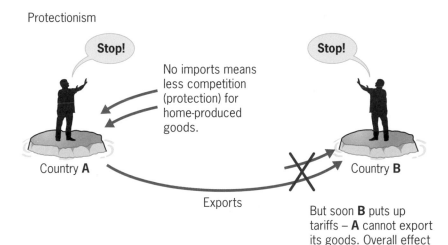

The effects of free trade and protectionism.

Key terms

Protectionism: economic policies followed by a country to protect its own industries and products from overseas competition – for example, by charging import duties on goods from abroad.

Comment

The Depression had very severe economic effects. However, these economic effects (especially unemployment) in turn caused political problems and tensions between countries. As a result, it is very difficult to separate the economic impact from the political impact of the Depression.

Revision tasks

1 Why and how did the Depression in the USA cause economic problems in Europe? Answer this question using four to six key words.

2 Why did unemployment continue to be such a problem throughout the 1930s?

3 Use six key words to explain why countries adopted protectionist policies.

4 Use the information on pages 72–73 (in chapter 7) to show how the Depression affected Germany in particular.

2.6 The League in the 1930s: failures in Manchuria and Abyssinia

Manchuria, 1931

The first major blow to the authority of the League came in 1931 when Japan invaded Chinese Manchuria. The Chinese Government appealed immediately to the League for assistance, but instead of using economic or military sanctions the League sent a commission to investigate Japanese aggression. The Lytton Commission concluded that the Japanese had acted unreasonably, and the League demanded the Japanese withdraw from Manchuria. But it was too late. When the League condemned Japanese aggression in 1933, Japan simply left the League of Nations and continued its occupation of Manchuria. The League had been completely humiliated.

The Manchurian affair was the first real test for the League of Nations and proved to be a turning point in its history. Neither Britain nor France was prepared to give the League the support it needed over Manchuria. Most European countries were preoccupied by the effects of the Depression and were unwilling to become involved. The failure of the League to act was decisive. The European dictators, such as Mussolini and Hitler, realised that the West would not stand up to determined military action.

Abyssinia, 1935

If the Manchurian affair was the turning point for the League, the Abyssinian crisis was the final and fatal blow. Abyssinia was one of the few countries in Africa not under the control of a European power. Italy had already tried to invade Abyssinia in 1896 and was humiliated by the poorly equipped Abyssinian tribes.

In 1935, a well-equipped Italian force led by Mussolini invaded Abyssinia.

- Haile Selassie, leader of Abyssinia, appealed to the League of Nations for assistance.
- The League condemned Italian aggression and imposed economic sanctions against Italy. The sanctions were not effective since Italy was still allowed to buy oil (vital fuel for her tanks, etc.).
- France and Britain were keen not to offend Mussolini in case he joined forces with Hitler.
- Mussolini completed his invasion of Abyssinia and left the League of Nations.

The Abyssinian crisis was a disaster for Britain and France as well as the deathblow to the League. The British and French Governments had been keen not to offend Mussolini in the hope that he would not ally himself with Hitler's Germany. Samuel Hoare, the British Foreign Secretary, and Pierre Laval, the French Prime Minister, even worked out a scheme to give most of Abyssinia to Mussolini in order to appease him. The plan did not work. The Hoare–Laval Pact was condemned when it became public in 1935, and Mussolini signed the Rome–Berlin Axis (a treaty of friendship) with Germany in 1936. Within three years, most of Europe was at war once again. The League had failed to maintain the peace.

> **Exam tip** This question tests your knowledge and understanding but it goes further. A question that starts 'How far …' is also inviting you to **evaluate**. In your exam, question 2c) or 3c) will include an element of evaluation like this.
>
> You need to describe the failures and also explain the reasons for them. To get the highest marks you need to evaluate whether the Great Depression was the most significant of these reasons.

> ## Exam practice
> 1 How far can the failure of the League in the 1930s be blamed on the Great Depression? Explain your answer? *(10 marks)*

Summary/revision plan

You need to have a good working knowledge of the following areas. **Tick off each item** once you are confident in your knowledge.

❑ **1 The aims of the League; its strengths and weaknesses**
- The structure and organisation of the League
- The strengths and weaknesses of the League
  - The League's power in theory
  - The League's power in practice
- Membership of the League
  - USA
  - Russia
  - Germany

❑ **2 Successes and failures in peacekeeping during the 1920s**
- Examples of successes
  - E.g. Bulgaria
- Examples of failures
  - E.g. Corfu

❑ **3 Disarmament**
- The Locarno Treaties, 1925
- The Kellogg–Briand Pact (Pact of Paris), 1928
- Attempts at disarmament in the 1930s

❑ **4 Achievements of the League's agencies and commissions**
- The International Labour Organisation (ILO)
- The special commissions

❑ **5 The impact of the World Depression on the work of the League after 1929**
- The effects of the Wall Street Crash
- The effects of the Depression

❑ **6 The failures of the League in the 1930s**
- Manchuria, 1931
- Abyssinia, 1935.

Check your knowledge online with our Quick quizzes at www.hodderplus.co.uk/modernworldhistory.

Chapter 3: Why had international peace collapsed by 1939?

By 1928, many countries seemed to be recovering well from the effects of the First World War. However, by 1939, much of the world was at war again. In this chapter, you will look at how the effects of the Depression and a series of international disputes and problems led to the outbreak of war. In particular, you will consider the role of the German leader, Adolf Hitler, in causing war.

Focus points

Each key question in the OCR course is divided into focus points. To do well in the examination, you will need a good understanding of each focus point.

- What were the long-term consequences of the peace treaties of 1919–1923?
- What were the consequences of the failures of the League in the 1930s?
- How far was Hitler's foreign policy to blame for the outbreak of war in 1939?
- Was the policy of appeasement justified?
- How important was the Nazi–Soviet Pact?
- Why did Britain and France declare war on Germany in September 1939?

Key content

In order to fully understand the focus points, you will need to have a good working knowledge of:

- the underlying problems: the long-term consequences of the peace treaties, and effects of the Depression
- the foreign policies of Italy and Japan and the failures of the League of Nations in Abyssinia and Manchuria
- the foreign policies of Britain and France (especially appeasement)
- Hitler's foreign policy up to 1939: including the Saar, remilitarisation of the Rhineland, Austria, Czechoslovakia, Poland and the Nazi–Soviet Pact
- the end of appeasement and the outbreak of war, September 1939.

3.1 Underlying problems

Long-term consequences of the peace treaties

Soon after the Treaty of Versailles was signed in 1919, it began to cause major problems in Germany and for the new democratic German leaders. The Treaty of Versailles was hated by the German people and this was used very effectively by Hitler to help him become German leader in 1933.

The most important consequences of the Treaty of Versailles on Germany were:

- *Weimar Government*: The new German democratic Government was seen as weak and unpopular because it had been created by the Treaty of Versailles
- *Reparations*: Germany had to pay huge **reparations** at the end of the war. This caused much hardship, the collapse of the German currency in 1923, hyperinflation, and the invasion of the Ruhr by French troops.
- *Loss of territory*: Germany lost all her colonies and territory in Europe at the end of the First World War. This was seen as humiliating and was an important reason why the German people hated the Treaty of Versailles.
- *Limited armed forces*: The German armed forces were severely limited by the Treaty of Versailles. This made Germany appear weak when it had been a great power. This seemed unjust when Germany's rivals kept their military strength.

There were consequences of other peace treaties, too. In the Treaty of St Germain, Austria lost territory to Poland, Romania and Italy. After this Treaty, Austria was no longer a leading power in Europe. Austria also suffered severe economic problems since much of its industry had gone to Czechoslavakia. The Italian Government was not happy with the Treaty of St Germain as it felt Italy should have received more land from Austria. The Treaty of St Germain also gave millions of people in eastern Europe **self-determination** and the freedom to rule themselves.

> **Key terms**
>
> **Reparations:** repair, or compensation for damage caused by the war.
> **Self-determination:** the right of nations to rule themselves.

The effects of the Depression

The Wall Street Crash in 1929 and the Depression that followed had a major effect upon the stability of many nations across the world. As world trade decreased and unemployment rose to record levels, many people began to turn away from the moderate democratic parties to support extreme groups, such as the Nazi Party in Germany.

3.2 The foreign policies of Italy and Japan

Italy

From 1922 to 1943, Italy was a **fascist** dictatorship led by Benito Mussolini. Mussolini's aim was to increase the status of Italy as a major power. He signed the Locarno and Kellogg–Briand treaties, for example, not because he believed in compromise or negotiation but because he thought Italy should be playing a more important role in world affairs.

In the early 1930s, Mussolini was very suspicious of his main fascist rival, Adolf Hitler. He opposed Hitler's attempted takeover of Austria in 1934 and seemed to be drawing closer to Britain and France. Mussolini even joined Britain and France in the Stresa Front, aimed at supporting the terms of the Treaty of Versailles.

From 1935, however, Italy's foreign policy changed. Mussolini:

- began to look for ways to increase Italian territory overseas
- decided to attack Abyssinia to extend Italian land in Eritrea and Somaliland.

The invasion of Abyssinia ruined Italy's relationship with Britain and France and undermined the Stresa agreement. From this point onwards, Italy drew closer to Germany. In 1936, Mussolini signed the Rome–Berlin Axis with Hitler, and in 1939 ties were strengthened with the signing of the Pact of Steel.

> **Key terms**
>
> **Foreign policy:** a set of objectives outlining how a country will interact with other countries.
> **Fascism:** a right-wing system of government generally led by a single strong leader or dictator who uses physical force and intimidation to maintain control and power.

> **Comment**
>
> *In the 1920s, Mussolini was the most important fascist leader in Europe. By the late 1930s, he had fallen under the influence of Hitler, rejected offers of friendship from Britain and France, and allied himself with the Nazis.*

Japan

Japan was one of the victorious powers at the end of the First World War and was rewarded with the takeover of the Mariana, Marshall and Caroline Islands in the Pacific Ocean. Japan developed very quickly into a modern trading nation and depended heavily on importing foreign goods and raw materials.

The Wall Street Crash and Depression had a major impact on Japanese economic growth. Its leaders felt let down by the western capitalist system and began to look for other ways to expand. In 1931, the Japanese decided to attack the Chinese province of Manchuria, to the north of Korea. Manchuria was rich in natural resources and raw materials and would provide a larger market for Japanese goods.

- Despite the attempted intervention of the League of Nations, the Japanese successfully conquered Manchuria and renamed it Manchukuo.
- They installed the former Chinese emperor as head of state.

The expansionist foreign policy continued in 1937 when Japanese forces attacked China. It was the beginning of a long struggle, which finally led to war with Britain and the attack on the US naval base at Pearl Harbor in December 1941.

Failures of the League of Nations

As you saw in the previous chapter these two invasions (Italy invading Abyssinia, and Japan invading Manchuria) also exposed the serious weaknesses of the League of Nations. In particular the failure of the League of Nations to prevent Mussolini invading Abyssinia gave Hitler in Germany confidence that the League of Nations would not try to stop his aggression towards other countries.

> ## Comment
>
> *Unlike Germany and Italy, Japan was never a one-man dictatorship. Moderates within the Government tried to stop the aggressive members within the army and navy. Moreover, the emperor, Hirohito, was not a keen militarist. Nonetheless, Japanese foreign policy was dominated by the need to expand and control much of South-East Asia. As with its European allies, this policy led to war and the defeat of the Japanese armed forces in 1945.*

Revision task

In what ways did the peace treaties, the Depression and the failure of the League of Nations lead to instability in Europe? Copy and complete the table below to show your understanding.

	The effects	How this caused instability
Peace treaties		
The Depression		
Failure of League of Nations		

> **Exam tip** It is important to see the link between the Depression, the failure of the League of Nations, and the aggressive actions of fascist dictators. Japan is a very good example of how all of these ideas are connected.

3.3 The foreign policies of Britain and France (appeasement)

Britain

After the First World War, the main aim of British foreign policy was to deal with the growing problems in Ireland and re-establish British authority in the British empire. Britain hoped that peace in Europe could be maintained by the League of Nations and by helping Germany recover from the war.

By the mid 1920s, there was a good deal of optimism that Europe had entered a new period of stability.

- Germany was admitted to the League of Nations in 1926.
- Tensions between Germany and France eased after the Locarno Treaties.

The World Depression, however, had a major effect on European stability. The Japanese invasion of Manchuria, and failure of the League to act, indicated that Britain would not go to war to support the League.

By the mid 1930s, British foreign policy was based on the idea of appeasing the dictators in Europe.

- They gave into Mussolini in the hope that Mussolini would not join with Hitler.
- British Prime Minister Neville Chamberlain and his government gave concessions to the Germans in the hope that this would maintain peace in Europe.

However by March 1939, when Hitler took over what was left of Czechoslovakia, it was clear that **appeasement** had failed and full-scale rearmament began.

It is easy to criticise the policies followed by Britain during the 1930s. Historians have the advantage of hindsight (knowing what happened). At the time, there were few people who were prepared to see Britain at war again, and the appeasement policy had plenty of backing from the public. British foreign policy failed to prevent war because the Government was not willing (until 1939) to risk going to war to save peace. The losses of the First World War had been so great that governments were willing to look at all alternatives rather than risk the prospect of another war against Germany.

> ### Key terms
>
> **Appeasement:** giving in to the demands of an aggressive country as a way of keeping the peace – for example, Chamberlain's concessions to Germany in the 1930s.

France

Although it was one of the victorious powers in 1918, France suffered heavily in the First World War. The northern part of the country was devastated by war and the country had 5 million dead or injured. A further blow came in 1919 when the USA refused to ratify the Treaty of Versailles and left the French Government no further support against future German aggression.

Successive French governments felt let down by their former allies who, after 1918, seemed to be encouraging German recovery. French foreign policy between 1918 and 1939 was dominated by the search for security against Germany. French policy aimed to protect its frontiers, secure agreement with countries that bordered Germany and avoid risking confrontation with Germany. So:

- Military agreements were signed with Yugoslavia, Czechoslovakia and Romania in the early 1920s.
- French and Belgian troops occupied the Ruhr industrial region of Germany in 1923 when reparations payments were not made.
- From 1929 to 1934, strong defensive fortifications, known as the Maginot Line, were built along the German border from Switzerland to the Belgium frontier.
- In the late 1930s, French policy followed that of Britain. Prime Minister Daladier, along with Neville Chamberlain, was a supporter of appeasement.
- Rather than honour its commitment to defend Czechoslovakia, France joined with Britain in appeasing Hitler at the Munich Conference in 1938.

France and Britain's support for appeasement encouraged Hitler to risk war in order to dismantle the Treaty of Versailles.

> ### Comment
>
> *Throughout the 1920s and 1930s, French foreign policy was based on protection from any future German attack. The building of the Maginot Line, reliance on Britain and alliances with eastern European countries meant that French foreign policy was of a defensive nature.*

3.4 Hitler's foreign policy up to 1939

German foreign policy between 1918 and 1939 falls into two convenient phases.

After the First World War, the priority of the Weimar Republic was to improve political stability at home.

- By the mid-1920s, Germany was recovering from the war. With the help of the Dawes Plan, it was receiving large amounts of financial support from the USA.
- Under Stresemann, German relations with France improved.
- In 1926, Germany was admitted as a member of the League of Nations.

This period of international co-operation did not last for long. The World Depression at the beginning of the 1930s undermined European economies and allowed an extremist group – the Nazis – to seize power.

From 1933, German foreign policy was controlled by Adolf Hitler. His foreign policy aims were to:

- dismantle and abolish the Treaty of Versailles
- create *lebensraum* in eastern Europe
- create union with Austria (*Anschluss*)
- defeat Communism.

The Spanish Civil War, 1936–1939

In 1936, civil war broke out in Spain between the nationalists (fascists) and republicans (Communists and Socialists). Hitler sent the Luftwaffe to assist the nationalists and bombed republican cities such as Guernica. The civil war ended in a nationalist victory in 1939.

The re-occupation of the Rhineland, 1936

One of Hitler's aims was to change parts, if not all of, the Treaty of Versailles.

- Under the Treaty, Germany was not allowed troops in the Rhineland.
- In 1936, France was occupied with domestic problems and Britain was keen not to provoke Germany.
- Hitler took the gamble of sending troops back into the Rhineland.
- German troops were under strict orders to retreat if the French army responded.
- Unwilling to act without the support of Britain, the French did nothing.

The re-occupation of the Rhineland was a clear breach of the Versailles and Locarno agreements and a propaganda triumph for Hitler.

Key terms

Lebensraum: the German word for living space – territory claimed by a country on the grounds that it needs more space to grow and survive (for example, Hitler's claim to land in eastern Europe).

Anschluss: German union with Austria to form a single country.

Comment

Hitler did not hide his hatred of the Treaty of Versailles and looked for every opportunity to strengthen Germany's position in Europe. His foreign policy was based on convincing Britain and France that once Germany had obtained territory lost at Versailles, no further demands would be made.

Comment

The successful re-occupation of the Rhineland by Hitler increased his belief that Britain and France would not stop him achieving his other objectives. To many smaller nations, particularly those in eastern Europe, collective security seemed to have failed. Britain and France began to rearm.

Exam tip

It is important to know the foreign policy aims of the major powers and how successful each country or leader was in achieving those aims.

Revision task

Draw a spider diagram like the one below to show the foreign policy aims of the major powers. You could add lines to show which policies might have alarmed other countries. Label these lines to explain what they show.

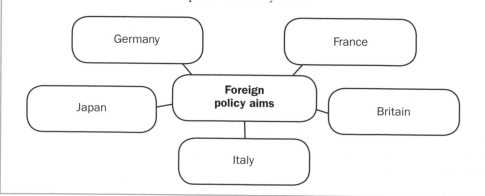

Anschluss, 1938 – the annexation of Austria

Hitler had been born in Austria and one of his objectives was to see Germany and Austria united as one country. He had already tried to take over Austria in 1934. Mussolini, however, was unwilling to see this happen and moved Italian troops to the Austrian border as a warning to Hitler not to act further. By 1938, Hitler and Mussolini had settled their differences and signed the Rome–Berlin Axis. Hitler's success in the Rhineland in 1936 encouraged him to reattempt *Anschluss*.

- Hitler invited the Austrian Chancellor, Schuschnigg, to Germany where he was bullied into accepting a Nazi, Seyss-Inquart, as Austrian Minister of the Interior.
- Schuschnigg retaliated by ordering a **plebiscite** to be held on 13 March to find out if the Austrian people really wanted union with Germany.
- Fearing a 'no' vote, Hitler decided to act quickly. He moved German troops to the Austrian border, and threatened to invade if Schuschnigg did not resign.

Under pressure, Schuschnigg resigned. Seyss-Inquart became Chancellor and invited German troops into Austria. On 12 March 1938, the German army entered Vienna. *Anschluss* was complete. The Nazis organised their own vote about union with Germany and, of those who voted, 99 per cent voted in favour. Austria immediately became a province of the new German *Reich*.

Sudetenland, 1938 – the Munich crisis

In 1919, Czechoslovakia was created out of parts of the old Austro-Hungarian empire. Part of the new Czech state consisted of German-speaking peoples in the area known as the Sudetenland.

- In 1933, when Hitler came to power, the leader of the Sudeten Germans, Konrad Henlein, called for the territory to become independent of Czechoslovakia.
- By 1938, with a number of diplomatic victories behind him, Hitler was ready to extend German territory into the Sudetenland.
- He ordered Henlein to provoke unrest in the area. Newspapers produced allegations of crimes apparently committed by Czechs against Sudeten Germans.
- Hitler threatened war if a solution was not found.

The British Prime Minister, Neville Chamberlain, believed that a peaceful solution could be worked out.

- Lord Runciman was sent to Czechoslovakia to persuade the Czech leader, Edvard Beneš, to accept self-government for the Sudetenland.
- Beneš reluctantly accepted the terms but then Hitler produced new demands in which he claimed the Sudetenland should be part of Germany.

On 22 September, at a meeting at Godesberg, Beneš refused to accept the German demands.

- Chamberlain appealed to Hitler to give him more time to find a settlement.
- The crisis was so grave that the Czech army was mobilised, French reservists were called up, and the British fleet was put on alert.

On 29 September, Chamberlain made one last effort to maintain peace.

- He met with Daladier, the French Prime Minister, Hitler and Mussolini in Munich in a last bid to resolve the Sudeten crisis.
- Neither the Czechs nor their Russian allies were invited to the meeting.

In the settlement, the Sudetenland was given to Germany and a commission was set up to decide which territory the Czechs would lose.

Chamberlain and Hitler had a further meeting in Munich in which both men agreed 'of the desire of our two peoples never to war with one another again'. Chamberlain returned to Britain a hero, having saved Europe from war.

Key terms

Plebiscite: a referendum, or vote, by the entire population on a single issue.
Reich: empire.

Comment

With Anschluss, Hitler's aggressive diplomacy had triumphed yet again and the western powers had shown themselves unwilling to support the terms of the Versailles treaty. Hitler now moved swiftly to achieve his next objective.

Comment

The Munich agreement was the critical point of Chamberlain's appeasement policy. Rather than risk war, Czechoslovakia was betrayed by the same countries (France and Britain) that had earlier guaranteed its frontiers from attack. With the loss of the Sudetenland, Czechoslovakia became a weak, unstable and divided country. Aggressive German foreign policy had once again given Hitler all he demanded. After Munich, few people believed that Hitler could be trusted again.

The Czechoslovakian Government was completely humiliated.

- The vital area of the Sudetenland and its natural raw materials were lost.
- In October and November, Hungary and Poland also occupied other parts of Czech territory without opposition.
- Beneš resigned as president and was replaced by Hacha.
- Hacha created a federal state out of what was left of Czechoslovakia.

The Czech crisis, 1939 – the end of appeasement

In March 1939, Czechoslovakia finally disappeared from the map of Europe. The Czechs were forced to agree to special terms for Germans living under their control. Before any action was taken, however, Hitler invaded what was left of Czechoslovakia. Bohemia and Moravia became a German **protectorate** and Slovakia a German **satellite state**. Ruthenia was handed over to Hungary.

Key terms

Protectorate: a state or territory completely or partly controlled by another state.
Satellite state: a country or region under the influence or control of another state.
Polish corridor: a strip of former German territory given to Poland in 1919 under the terms of the Treaty of Versailles; it provided Poland with access to the Baltic Sea.

Key

October 1938 Teschen taken by Poland

November 1938 to March 1939 Slovak border areas and Ruthenia taken by Hungary

October 1938 Sudetenland region given to Germany in the Munich Agreement

March 1939 Remainder of Czechoslovakia taken under German control

—— German border in 1939

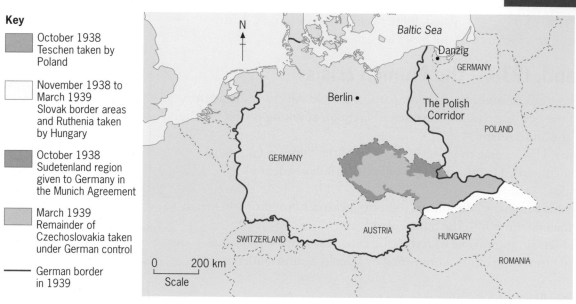

The destruction of Czechoslovakia, 1939.

The Pact of Steel, 1939

Mussolini followed Hitler's example in Czechoslovakia with his own occupation of Albania in May 1939. Hitler had also forced the Lithuanians to hand over Memel in March. In Spain, Madrid fell to fascist leader, Franco, and the nationalist forces supported by Germany and Italy.

It was at this point that Hitler and Mussolini drew their countries together more closely. In May, they signed the Pact of Steel in which they agreed to act 'side by side' in future events.

Poland, 1939

In 1939, Hitler turned his attention to his next target – Poland. In the Treaty of Versailles, German territory had been handed over to the Poles to give them access to the Baltic Sea (**Polish corridor**), and the German city of Danzig had been put under the control of the League of Nations. Following his success in Czechoslovakia, Hitler now demanded the return of Danzig and the 'corridor'.

Following the humiliation at Munich, the French and British Governments now acted firmly. New guarantees of support were given to the Polish, Greek and Romanian Governments and the production of arms increased. The prospect of a future war over Poland now partly hinged on the attitude of the Soviet Government.

Comment

The final occupation of Czechoslovakia in March 1939 had shown the emptiness of Hitler's promises made at Munich. By this time, Britain and France were rapidly rearming, their policy of appeasement having failed. It has been argued by some historians, however, that appeasement gave the French and British vital months in which to prepare their forces for an inevitable war against Germany.

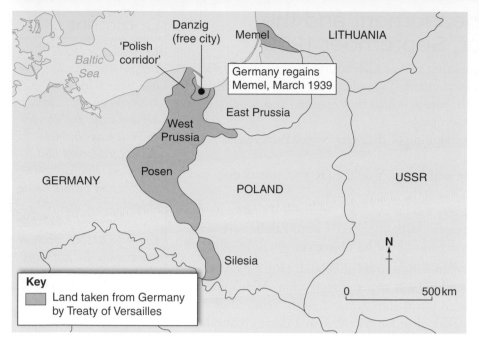

The Polish crisis, 1939.

The Nazi–Soviet Non-Aggression Pact, August 1939

On 23 August 1939, the German Foreign Minister, Ribbentrop, and Soviet Foreign Minister, Molotov, signed the Nazi–Soviet Non-Aggression Pact.

- The Soviets and Germans guaranteed not to fight each other in the event of war.
- In a secret agreement, both powers agreed to divide up Polish territory if war began.
- Hitler also gave Stalin a free hand to occupy Bessarabia in Romania and the Baltic states of Latvia, Estonia and Lithuania.

The news of the Nazi–Soviet Pact shocked the world. Since the beginning of the year, Britain and France had been trying to reach an agreement with Stalin. They hoped to entice him into an agreement so as to threaten Germany on her eastern frontier.

The Nazi–Soviet Pact removed the threat of war for Hitler on two fronts. It also gave him the opportunity he needed to deal with Poland, despite the assurances and threats coming from Britain and France.

Stalin had been suspicious of the British and French approaches; they had sent a low-level team of diplomats to negotiate with him. Hitler, on the other hand, had more to offer the Soviets and the Nazis had sent their high-ranking Foreign Minister, Ribbentrop, to Moscow.

Comment

Europe was now firmly divided into two camps. Both Britain and Germany began to look to the Soviet Union to safeguard their own security. Britain hoped that closer ties with the Soviet Union would threaten Hitler in eastern Europe. Hitler, on the other hand, saw an agreement with the Soviet Union as a means of achieving a solution to the Polish problem.

Comment

The Nazi–Soviet Non-Aggression Pact sealed Poland's fate. Hitler could now act against Poland without the threat of Soviet intervention.

Revision task

What were the main foreign policy aims of Adolf Hitler, and how much had he achieved by September 1939?

Copy and complete the table below.

Hitler's aims	Achievements by 1939
1) Destroy Treaty of Versailles	
2) *Lebensraum* in eastern Europe	
3) *Anschluss* with Austria	
4) Defeat Communism	

3.5 The end of appeasement and the outbreak of war, September 1939

The German occupation of the remaining part of Czechoslovakia in March 1939 (see page 36) marked the end of appeasement. The policy had not stopped Hitler. Now Britain and France increased the rate at which they rearmed and promised to defend Poland if it was invaded by Germany.

In late August 1939, soon after the signing of the Nazi–Soviet Pact, Hitler decided to invade Poland.

- Hitler did not believe that Britain and France would go to war, just as they had not done so over Czechoslovakia.
- Even if war was declared, Poland was too far away for Britain and France to provide practical support. If war came, Hitler decided it would all be over very quickly and he would have achieved another of his objectives.

At dawn on 1 September 1939, German troops invaded Poland. Hitler claimed that Poland had attacked Germany and his was an act of retaliation. After some hesitation, Britain sent the Germans an ultimatum demanding the removal of German forces from Polish territory. The ultimatum expired at 11a.m. on Sunday 3 September and Britain was once again at war with Germany. The French declared war at 5p.m. that afternoon.

Two weeks later, on 15 September, the Soviet Union also invaded Poland and took the Polish territory agreed in the Nazi–Soviet Pact. The Soviets also went on to attack Finland and occupy the Baltic states of Latvia, Estonia and Lithuania. Within six weeks, Poland had been defeated, and disappeared from the map of Europe.

Comment

Until March 1939, Britain and France had tried to appease Hitler by giving in to his demands. In March 1939, it was obvious that appeasement had failed. In response, Britain and France made agreements to defend Poland against potential German attacks, when in reality they did not have the actual means to save Poland from German aggression. This new British and French policy actually encouraged Hitler to threaten Poland since Britain and France would find it very difficult to protect Polish frontiers.

Revision task

Copy and complete the table below to summarise the evidence for and against the policy of appeasement.

Evidence supporting the policy of appeasement	Evidence to show that appeasement was the wrong policy

Here are some key points to consider on either side. You should be able to add others of your own.

- The British Government was more worried about the spread of Communism than they were about Hitler
- Appeasement depended on Hitler being trustworthy. He wasn't.
- Germany was rearming quickly. In the mid-1930s British was not as well armed as Germany
- Britain could not rely on the support of Allies such as the USA or the League of Nations in taking on Hitler
- The Depression had weakened Britain's economy
- Appeasement encouraged other countries to be aggressive
- Appeasement scared Stalin who knew that Hitler might one day want to invade the USSR. It led to the Nazi Soviet Pact.
- Many British politicians also felt that the Treaty of Versailles was unfair
- Delaying war with Germany gave Britain time to rearm

Exam practice

1 Study the source carefully and then answer the questions which follow.

SOURCE A

'Someone is taking someone for a walk'
A cartoon published in the British Sunday newspaper,
The Observer on May 24, 1964.

a) What is the message of this cartoon? Use the details of the cartoon and your own knowledge to explain your answer. *(4 marks)*

b) Explain why Hitler and Stalin signed a non-aggression pact in 1939. *(6 marks)*

Exam tip These are typical of the questions you will face in question 1.

Question a)
This is a starter question. It tests your **factual knowledge and your ability to interpret sources**. Try to show your knowledge and understanding of the period when the cartoon was produced.

Question b)
This tests your knowledge *and* **understanding**.
- A low level answer (worth 1–3 marks) will simply describe one or several reasons why the pact was advantageous for Hitler and Stalin.
- A top level answer (worth 4–6 marks) will explain several reasons why the pact had advantages for Hitler and Stalin and show what each hoped to gain.

Summary/revision plan

You need to have a good working knowledge of the following areas.
Tick off each item once you are confident in your knowledge.

❏ **1 Underlying problems**
- Long-term consequences of the peace treaties
- the effects of the Depression

❏ **2 The foreign policies of Italy and Japan**
- Manchuria
- Abyssinia

❏ **3 The foreign policies of Britain and France**
- appeasement

❏ **4 Hitler's foreign policy up to 1939**
- The Spanish Civil War, 1936–1939
- The re-occupation of the Rhineland, 1936
- *Anschluss*, 1938 – the annexation of Austria
- Sudetenland, 1938 – the Munich Crisis
- The Czech crisis, 1939 – the end of appeasement
- The Pact of Steel, 1939
- Poland, 1939
- Nazi–Soviet Non-Aggression Pact, August 1939

❏ **5 The end of appeasement and the outbreak of war, September 1939.**

Check your knowledge online with our Quick quizzes at www.hodderplus.co.uk/modernworldhistory.

During the Second World War, the USA and the USSR fought on the same side. When the war ended in 1945, relations between the Allies got worse. Soon a new type of conflict developed between the USA and the USSR – the Cold War. In this chapter, you will look at how and why this happened.

Focus points

Each key question in the OCR course is divided into focus points. To do well in the examination, you will need a good understanding of each focus point.

- Why did the USA–USSR alliance begin to break down in 1945?
- How had the USSR gained control of eastern Europe by 1948?
- How did the USA react to Soviet expansionism?
- Who was more to blame for the start of the Cold War, the USA or the USSR?

Key content

In order to fully understand the focus points, you will need to have a good working knowledge of:

- the beginnings of the Cold War
- the Allied conferences at Yalta and Potsdam in 1945 and the roles of Churchill, Roosevelt and Stalin
- the breakdown of the USA–USSR alliance, 1945–46
- Soviet expansion in eastern Europe; the Iron Curtain
- US policy on eastern Europe: the Truman Doctrine and the Marshall Plan
- the Berlin Blockade and its immediate consequences.

4.1 The beginnings of the Cold War

Damage caused by the Second World War

During the Second World War, millions of lives were lost on all sides as the table on the right shows. This does not include the millions of people who were killed in the Holocaust.

Bombing and fighting on the ground had destroyed houses, factories, shops and entire cities. By 1945, there were millions of sick, hungry and homeless refugees throughout Europe and the rest of the world.

Country	Military deaths	Civilians deaths
Britain	326,000	62,000
France	340,000	470,000
Germany	3,250,000	3,810,000
Japan	1,380,000	933,000
Italy	330,000	80,000
USSR	13,600,000	7,700,000
USA	500,000	5,662

The disruption to all countries at the end of the war meant it was very difficult to be sure about the numbers of killed and wounded. What is certain is that the USSR lost millions of its people as a result of the war with Germany, and Stalin was determined to make the USSR secure in future. In addition, China also suffered millions of civilian casualties owing to its war with Japan.

The rise of the superpowers

Perhaps the most important change brought about by the Second World War was the rise of the superpowers. Before the war, there had been many countries in the world that could claim to be great powers, such as the USA, the USSR, Britain, France, Germany and Japan. By 1945, it had become clear that the military strength of the USA and the USSR put them in a league of their own as superpowers.

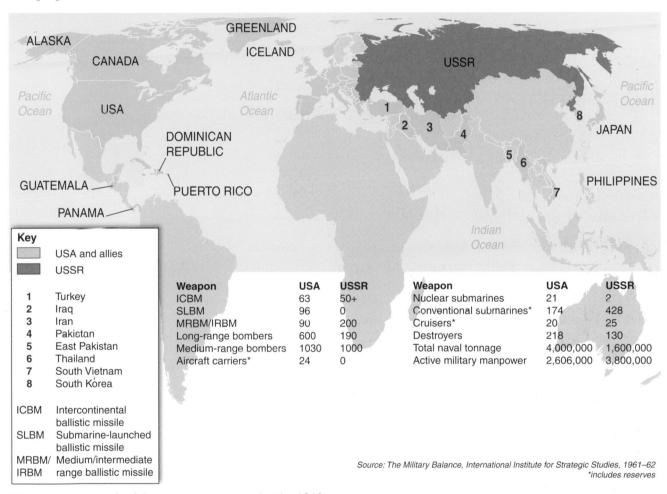

Key

	USA and allies
	USSR

1	Turkey
2	Iraq
3	Iran
4	Pakistan
5	East Pakistan
6	Thailand
7	South Vietnam
8	South Korea

ICBM	Intercontinental ballistic missile
SLBM	Submarine-launched ballistic missile
MRBM/ IRBM	Medium/intermediate range ballistic missile

Weapon	USA	USSR	Weapon	USA	USSR
ICBM	63	50+	Nuclear submarines	21	2
SLBM	96	0	Conventional submarines*	174	428
MRBM/IRBM	90	200	Cruisers*	20	25
Long-range bombers	600	190	Destroyers	218	130
Medium-range bombers	1030	1000	Total naval tonnage	4,000,000	1,600,000
Aircraft carriers*	24	0	Active military manpower	2,606,000	3,800,000

Source: The Military Balance, International Institute for Strategic Studies, 1961–62
*includes reserves

The military strength of the two superpowers by the 1960s.

Conflicting ideologies: Communism and Capitalism

During the war, the Communist superpower, the USSR, had united with the capitalist superpower, the USA, to defeat **fascism**. However, Communism and Capitalism were very different **ideologies** and economic systems strongly opposed to one another.

Key terms

Fascism: a right-wing system of government generally led by a single strong leader or dictator who uses physical force and intimidation to maintain control and power.

Ideology: a set of beliefs and characteristics.

The USA

What were the main political and economic features of the USA?

- A democratic system of government. The President and **Congress** of the USA were chosen in free democratic elections.
- A capitalist economy. Business and property were privately owned. Individuals could make profits in business or move jobs if they wished.
- The USA was the world's wealthiest country, but under capitalism there were always great contrasts – some people were very rich, others very poor.
- Americans believed in the freedom of the individual and in government by consent.

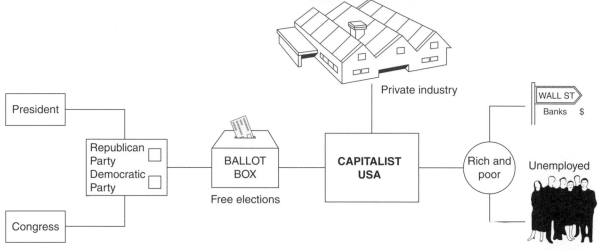

The main political and economic features of the USA.

In the 1920s and 1930s, the USA had followed a policy of **isolationism**. Now faced by Communism extending into eastern Europe, the US Government was prepared to help and support people and countries that wanted to become democracies with capitalist economies. This was seen as simply the defence of people's freedom against a system they did not want.

The USSR

The USSR was a Communist state under Stalin's dictatorship.

- People could vote in elections for the **Supreme Soviet**. But they could only vote for members of the Communist Party, and the Supreme Soviet had no real power. The USSR was governed by Stalin and committees of the Communist Party.
- In the Communist system, people's lives were closely controlled. The rights of individuals were seen as less important than the good of society as a whole.
- It had a planned economy. The Government owned all industry and planned what every factory should produce.
- The standard of living in the USSR was much lower than in the USA, but unemployment was low, and there were not the extremes of wealth and poverty as in the USA.
- Unlike the USA, the USSR had been attacked many times in the past. Stalin was determined that this would never happen again. In his view, the USSR could only be safe if the countries on its borders were controlled by Communist governments. He believed that if he did not set up other Communist governments, the USA would set up hostile countries on his borders.

Key terms

Congress: the American representative assemblies (the equivalent of Parliament in Britain). There are two houses, the Senate and the House of Representatives.

Isolationism: withdrawing from international politics and policies.

Supreme Soviet: an elected body of representatives (the equivalent of the British Parliament), but which had no real power. It only met for two weeks a year. It was the Communist Party under Stalin that made the important decisions.

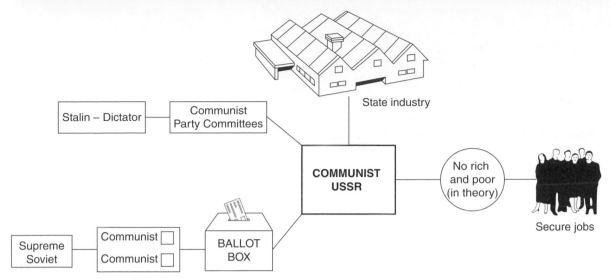

The main political and economic features of the USSR.

Revision tasks

1 Use six key words to summarise the USA's system of government. Then choose six key words to contrast the USSR's system. Compare the two in a table like the one below.

USA	USSR

2 Explain why Stalin was determined to keep control of eastern Europe.

While the two countries had Hitler as a common enemy they could work together. Once Hitler was defeated the relationship would be severely tested.

4.2 The Allied conferences at Yalta and Potsdam and the roles of Churchill, Roosevelt and Stalin

By early 1945, it was clear that Germany would be defeated. The minds of the Allied leaders turned to the problems that peace would bring. To discuss these matters, they met for conferences at Yalta and Potsdam.

The aim of the conferences at Yalta and Potsdam was to discuss the challenges that the defeat of Germany would bring. These were:
- what to do with Germany and its leaders once Germany had surrendered
- what was to happen to the occupied countries after they had been liberated, especially the countries of eastern Europe
- how to bring the war with Japan to a speedy end
- how to create and maintain a peace that would last.

The Yalta Conference, February 1945

At the Yalta Conference, the Allied leaders (Churchill, Roosevelt and Stalin) got on well together, despite their differences. The following points were agreed.
- Germany would be divided into four zones. These would be run by the USA, France, Britain and the USSR.
- Germany's capital city, Berlin (which was in the Soviet zone), would also be divided into four zones.
- The countries of eastern Europe would be allowed to hold free elections to decide how they would be governed.
- The USSR would join the war against Japan in return for territory in Manchuria and Sakhalin Island.

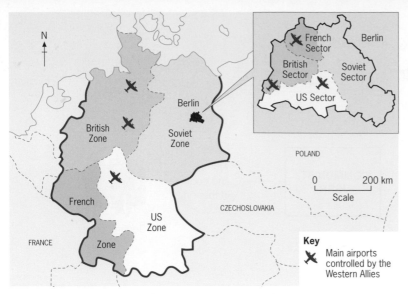

The division of Germany after the Second World War.

The only real disagreement was about Poland. Stalin wanted to move Poland's frontier westward into German territory. Churchill and Roosevelt were unhappy about this, but with thousands of Soviet troops still in Poland there was little alternative but to agree. To compensate, Stalin agreed not to support the Communist rebels in Greece.

The Potsdam Conference, July–August 1945

A second conference was arranged in the Berlin suburb of Potsdam in July 1945, two months after the war in Europe had ended. By the time this second conference was held, five months after Yalta, a number of changes had taken place that would significantly affect the relationship between the Allied powers.

- *Changing leaders*: In April 1945, President Roosevelt died suddenly and was succeeded by Vice-President Harry Truman. He was much more anti-Communist than Roosevelt and very suspicious of Stalin's intentions. During the conference, there was a general election in Britain and Clement Attlee replaced Churchill as Prime Minister.

Attlee   **Truman**   **Stalin**

- *Victory in Europe and the Soviet army*: Germany surrendered on 8 May 1945. Britain and the USA immediately began to reduce their forces in Europe, but the Soviets, who occupied much of eastern Europe, did not. Stalin ignored British and American protests about the creation of a Communist government in Poland, saying that he needed to protect the USSR's borders.
- *The atom bomb*: At the Potsdam Conference, Truman informed Stalin about a new weapon he was about to use against Japan. The successful testing of the atom bomb in July 1945 began a new arms race between the USA and USSR.

Potsdam continued the discussions left over from the Yalta Conference. There was agreement on some points.

- The Nazi Party was to be banned and its leaders would be tried as war criminals.
- The Oder–Neisse line (two rivers) was to form part of the future border between Poland and Germany.

However, on other issues there were disagreements. There were clear signs that Stalin did not trust Truman and Attlee and that they did not trust him.

Exam practice

1 What were the aims of the Allied leaders at the Yalta and Potsdam Conferences in 1945? *(4 marks)*

Exam tip This is typical of the questions you will face in questions 2 or 3.

This is a starter question. It tests your **factual knowledge**. Try to include four details about what the Allied leaders were trying to achieve.

Tensions at Potsdam

1 Britain and the USA denied Stalin a naval base in the Mediterranean.
   - They saw no need for Stalin to have such a base.
   - Stalin saw this as evidence that his allies mistrusted him.

2 Stalin wanted to take more **reparations** from Germany than Britain and the USA thought was necessary.
   - The USA and Britain did not wish to cripple Germany; they had seen the results of reparations after the First World War.
   - Stalin was suspicious about why his allies seemed to want to protect Germany and even help it recover.

3 Stalin had set up a Communist government in Lublin, then the capital of Poland. Britain preferred the non-Communist Polish Government, which had lived in exile in Britain throughout the war. Truman and Attlee were very suspicious of Stalin's motives in setting up a Communist government.

Comment

It was almost inevitable that tensions and differences in policy between the new superpowers would lead to resentment and mistrust. The factors that had made them friends had disappeared. There was no common enemy and no reason to work together any longer. The build-up of arms, growing self-interest and differences over eastern Europe, in particular, created tension and suspicion.

Revision tasks

1 Make a copy of the table below and add notes on what was agreed and the areas of disagreement.

Conference	Points agreed	Areas of disagreement
Yalta		
Potsdam		

2 What important changes had occurred between the Yalta and Potsdam Conferences and how did these changes affect relations between the allies?

Exam practice

1 Explain why the USA–USSR alliance began to break down in 1945.   *(6 marks)*

Exam tip This tests your knowledge *and* **understanding**.
- A low level answer (worth 1–3 marks) will simply describe one or two reasons why the Americans and Soviets began to fall out in 1945.
- A better answer (worth 4–6 marks) will need to describe AND explain the different objectives of the Americans and Soviets at the end of the war and how each hoped to strengthen their position as world powers.

4.3 Soviet expansion in eastern Europe

	Troops in Europe (millions)	
	1945	1946
USA	3.1	0.4
UK	1.3	0.5
USSR	6.0	6.0

The Soviet army advanced through large areas of eastern Europe whilst driving back the Germans. One year after the war, many Soviet troops remained in much of eastern Europe, as the table on the right shows. Communist governments were elected or imposed on each country.

'The Iron Curtain'

In a speech in March 1946, the former British Prime Minister, Winston Churchill, claimed that an 'Iron Curtain' had descended across Europe, separating the democratic nations of the West from the Communist controlled states of eastern Europe.

Creating satellites

Elections were held in each eastern European country as promised at Yalta in 1945, but the evidence suggests that they were rigged to allow the USSR-backed Communist parties to take control. In Bulgaria, Albania, Poland, Romania and Hungary, opponents of the Communists had been beaten, murdered or frightened into submission. By May 1948, all eastern European states had Communist governments.

Stalin created Cominform and later Comecon – a trading alliance of Communist countries – to help him keep a tight grip on his neighbours. These countries became known as **satellite states** because their governments and economies depended so heavily on the USSR.

> **Comment**
>
> *Stalin was simply carrying out his policy to ensure he had friendly governments on his doorstep to reduce the risk of future invasion. However, to the British and Americans Stalin seemed to be trying to build up a Communist empire.*

Cominform, 1947

Stalin set up the Cominform – an alliance of Communist countries – in 1947, probably as a response to Marshall Aid (see page 47). Its aim was to spread Stalin's Communist ideas. Cominform helped Stalin tighten his hold on his Communist allies because it restricted their contact with the West.

Only one Communist leader, Marshall Tito of Yugoslavia, was not prepared to accept Stalin's leadership and he split with Moscow. However, Yugoslavia remained Communist, but was cut off from any type of support from the USSR.

Comecon, 1949

Comecon was set up by Stalin to co-ordinate the production and trade of the eastern European countries. It was rather like an early Communist version of the European Economic Community. However, Comecon favoured the USSR far more than any of its other members.

4.4 US policy on eastern Europe: the Truman Doctrine and the Marshall Plan

Greece

You can see from the map on page 47 that Greece appeared to be the next country likely to fall under Communist control. Greek resistance to the Germans had been divided into two movements – the royalists (who wanted the return of the king) and the Communists. After the war, the royalists restored the king with the help of British troops. However, they came under attack from Communist forces and asked the USA for help in 1947.

Truman was already very worried about the spread of Communism. Under a **foreign policy** initiative that became known as the Truman **Doctrine**, the USA provided Greece with arms and money. The Communists were eventually defeated in 1949 after a civil war.

> **Key terms**
>
> **Satellite state:** a country or region under the influence or control of another state.
> **Foreign policy:** a set of objectives outlining how a country will interact with other countries.
> **Doctrine:** a statement of ideas.

The Truman Doctrine, 1947

Events in Greece convinced Truman that unless he acted, Communism would continue to spread. He therefore explained the Truman Doctrine to the world. Truman said:

> *I believe it must be the policy of the USA to support all free people who are resisting attempted subjugation by armed minorities or by outside pressure.*

- The USA would not return to isolationism – it would play a leading world role.
- The aim was to contain (stop the spread of) Communism but not to push it back. This was the policy of **containment**.

Under the Truman Doctrine, the USA provided military and economic aid to Turkey as well as Greece.

At this point, it became clear that a **cold war** – the term was first used by one of President Truman's advisers in 1947 – had started. The two sides believed in totally different political ideas. Each side feared the spread of the other idea. When one tried to extend its influence or support (for example, the USSR in eastern Europe), this was seen as a threat by the other side.

Greece and the spread of Communism.

Marshall Aid, 1947

Truman believed that poverty and hardship provided a breeding ground for Communism, so he wanted to make Europe prosperous again. It was also important for American businesses to have trading partners in the future, yet Europe's economies were still in ruins after the war.

The American Secretary of State, George Marshall, therefore visited Europe and came up with a European recovery programme – usually known as the Marshall Plan or Marshall Aid. This had two main aims:
- to stop the spread of Communism (although Truman did not admit this at the time)
- to help the economies of Europe to recover (this would eventually provide a market for American exports).

Billions of dollars poured into Europe in the years 1947–51, providing vital help for Europe's economic recovery. However, Marshall Aid also caused tensions.
- Only sixteen European countries accepted it – and these were all western European states.
- Stalin refused Marshall Aid for the USSR and banned eastern European countries from accepting it.

The Communist takeover in Czechoslovakia, 1948

The only eastern European country that considered accepting Marshall Aid was Czechoslovakia. Czechoslovakia was not fully part of Stalin's 'eastern bloc' of countries – Communists were not fully in control. In the spring of 1948, elections were due and it seemed likely that the Communists (who were opposed to accepting Marshall Aid) would do badly, while the opposition (who were in favour) would do well.

Key terms

Containment: a foreign policy aimed at containing the political influence or military power of another country – for example, US policy to stop the spread of Communism during the Cold War.

Cold War: political hostility between countries that stops short of actual armed conflict.

Comment

Marshall Aid was a generous gesture by the USA but it was not entirely an act of kindness. Stalin saw it as an attempt by American business to dominate western Europe. If the USA was determined to 'buy' western Europe with its dollars, then he was determined to control eastern Europe with his Communist allies and the Red Army.

Communists organised marches and protests. Non-Communist ministers resigned and Foreign Minister Jan Masaryk died under suspicious circumstances. In May 1948, elections took place but only Communists were allowed to stand. Czechoslovakia was now fully part of the Communist eastern bloc.

Comment

East and West were now completely divided. Czechoslovakia had been a link between them. Although there is no definite proof, historians believe that Stalin did not want a link between East and West and that the USSR was behind the takeover in Czechoslovakia.

Revision task

Copy and complete the table below to explain why relations between the USSR and USA had broken down by 1947.

Contributing factor or event	How this undermined relations between the USSR and the USA
Yalta Conference	
Potsdam Conference	
Post-war aims of the USA and the USSR	
Events in Greece and eastern Europe	
Truman Doctrine and Marshall Plan	

4.5 The Berlin Blockade and its immediate consequences

This was the first major crisis of the Cold War.

Causes

At the end of the war, the Allies divided Germany and Berlin into zones (see map on page 44). Germany's economy and government had been shattered by the war and the Allies were faced with a serious question: should they continue to occupy Germany or should they try to rebuild it?

- Britain and the USA wanted Germany to recover – they could not afford to keep supporting Germany and they felt that punishing Germany would not help future peace.
- The French were unsure about whether to help German economic recovery or keep Germany weak.
- The USSR did not want to rebuild Germany and Stalin was suspicious about American and British intentions.

In 1948, the French, American and British zones merged to become one zone, 'Trizonia'. With the help of Marshall Aid, West Germany began to recover and prosper. It was a very different story in East Germany. In this area, controlled by the USSR, there was poverty and hunger.

To Stalin, it seemed that the Allies were building up West Germany in order to attack him. When they introduced a new West German currency (the Deutsche Mark), it was the last straw.

The Berlin Blockade

Stalin could not stop the introduction of a new currency or the merging of the western zones into one zone, but because Berlin itself was deep in the Soviet-controlled zone, he could cut West Berlin's physical links with the West. In June 1948 Soviet troops set up road and rail blocks to prevent any goods reaching Berlin. He hoped to force the Allies to withdraw. Many people feared that this could provoke war.

The Berlin Airlift

The Allied response was to fly in supplies by air. The early flights were tense. People feared Soviet troops might try to shoot down the planes, but they did not. And for the next ten months the Allies supplied West Berlin with everything it needed by air. One plane landed every three minutes day and night. By May 1949 when it was clear the Blockade had failed, Stalin reopened communications.

The effects of the Berlin Blockade

The success of the western powers in preventing a Communist takeover of West Berlin had far reaching consequences.

- In May 1949, the British, French and US zones became the Federal Republic of Germany, known as West Germany.
- In October 1949, the Soviet-occupied zone in Germany became the German Democratic Republic (GDR).

NATO (The North Atlantic Treaty Organisation), 1949

This military alliance contained most of the states in western Europe as well as the USA and Canada. Its main purpose was to defend each of its members from attack. If one member was attacked, all the others would help to defend it.

The Warsaw Pact, 1955

In 1955, West Germany joined NATO. The Soviet response was to set up the Warsaw Pact – a Communist version of NATO. The Soviets had not forgotten the damage that Germany had done to the USSR in the Second World War.

Comment

The Berlin Blockade had shown that the USA and USSR were not prepared to go to war with each other despite their differences. Each country used propaganda to undermine the other, but their leaders knew that actual conflict with the use of nuclear weapons could leave both countries in ruins.

Berlin, however, continued to remain a flashpoint for superpower conflict. The Cold War was to deepen further during the 1950s and early 1960s before a thaw began.

Revision task

Copy and complete the table below to help you to answer the following question:

Was the USSR or the USA more to blame for the Cold War? What is the evidence that supports your answer? (You may not fill in all the cells)

	Evidence that the USSR was to blame	Evidence that the USA was to blame	Evidence that neither the USSR or the USA was to blame
Relations between the USA and the USSR before and during the Second World War			
Changing relationships between the leaders of the USA and the USSR			
Yalta and Potsdam conferences			
Soviet and American policies on Greece and eastern Europe			
Berlin Blockade and Airlift 1948–9			
Creation of NATO and the Warsaw Pact			

Exam practice

1 How far was the USSR able to dominate eastern Europe by 1955? *(10 marks)*

Exam tip Exams often ask about the factors that caused the Cold War and which were the most important.

Exam tip This question tests your knowledge and understanding but also goes further. A question that starts 'How far …' is also inviting you to **evaluate**. In your exam, question 2c) or 3c) will usually include an element of evaluation like this.

You know that the USSR had its army in many countries at the end of Second World War but this question is also asking you to evaluate how successful were the Soviets in dominating these countries. For example, does the Berlin Blockade and Airlift in 1949 tell us anything about the extent of Soviet domination of eastern Europe?

Summary/revision plan

You need to have a good working knowledge of the following areas. **Tick off each item** once you are confident in your knowledge.

❑ **1 The beginnings of the Cold War**
- Damage caused by the Second World War
- The rise of the superpowers
- Conflicting ideologies: Communism and Capitalism

❑ **2 The Allied conferences at Yalta and Potsdam and the roles of Churchill, Roosevelt and Stalin**
- The Yalta Conference, February 1945
- The Potsdam Conference, July–August 1945

❑ **3 Soviet expansion in eastern Europe**
- The Iron Curtain
- Creating satellites
- Cominform, 1947
- Comecon, 1949

❑ **4 US policy on eastern Europe: the Truman Doctrine and the Marshall Plan**
- Greece
- The Truman Doctrine, 1947
- Marshall Aid, 1947
- The Communist takeover in Czechoslovakia, 1948

❑ **5 The Berlin Blockade and its immediate consequences**
- The Berlin Blockade and Airlift, 1948–49
- The effects of the Berlin Blockade
- NATO (The North Atlantic Treaty Organisation), 1949
- The Warsaw Pact, 1955.

Check your knowledge online with our Quick quizzes at www.hodderplus.co.uk/modernworldhistory.

Chapter 5: Who won the Cuban missile crisis?

In October 1962, the world was brought to the brink of nuclear war as the USA and USSR faced each other in a conflict over the island of Cuba. The USA was trying to contain the spread of Communism but faced problems in Cuba where Communists had seized power. In this chapter, you will learn how the USA reacted to the Cuban revolution and why the Cuban missile crisis almost led to a nuclear war.

Focus points

Each key question in the OCR course is divided into focus points. To do well in the examination, you will need a good understanding of each focus point.

- How did the USA react to the Cuban revolution?
- Why did Khrushchev put missiles into Cuba?
- Why did Kennedy react as he did?
- Who won the Cuban missile crisis?

Key content

In order to fully understand the focus points, you will need to have a good working knowledge of:

- the Cuban revolution and the reaction of the USA
- the Bay of Pigs invasion
- the beginnings of the missile crisis
- the missile crisis – day by day
- the end of the crisis and its consequences.

5.1 The Cuban revolution and the reaction of the USA

Cuba is a large island in the Caribbean Sea. It is only 144 km from the coast of the USA. For many years, the USA was very happy with the political and economic situation in Cuba.

- US businesses dominated Cuba. They owned its major industries (sugar and tobacco).
- US tourists enjoyed holidays in Cuba, especially in the capital, Havana.
- The USA dominated Cuba militarily – there was a large US naval base at Guantanamo.

The USA supported the leader of Cuba, Fulgencio Batista. The USA knew Batista was a corrupt and unpopular dictator. Despite this, it supported him because he was anti-Communist.

In 1959, US policy went terribly wrong. From 1956, a young Communist called Fidel Castro had led a campaign of guerrilla warfare against Batista and eventually overthrew him in 1959.

- Castro took over many US-owned businesses.
- He also took over much US-owned land.
- He gave the land to ordinary Cuban farmers.
- He forged close links with the USSR (led by Nikita Khrushchev).
- Khrushchev sent him advisers, economic aid and military equipment.

5.2 The Bay of Pigs invasion

The USA was furious at Castro's actions (and Khrushchev's support for Castro). From 1959 to 1961, there was a tense, frosty relationship between the USA and Cuba. During this time, the USA gave support to Cubans who had left Cuba to get away from Castro.

In January 1961, US President Eisenhower broke off diplomatic relations with Cuba, and this policy continued under Eisenhower's successor, President Kennedy. He supplied weapons and transport for 1,500 Cuban exiles to land in Cuba and overthrow Castro. They landed at the Bay of Pigs and were met by 20,000 Cuban troops with weapons supplied by the USSR. The Bay of Pigs was a humiliating disaster for Kennedy.

The failure at the Bay of Pigs was bad enough for Kennedy, but he also feared that it would encourage other countries to become Communist and risk becoming enemies of the USA. The crisis also further strengthened Castro's position in Cuba. Khrushchev had already decided that Kennedy was weak and unwilling to use force over Cuba. He met Kennedy in June 1961 in Vienna, but the talks did not go well and gave Khrushchev the view that the USA would not back up its **containment** policy by using force. This led directly to the Cuban missile crisis in October 1962.

5.3 The beginnings of the missile crisis

After the Bay of Pigs, Khrushchev gave Castro large amounts of Soviet military equipment to prevent a follow-up American-supported invasion of Cuba.

The Americans became increasingly alarmed about the Soviet military build-up in Cuba. In September 1962, the Soviets told Kennedy they had no intention of placing nuclear missiles in Cuba; it was a lie.

Why did Khrushchev put missiles in Cuba?

The USSR supplied many of its allies with non-nuclear weapons, but the Cuban crisis was the first time that nuclear weapons were installed outside Soviet boundaries. There were several reasons for Khrushchev's actions.

- Khrushchev wanted to produce more nuclear warheads and close the 'missile gap' between the USA and the USSR.
- The USA had missiles in Western Europe and Turkey, well within range of the USSR. Placing missiles in Cuba would help restore the missile balance.
- The USSR had many more cheap, medium-range missiles than the USA so a launch site in Cuba, close to the US coast, was an ideal place to put missiles.
- Soviet missiles in Cuba would strengthen Khrushchev's bargaining position against the USA.
- Khrushchev was very keen to defend Castro. Cuba was the only Communist country in the **western hemisphere** and had just survived the Bay of Pigs attack.
- Khrushchev was keen to strengthen his own political position in the USSR. Missiles in Cuba would be seen as another major propaganda victory against the USA.

Exam practice

1 Describe the main events in the Bay of Pigs invasion in 1961. *(4 marks)*

Exam tip These are typical of the questions you will face in questions 2 or 3.

This is a starter question. It tests your **factual knowledge**. Try to include four details about the Cuban exiles' attempted invasion of Cuba and who supported them.

Key terms

Containment: a foreign policy aimed at containing the political influence or miilitary power of another country – for example, US policy to stop the spread of Communism during the Cold War.
Western hemisphere: the area of the world that includes North America, South America and Central America.

Exam tip History is often about cause and effect, and explaining why people did what they did. In this case, it is really important that you understand the reasons why Khrushchev allowed Soviet missiles to be placed in Cuba and the effect this had on the USA.

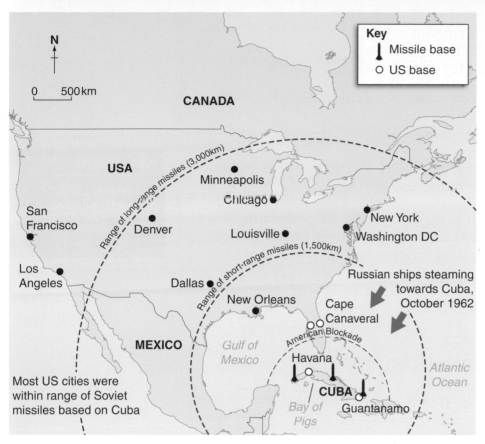

The location of missile sites in Cuba and the threat posed to US cities.

How could the US respond?

On 14 October 1962, a US spy plane photographed the construction of nuclear missile sites on Cuba. In the days that followed, Kennedy and his advisers had several options. They were:

Do nothing

For: The USA still had a much larger nuclear force than the USSR. Overreacting to the Cuban missiles might lead to a nuclear war between the USA and USSR.

Against: To do nothing would be seen as a sign of weakness and encourage the Soviets to challenge the USA elsewhere in the world, possibly in Berlin.

Surgical air strike: an immediate air strike against missile sites in Cuba.

For: Destroy the missiles before they became operational.

Against: The US air force could not guarantee to destroy all the missiles. Some might be launched against US cities and kill millions of people. Bombing Cuban missile sites would inevitably kill Soviet soldiers, too, and this would cause Khrushchev to respond. Bombing a small country such as Cuba without warning would be seen as a very aggressive act by many other countries.

Invasion: a full-scale US invasion of Cuba.

For: Remove the missile bases and Castro from power.

Against: This would cause an inevitable Soviet response – possibly an invasion of West Berlin and nuclear war.

Diplomatic pressure: to involve the United Nations and other international organisations to resolve the dispute.

For: Involvement of other countries might force the Soviets to remove the missiles.

Against: It was very unlikely that diplomacy would cause Khrushchev to give way, so this option was seen as very weak.

Blockade (quarantine): US navy to stop Soviet ships delivering any further weapons to Cuba, along with a demand for missiles already in Cuba to be removed.

For: This would show firm action by the USA without using immediate force. It would give Khrushchev time to consider his next actions, and the USA the option of an air strike or invasion later if the blockade did not work.

Against: A blockade would not remove the weapons already in Cuba. Action was likely to be slow in producing results. It did not rule out Soviet retaliation in other parts of world – for example, Berlin.

5.4 The missile crisis – day by day

9 October 1962	Kennedy orders a US U-2 spy plane reconnaissance flight over Cuba. The flight was delayed until 14 October because of bad weather.
14 October 1962	A U-2 flying over western Cuba takes photographs of missile sites under construction.
15 October 1962	US intelligence agencies analyse the photos and confirm that Soviet nuclear missiles have been placed in Cuba.
16 October 1962	Kennedy forms a group of advisers called EX-COMM, which begins to discuss in secret how to respond to the crisis.
17 October 1962	Kennedy continues his normal duties as President so as not to arouse suspicion while EX-COMM works on possible options.
18 October 1962	Soviet Foreign Minister, Gromyko, and Kennedy meet but Gromyko denies that there are any 'offensive' missiles in Cuba, and Kennedy does not tell him of his discovery.
21 October 1962	Kennedy's military advisers tell him that an air strike could not guarantee to destroy all Soviet missiles in Cuba. Kennedy decides on a blockade (quarantine) of Cuba.
22 October 1962	Kennedy broadcasts live on US TV and tells the American public about the existence of the missiles and his intention to quarantine Cuba as the first step to getting them removed.
23 October 1962	The Organisation of American States (OAS) unanimously supports the blockade of Cuba by the USA.
24 October 1962	The US blockade of Cuba begins. Soviet ships sailing to Cuba with questionable cargo either slow down or turn around, except for one. American military forces are put on alert and go to DEFCON 2, one step short of war.

26 October 1962	Kennedy is informed that evidence from reconnaissance flights shows that the missile sites are nearing completion. Khrushchev sends a private letter to Kennedy proposing to remove Soviet missiles if Kennedy publicly announces that he will never invade Cuba.
27 October 1962	A new official letter from Khrushchev arrives, proposing a public trade of Soviet missiles in Cuba for US missiles in Turkey. An American U-2 spy plane is shot down over Cuba, killing the pilot Major Rudolf Anderson. Kennedy decides to delay an attack on Cuba. He ignores Khrushchev's second letter and agrees to the terms in the first letter. Kennedy sends his brother Robert, one of his advisers, to meet the Soviet ambassador in Washington DC. The Soviets are told secretly that the USA will not invade Cuba and will remove its missiles from Turkey within 6 months. If the Soviets do not agree to this deal, Kennedy informs them that the USA will invade Cuba immediately.
28 October 1962	Khrushchev announces on Radio Moscow that he has agreed to remove the missiles from Cuba.

Why did Kennedy react as he did?

There was no doubt as to the seriousness of the Cuban missile crisis.

- Kennedy was under serious pressure from US military leaders to bomb and invade Cuba immediately. This would have almost certainly led to a war with the USSR.
- Instead, Kennedy tried to give himself and Khrushchev a means of solving the crisis without immediate conflict. This is why he chose a blockade.
- Kennedy also realised that he needed to give Khrushchev a way out without appearing to humiliate the Soviet leader – that is why, in private, he agreed not to invade Cuba and later remove US missiles from Turkey.
- Kennedy used the opportunity of Khrushchev's first letter to explore ways to solve the crisis whilst at the same time convincing the Soviets that he was prepared for war.

Revision task

How far was the Cuban missile crisis a real threat to world peace?

Copy and complete the table below to show how far the events of the crisis and the actions of the leading figures caused a real threat.

Reasons it was a real threat to peace	Reasons it was a little threat to peace

Revision task

Using the calendar on pages 54–55, draw a very simple timeline of your own to show the key events in the Cuban missile crisis. Highlight what you consider to be the most important events during the crisis.

Exam practice

1 Explain why President Kennedy chose to blockade rather than invade Cuba in October 1962. *(6 marks)*

Exam tip This tests your knowledge *and* **understanding**.
- A low level answer (worth 1–3 marks) will simply describe one or two reasons why President Kennedy chose blockade instead of invasion.
- A better answer (worth 4–6 marks) will need to describe AND explain the advantages and disadvantages of the different options facing President Kennedy in his attempt to remove Soviet nuclear missiles from Cuba.

5.5 The end of the crisis and its consequences

On the morning of 28 October, Radio Moscow broadcast that the USSR was prepared to remove the missiles from Cuba. The missile crisis was over, but important lessons had been learned by both sides.

- Firstly, it is widely agreed that the Cuban missile crisis was the closest that the USA and USSR came to nuclear conflict throughout the whole of the **Cold War**. There was general agreement that future disputes like this had to be avoided, so the missile crisis actually helped improve US–Soviet relations.
- Secondly, the USA and USSR decided to set up a telephone link (hotline) between Moscow and Washington DC so that problems could be discussed to avoid future crises.
- Thirdly, nuclear arms talks began and, in 1963, a Test Ban Treaty was signed by the USSR, the USA and Britain.

So who won the Cuban missile crisis and what were the outcomes for the USA, the USSR and Cuba?

The USA

- Kennedy was immediately seen by world opinion as the 'victor' in the Cuban missile crisis. He had stood up to the Soviets and they had backed down.
- Kennedy had also successfully stood up to some of his hard-line military advisers who wanted to invade Cuba. The crisis showed how dangerous their ideas were.

BUT

- Kennedy also agreed in secret not to invade Cuba and, more controversially, to remove NATO missiles from Turkey at a later date.
- Castro remained in power in Cuba and so the Communist threat remained.
- Kennedy had made plenty of enemies. He was now distrusted by some key generals, who thought he was not really prepared to fight the spread of Communism. He was hated by Cuban exiles in the USA since Castro had survived the Bay of Pigs and the missile crisis.

The USSR

- Khrushchev had prevented a US invasion of Cuba and had a guarantee that no further invasion attempts would take place.
- In public, he could claim to have acted reasonably and as a peacemaker by agreeing to remove the missiles from Cuba.
- Khrushchev had US agreement that NATO missiles in Turkey would also be removed, although this was a secret agreement and unknown at the time.

BUT

- The USSR was shown to have lied to the UN and the world about nuclear missiles in Cuba.
- Khrushchev had been forced to back down in the face of US pressure. Soviet missiles were removed and many in the USSR felt humiliated.
- Khrushchev was unable to make public his secret agreements with the USA.
- In 1964, Khrushchev was replaced as Soviet leader. Historians consider the outcome of the missile crisis contributed to his downfall.

Key terms

Cold War: political hostility between countries that stops short of actual armed conflict.

Comment

The Cuban missile crisis is now seen by historians as the event that nearly triggered a nuclear war between the USA and USSR. Recent evidence shows that Soviet nuclear submarines were stationed off the US east coast ready to launch their missiles if instructed by Khruschev. Kennedy also had the American military ready for war. In the end, both Kennedy and Khrushchev managed to achieve at least some of their objectives and remain in control of their military commanders who were urging the use of force.

Cuba

- Castro remained in power and the USA agreed not to attempt further invasions.
- Cuba remained heavily armed, although not with nuclear weapons, and became a focus for other Communists in South America.
- Castro maintained his control of former US industries.

BUT
- Cuba remained poor and isolated in the western hemisphere, unable to trade with the USA and therefore dependent on the USSR for supplies and equipment.

Revision task

Copy and complete the table below to show who gained most from the missile crisis. Who most achieved his objectives?

	Objectives	Success or failure?
Kennedy		
Khrushchev		
Castro		

Exam practice

1 'The Cuban missile crisis was won by the United States of America?' How far do you agree with this statement? Explain your answer.

(10 marks)

Exam tip This question tests your knowledge and understanding but also goes further. A question that starts 'How far …' is also inviting you to **evaluate**. In your exam, question 2c) or 3c) will usually include an element of evaluation like this.

You know that the USSR removed its nuclear missiles from Cuba at the end of the crisis but was this because Soviet leader Khrushchev was admitting defeat or was it because he had won a secret victory because President Kennedy had secretly agreed to remove old missiles from American bases in Turkey? Your task is to evaluate the evidence and judge who won and for what reasons.

Summary/revision plan

You need to have a good working knowledge of the following areas. **Tick off each item** once you are confident in your knowledge.

- ❑ 1 **The Cuban revolution and the reaction of the USA**
- ❑ 2 **The Bay of Pigs invasion**
- ❑ 3 **The beginnings of the missile crisis**
  - Why did Khrushchev put missiles in Cuba?
  - Kennedy's options
- ❑ 4 **The missile crisis**
  - day by day, the main events
  - Why did Kennedy react as he did?
- ❑ 5 **The end of the crisis and its consequences for**
  - the USA
  - the USSR
  - Cuba.

Check your knowledge online with our Quick quizzes at www.hodderplus.co.uk/modernworldhistory.

Chapter 6: Why did the USA fail in Vietnam?

Americans' fear of Communism meant that American governments in the 1950s and 1960s used their economic and military strength to support anti-Communists around the world. In South-East Asia, the USA became heavily involved in the defence of South Vietnam. In the early stages of the Vietnam War, many Americans supported US government policy. By 1968, however, over half a million US soldiers and marines were fighting in the jungles of South Vietnam and there had been thousands of US casualties. The Vietnam War turned into a major American defeat and helped change US policy in containing Communism.

Focus points

Each key question in the OCR course is divided into focus points. To do well in the examination, you will need a good understanding of each focus point.

- Why did the USA get increasingly involved in Vietnam?
- What were the different ways that the USA and the Communists fought the war?
- Whose tactics were the most effective – the USA's or the Communists'?
- Why did the USA withdraw from Vietnam?

Key content

In order to fully understand the focus points, you will need to have a good working knowledge of:

- US involvement in Vietnam under Presidents Eisenhower, Kennedy and Johnson
- the main events of the war
- the tactics used by the two sides
- reasons for the American withdrawal from Vietnam

6.1 Reasons for increasing American involvement in Vietnam

The origins of the Vietnam War

The Vietnamese had a long history of fighting occupying foreign forces.

Before the Second World War, Vietnam was ruled by France. In 1942, Japan invaded and occupied French Indochina and treated the Vietnamese in a brutal and savage way. A strong Vietnamese resistance movement was set up by Ho Chi Minh. He had lived in Europe and the USA and studied Communism in the USSR.

In August 1945, Japan was defeated and the French returned to rule Vietnam, but Ho Chi Minh and his Communist supporters continued to fight for independence. Despite American assistance, the French army was defeated by the Communists at Dien Bien Phu in 1954. A peace treaty was signed and France pulled out of Vietnam.

After the French withdrawal, Vietnam was divided into two – Communist North Vietnam and non-Communist South Vietnam.

How did the USA first get involved?

Under the terms of the 1954 peace treaty, which also aimed to unite Vietnam, elections were to be held within two years. However, the Americans, led by President Eisenhower, were concerned that the Communists might win so they helped the anti-Communist Ngo Dinh Diem set up the Republic of South Vietnam.

Diem's Government was corrupt. He put many of his relatives in positions of power and refused to hold elections. The Vietnamese peasants were treated badly by Diem and many began supporting the Communist National Liberation Front for South Vietnam, known as the Vietcong. Supported by Communist North Vietnam, the Vietcong began a **guerrilla war** against the South Vietnamese Government.

Diem's Government was weak and needed US support if it was to survive. To start with the US only supplied materials, money and advice to Diem's government. But from 1961, under the leadership of President Kennedy, US military support for South Vietnam increased. In 1961, 16,000 US 'advisers' were sent to assist the South Vietnamese army.

After Kennedy was assassinated in November 1963, his successor, President Johnson, sent large numbers of combat troops to Vietnam. In August 1964, North Vietnamese patrol boats fired on US ships in the Gulf of Tonkin. In response, the US Congress gave President Johnson sweeping powers to retaliate, and he sent thousands more troops to fight in the jungles of South Vietnam. The Vietnam War was now well underway.

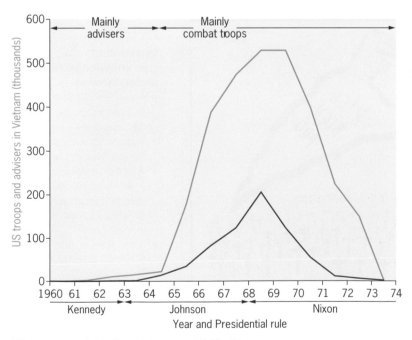

US troops and deaths in Vietnam, 1960–74.

Key terms

Guerrilla war: ambushes, raids and hit-and-run operations carried out behind enemy lines.

Containment: a foreign policy aimed at containing the political influence or military power of another country – for example, US policy to stop the spread of Communism during the Cold War.

Domino theory: the political theory that if one nation comes under Communist control then neighbouring nations are likely to fall to Communism as well. The phrase was popularised by US President Eisenhower in 1954.

Military industrial complex: the US military establishment and industries producing military equipment. Together, they exerted a powerful influence on US foreign and economic policy. (This term was first used by President Eisenhower in his last speech as US President.)

Why did the USA get increasingly involved in Vietnam?

- During the Cold War, US policy was based on the idea of **containment**. The USA, therefore, supported the French in Vietnam in the 1950s in order to stop the spread of Communism and gain support from its allies.
- US President Eisenhower and others believed in the **domino theory**. They believed that the USSR was trying to spread Communism throughout the world. So if one country was allowed to fall to the Communists, others would follow.
- Some historians believe that a combination of high-ranking officers and large arms manufacturers actually wanted a war with the USSR. War meant that more money would be spent on arms and equipment. In his last speech as president before he retired in January 1960, President Eisenhower warned the American people not to let this '**military industrial complex**' become too powerful.

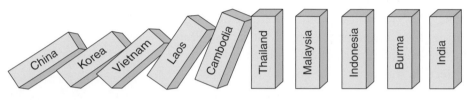

The domino theory and the potential spread of Communism.

Comment

It was never the intention of the US Government to become involved in a full-scale war in Vietnam. Eisenhower, Kennedy and Johnson steadily increased the number of advisers, and later troops, as they tried to contain the spread of Communism throughout South-East Asia. By 1964, President Johnson was caught between sending thousands more US troops to prop up a corrupt, unpopular but pro-American Government in South Vietnam and allowing a Communist takeover.

Revision task

Create a timeline showing the key events in increasing American involvement in Vietnam. Use key words to summarise what happened in 1945, 1954, 1961, 1963.

Exam practice

1 Study the source carefully and then answer the questions which follow.

SOURCE A

'Go away! I don't believe in ghosts!'

A cartoon published in the British Sunday newspaper, *The Observer* on May 24, 1964.

a) What is the message of this cartoon? Use the details of the cartoon and your own knowledge to explain your answer. *(4 marks)*

b) Explain briefly why the USA became involved in Vietnam. *(6 marks)*

Exam tip These are typical of the questions you will face in question 1.

Question a) is a starter question. It tests your **factual knowledge** and your ability to **interpret sources**. Try to show your knowledge and understanding of the period when the cartoon was produced.

Question b) tests your **knowledge and understanding**.
- A low level answer (worth 1–2 marks) will simply describe one or two reasons for American involvement in Vietnam.
- A better answer (worth 3–4 marks) will describe several reasons why America became involved in Vietnam.
- A top level answer (worth 5–6 marks) will explain several reasons why America became involved in Vietnam and show which reasons were most important.

6.2 The main events of the Vietnam war

Timeline

1960	Vietcong formed (National Liberation Front for South Vietnam).
1961	Vice-President Lyndon B. Johnson tours Saigon (capital of South Vietnam).
1962	America's first combat mission against the Vietcong.
1963	President Kennedy assassinated in Dallas, Texas; Johnson becomes US President.
	South Vietnamese Buddhist monks start setting themselves on fire in public places in protest against the South Vietnamese Government.
1964	The Gulf of Tonkin incident.
	Congress authorises President Johnson to 'take all necessary measures to repel any armed attack against forces of the United States and to prevent further aggression'. The US wages total war against North Vietnam.
1965	Over 200,000 US troops are sent to Vietnam.
	Bombing raids on North Vietnam commence under the code name, 'Operation Rolling Thunder'. The air raids continue for three years.
1966	American B-52 heavy bombers strike North Vietnam.
1967	The US Secretary of Defence, Robert McNamara, admits that the US bombing raids had failed to meet their objectives.
1968	The Tet Offensive.
	My Lai Village massacre by US troops.
	Peace talks take place in Paris between the North Vietnamese and the USA.
	President Johnson decides not to seek re-election and Richard Nixon is elected US President.
1969	The news coverage of the massacre in My Lai by US troops is published. It shocks the American public and leads to numerous anti-war demonstrations.
1970	President Nixon extends the Vietnam War to Cambodia in order to prevent the Vietcong from using Cambodia as a base to strike US forces.
1972	Pressure on Nixon to end US involvement in Vietnam increases and secret peace talks begin. US forces apply pressure on North Vietnam to make an agreement by heavy bombing of major cities, such as Hanoi and Haiphong.
1973	A ceasefire agreement is signed in Paris.
	US conscription to fight in Vietnam ends.
	All remaining US troops leave Vietnam.
1974	Major North Vietnamese offensive against South Vietnam.
1975	South Vietnamese capital, Saigon, falls to Communists; US Embassy staff are airlifted to safety by helicopter.

6.3 Tactics used in the Vietnam War

Vietcong tactics – guerrilla warfare

The Vietcong and its ally, North Vietnam, were no match for the superior forces of the USA and South Vietnamese. The Vietcong had about 170,000 soldiers with weapons supplied by Communist China and the USSR. The USA had 500,000 troops in South Vietnam by 1968. In response, the Vietcong used guerrilla warfare.

The North Vietnamese leader, Ho Chi Minh, had seen guerrilla tactics used successfully by the Communist leader Mao Zedong to gain power in China. The methods of guerrilla warfare were simple.

- Retreat when the enemy attacks.
- Launch surprise attacks on enemy camps.
- Pursue the enemy when he retreats.
- Wear the enemy down by ambushing troops and laying booby traps and mines.
- Use the local terrain, tunnels or jungle to hide.
- Live amongst civilians for protection.
- Decide not to wear uniform to make it difficult to separate fighters from innocent civilians.

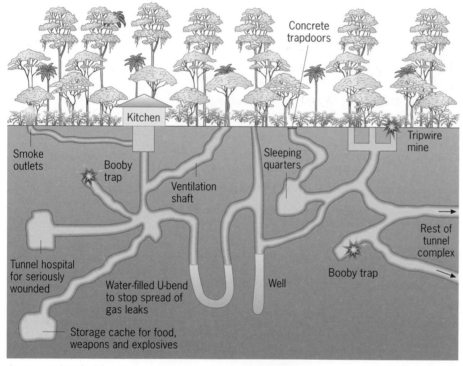

An example of a Vietcong underground tunnel system.

Guerrilla tactics were very effective and US soldiers lived in constant fear of attack or ambush. The Vietcong was difficult to identify, difficult to find and difficult to fight. These tactics wore down the morale of the US soldiers and was a major factor in the US defeat in Vietnam.

The Vietcong was also helped by Vietnam's neighbours, Cambodia and Laos. Vietcong guerrillas were able to retreat across the border to Cambodia and US troops were unable to follow them. This gave the Vietcong a huge advantage and caused serious problems for US soldiers.

US tactics

a) Bombing

Bombing Vietcong strongholds, supply lines and key cities in North Vietnam was a major part of the US strategy during the Vietnam War.

Bombing Vietcong targets and North Vietnam achieved some objectives.

- Vietcong supply lines were disrupted.
- North Vietnam's industry and military production was badly damaged.
- Extensive bombing of North Vietnam encouraged the Communist leaders to seek a negotiated end to the war.

Bombing alone, however, could not win a war.

- The North Vietnamese war effort was disrupted and slowed down but not stopped. Vietcong supply lines continued to operate and South Vietnamese towns and cities were still attacked.
- The Vietcong used a system of tunnels and underground passages that bombing did not affect (see diagram on page 62).
- The cost of the bombing was huge. The Communists destroyed approximately 14,000 US and South Vietnamese aircraft.

b) Chemical weapons

Whilst North Vietnam was bombed with high explosives, much of the jungle in South Vietnam was bombed with chemical weapons. The US developed Agent Orange, which was used to destroy jungle foliage in order to help find Vietcong fighters. The Americans also used napalm. Napalm was highly inflammable and burnt everything with which it came into contact. Its use was very controversial since many civilians suffered extensive burns.

c) Search and destroy

The Vietcong used **guerrilla tactics** against the Americans so there were few large-scale battles. Instead, Vietcong soldiers would make hit-and-run attacks against American bases and quickly disappear into the jungle. In order to deal with guerrilla warfare, US General Westmoreland developed search-and-destroy tactics. US and South Vietnamese forces would use helicopters to land quickly near Vietnamese villages and kill hiding Vietcong fighters.

This method of warfare did have positive outcomes but it also had drawbacks.

- The Vietcong often set traps for inexperienced US soldiers.
- Sometimes, the wrong villages were attacked and burned as intelligence was often inadequate and out of date.
- There was a large number of Vietnamese civilian casualties.
- Search-and-destroy tactics made US soldiers very unpopular with local civilians and encouraged many to join the Vietcong.

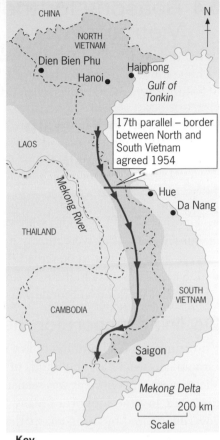

Key

Communist-controlled areas in the mid-1960s

Ho Chi Minh trail (route used by Vietcong to supply their troops)

Comment

It has been estimated that between 1965 when Operation Rolling Thunder (bombing raids on North Vietnam) began and 1972, approximately twice as many bombs were dropped in Vietnam and Cambodia than were used by the USA in Europe and the Pacific during the whole of the Second World War.

Revision tasks

1 Draw a mind map to show the different tactics used by the USA and the Vietcong during the Vietnam War.
2 On a scale of one to five, how effective were Vietcong and USA tactics? Pick out any key words from your mind map to justify your score.

Key terms

Guerrilla tactics: hit-and-run tactics against an enemy that is more powerful in terms of weapons if they were to meet in a face-to-face battle.

6.4 Reasons for the US failure in the Vietnam War

In the early years of the Vietnam War, it seemed that the USA would be able to use its huge military power to defeat the Vietcong and prevent a Communist takeover of South Vietnam. However, this did not happen. Why?

Problems in Vietnam

Tactics and morale

- US tactics were no match for the Vietcong's. US bombing and 'search and destroy' could not defeat a committed guerrilla army.
- Up to 1967 all US troops were volunteers but after 1967 many were conscripted. They were mostly inexperienced young men who served only one year, and then left to be replaced by yet more inexperienced conscripts.
- US casualties were high and many of the US troops could see that the tactics were not working so morale was low.

Declining support for the USA in South Vietnam

Unfortunately, US bombing of key targets and use of weapons to destroy jungle camouflage also killed thousands of innocent civilians. In addition, the South Vietnamese Government was seen as corrupt by many of its people. The USA, therefore, lost the support of many South Vietnamese by supporting an unpopular government and by using tactics that killed innocent civilians.

The Tet Offensive, January 1968

In January 1968 the Vietcong launched a major attack on about 100 Vietnamese cities during the New Year ('Tet') holiday. The Vietcong had hoped that ordinary Vietnamese would join them in the rebellion but this did not happen. It lost about 10,000 experienced fighters during the offensive and its power was severely weakened.

However, despite these setbacks for the Vietcong, the Tet Offensive was a major turning point for the USA in Vietnam.

- Before the Tet Offensive, American leaders were convinced that they could win the war.
- After the offensive, it became clear it would take many more troops, and therefore more casualties, to win military victory.
- Americans were not expecting such a co-ordinated and effective response from the Vietcong.

Problems at home

Against this background events in the USA became more important to the outcome of the war than what was going on in Vietnam itself.

The US media

The American press and TV news was often accused of undermining the Government in its effort to win in Vietnam. The reality is a little more complex.

In the early stages of the Vietnam War, from 1964 to 1968, most American newspapers and TV news journalists did not criticise US involvement in Vietnam. Most editors did not want to be seen to be undermining the Government's anti-Communist policies.

After 1967, however, the content of news reports from Vietnam began to change.

- Television began to take over from newspapers as the means by which the American public received news from Vietnam. Reports often showed graphic and shocking violence.

Key terms

Conscription: compulsory military service in the armed forces. In the USA men between 18 and 26 had to register for two years' military service.

- By 1968, concern was increasing about the huge number of Americans (500,000) fighting in Vietnam. After the surprise of the Tet Offensive very well-respected TV reporters, such as Walter Cronkite of CBS News, publicly suggested that the Vietnam War was unwinnable. This had a significant effect on American public opinion.

The My Lai Massacre

In March 1968, a group of American soldiers on a search-and-destroy mission was informed that Vietcong fighters were hiding in the village of My Lai in Quang Ngai province. Within four hours nearly 400 civilians, mostly women, children and old men, had been killed and no Vietcong found. The incident only became known when one of the soldiers gave an account of the events on US television in 1969. An investigation was launched and the soldiers in charge of the My Lai operation were put on trial for mass murder. Only one officer, Lieutenant William Calley, who led the US unit at My Lai, was found guilty. He was given a twenty-year prison sentence, but only served three years in custody. The My Lai massacre and the investigation that followed deeply shocked the American public and further undermined the war effort.

Protests against the Vietnam War

As American problems in Vietnam worsened, protests against the war increased. In 1968, there were protests across the USA about several issues – civil rights for African Americans, the problems of poverty and the Vietnam War.

- The Vietnam War showed the inequalities in American society. Many white young men were able to avoid conscription by joining universities, but this did not apply to as many African Americans. Therefore, the number of African Americans in Vietnam was proportionally much higher than white Americans. In addition, 22.5 per cent of casualties were African Americans but only 11 per cent were white.
- There were further protests about the war at many universities across the United States. The worst events occurred in 1970 at Kent State University in Ohio when nervous US national guardsmen fired into a group of unarmed students protesting about the extension of the Vietnam War into neighbouring Cambodia. Four students were killed in the protest and eleven others injured.

By 1969, half a million US troops and thousands of bombing raids had not defeated a determined, resourceful and well-motivated Vietcong. As one of the only two superpowers, the USA, with its huge military capability, was being humiliated in the jungles of South-East Asia. Despite the lessons of history, American military planners were convinced that modern technology and weaponry would always deliver a victory. By 1969, it was clear that a military solution alone was not possible.

US withdrawal

With the above problems, all the US political parties campaigning in the 1968 presidential campaign realised that they had to support a policy to end the Vietnam War or lose the election. President Johnson decided in 1968 not to seek re-election; the Vietnam War had defeated him. His successor, Richard Nixon, now looked for a way to end the Vietnam War without it looking like an American defeat.

Comment

The Vietnam War was a case of Cold War tension causing a local conflict to escalate into a larger conflict. The USA's massive firepower was able to cause much heavier damage to the Vietcong than it received, but this was not enough to defeat the Vietcong. Vietnam was a fully Communist state by 1975.

Exam tip Prior to Vietnam, the USA had never lost a war so examiners often want you to explain why the Americans lost in Vietnam. For example, did the Americans finally pull out because the tactics of the Vietcong were so successful? Or did US public opinion force the US Government to look for a way out before a military victory could be won?

Revision task

Draw a mind map to explain why the Americans could not win the Vietnam War. Include the following points. Show connections between the points. Highlight the most important reasons.

- US military tactics
- the role of the US media
- protests in the USA
- Vietcong military tactics
- US public opinion
- key military events, e.g. the Tet Offensive
- other events, e.g. the My Lai Massacre

Summary/revision plan

You need to have a good working knowledge of the following areas. **Tick off each item** once you are confident in your knowledge.

- ❑ 1 **Reasons for increasing American involvement in Vietnam**
  - The origins of the Vietnam War
  - Eisenhower's actions
  - Kennedy's actions
  - Johnson's actions
- ❑ 2 **The main events of the Vietnam war**
- ❑ 3 **Tactics used in the Vietnam War**
  - Vietcong tactics
  - US tactics
    - Bombing: strategic
    - Bombing: chemical weapons
    - Search and destroy
- ❑ 4 **Reasons for the US failure in Vietnam**
  - Problems in Vietnam
    - Tactics and morale
    - Declining support in South Vietnam
    - The Tet Offensive
  - Problems at home
    - The US media
    - The My Lai Massacre
    - Protests against the Vietnam War
  - US withdrawal

Check your knowledge online with our Quick quizzes at www.hodderplus.co.uk/modernworldhistory.

At the end of the First World War, Germany's old political system collapsed and was replaced by a democracy. In this chapter, you will examine how successful that democratic regime was, and why and how it was overthrown by the Nazis.

Focus points

In the OCR course, each Paper 1 depth study option is divided into key questions, and each key question is divided into focus points. To do well in the examination, you need to have a well-thought-out view on each of the key questions and focus points.

Key question 1: Was the Weimar Republic doomed from the start?
Focus points

- How did Germany emerge from defeat in the First World War?
- What was the economic and political impact of the Treaty of Versailles on the Weimar Republic?
- To what extent did the Republic recover after 1923?
- What were the achievements of the Weimar period?

Key question 2: Why was Hitler able to dominate Germany by 1933?
Focus points

- What did the Nazi Party stand for in the 1920s?
- Why did the Nazis have little success before 1930?
- Why was Hitler able to become Chancellor by 1933?
- How did Hitler consolidate his power in 1933?

Key question 3(a): The Nazi regime: how effectively did the Nazis control Germany, 1933–1945?
Focus points

- How much opposition was there to the Nazi regime?
- How effectively did the Nazis deal with their political opponents?
- How did the Nazis use culture, propaganda and the mass media to control the people?
- Why did the Nazis persecute many groups in German society?

Key question 3(b): The Nazi regime: what was it like to live in Nazi Germany?
Focus points

- What was the purpose of the Hitler Youth?
- How successful were Nazi policies towards women and the family?
- Were most people better off under Nazi rule?
- How did the coming of war change life in Germany?

Key content

In order to fully understand the focus points, you will need to have a good working knowledge of:

- the origins of the Weimar Republic and revolution of 1918–19
- economic and political problems in Germany during the 1920s
- German recovery in the 1920s under Stresemann
- the effects of the Depression on Germany
- how the Nazis took power in 1933
- life in Nazi Germany
- Nazi treatment of the Jews
- opposition to the Nazis
- Nazi economic and foreign policy
- Germany and the Second World War.

7.1 The origins of the Weimar Republic and revolution of 1918–19

When Germany was clearly losing the First World War, the German **Kaiser** Wilhelm II abdicated. In November 1918, the Government of Germany was left in the hands of a new **Chancellor**, Friedrich Ebert. Ebert and his colleagues drew up a new democratic **constitution** for Germany, and in the summer of 1919, he was elected the first President of the new **Weimar Republic**.

A democratic Germany

In theory, the new Weimar constitution gave Germany a nearly perfect democratic system.
- The 'lower house', or Reichstag, was elected by **proportional representation**. The vote was by secret ballot and universal suffrage (every adult could vote). Elections were to be held at least every four years.
- The 'upper house', or Reichsrat, was made up of representatives from each of the German states. It could delay new laws.
- The President was also the head of state and was elected every seven years. The President appointed a chancellor (usually the head of the largest party in the Reichstag) to form a government. The Chancellor's role was therefore similar to the Prime Minister's role in Britain.

In practice, it proved very difficult to get one party into power. Governments were usually coalitions of different parties and they tended not to last very long.

Problems in the new Republic

In the years immediately after the First World War, the new Weimar Republic was constantly under threat from extreme political groups.

Spartacist Revolt, 1919 – opposition from the left

- In November 1918, an independent socialist state was created in Bavaria under the leadership of Kurt Eisner.
- Communists in Germany, known as Spartacists, wanted a revolution similar to the one in Russia in 1917. In January 1919, Communist activists led by Karl Liebknecht and Rosa Luxemburg seized power in Berlin and the Baltic ports.
- Within weeks, however, all the revolts had been crushed by regular troops and the Freikorps (groups of ex-soldiers). The Communist leaders were assassinated.

The Kapp putsch, 1920 – opposition from the right

German nationalists saw democracy as weak. For many nationalists, the new Weimar Republic was a symbol of Germany's defeat in the war. They were

Key terms

Kaiser: emperor.
Chancellor: chief minister (equivalent of Prime Minister in Britain).
Constitution: an agreement method of governing a country, with the details usually written down and agreed on by those being governed.
Weimar Republic: a republic is a country without a hereditary ruler, such as a king or emperor. The new Government first met in the town of Weimar.
Proportional representation: the number of representatives from a given party is determined by the share or proportion of votes that party gains nationally.
Putsch: a revolt, rebellion or uprising aimed at overthrowing the current government.

Exam practice

1 Describe the main features of the Weimar Constitution.
(4 marks)

Exam tip This is typical of the questions you will face in questions 8 or 9.

This is a starter question. It tests your **factual knowledge**. Try to include four details about the Weimar Constitution.

furious with the Government for signing the hated Treaty of Versailles (see pages 12–14).

Source 1 below expresses what many people in Germany felt about the treaty at the time. They associated the Weimar government with Germany's defeat in the war.

SOURCE 1

Deutsche Zeitung, 28 June 1919.

Vengeance, German nation!
Today in the Hall of Mirrors, the disgraceful treaty is being signed. Do not forget it
The German people will reconquer the place among the nations to which they are
entitled. Then will come vengeance for the shame of 1919.

Many Germans wanted a strong government to make Germany great again.

- In March 1920, Wolfgang Kapp, an extreme nationalist, and a group of Freikorps units seized power in Berlin.
- Kapp was not supported by the workers in the factories. The workers organised a strike in Berlin in support of the Government. Within hours, the German capital came to a halt and supplies of gas, water and coal stopped.
- After four days, Kapp and his supporters gave up and fled Berlin. Ebert and the Weimar Government returned to power.

Source 2 below gives us Kapp's view of the new Weimar Republic:

SOURCE 2

Wolfgang Kapp, March 1920.

The nation is in grave danger. We are approaching the collapse of law and order.
Hardship is growing. Starvation threatens. The government has no authority and is
corrupt. We are threatened with Bolshevism. We shall get rid of this weak republic
and replace it with a strong government.

Kapp was obviously biased against the Weimar government. Even so, the source shows that some people viewed the government in 1920 as weak, corrupt and without authority.

7.2 Economic and political problems in Germany during the 1920s

Reparations and the invasion of the Ruhr

According to the terms of the Treaty of Versailles, Germany had to pay for the damage caused during the First World War. These payments were known as **reparations** and were a major burden to the new state.

- The Reparations Commission announced that Germany would be required to pay 132,000 million gold marks in annual instalments.
- In 1922, the German Government announced it would not be able to pay the annual instalment and asked for more time.

The British Government agreed to this, but the French Government insisted that Germany must pay. In January 1923, the French and Belgian Governments sent troops to the Ruhr, the centre of German industry. The results were disastrous for Germany.

- German workers used 'passive resistance' against the invaders (they did not fight but they refused to co-operate-workers went on strike).
- Factories closed and the German economy ground to a halt.

Exam practice

1 Explain the reasons why the period 1918–25 nearly caused the collapse of the Weimar Government.

(6 marks)

Exam tip This tests your **knowledge and understanding**.

- A low level answer (worth 1–2 marks) will simply state or two reasons.
- A better answer (worth 3–4 marks) will describe several reasons why the Weimar Government nearly collapsed and explain each more fully.
- A top level answer (worth 5–6 marks) will do all the above but also explain and evaluate the importance of each reason.

Revision tasks

1 Make a list of key words to show that the new Republic was not popular in Germany.

2 Give two examples of threats to the new Republic and explain why they were a threat.

Key terms

Reparations: repair, or compensation for damage caused by the war.

Hyperinflation, 1923

The Weimar Government printed more and more money to pay off its debts payments. However, printing money simply caused prices to rise out of control and cause **hyperinflation**. The German Mark became virtually worthless.

Key terms

Hyperinflation: rapidly rising prices so that money becomes worthless.

Value of the German mark against the US dollar, 1914–23	
1914	$1 = 4 marks
1922	$1 = 7,000 marks
July 1923	$1 = 160,000 marks
November 1923	$1 = 4,200,000,000 marks

- As prices rose, people's savings became worthless (this caused particular hardship to the middle classes). In 1923, prices in shops were increased almost every hour.
- At times, workers were paid twice a day so they could buy food before prices rose.
- People on fixed incomes, such as pensioners, suffered badly.
- Prices rose much faster than incomes and many people starved as they were unable to afford food or fuel.

Crisis under control

In September 1923, at the height of the economic crisis, a new government was formed by Gustav Stresemann.
- He stopped the printing of worthless paper money in November 1923.
- He created a new currency called the Rentenmark.
- He also called off the resistance against the French occupation by German workers in the Ruhr. The German economy began to recover slowly, although French troops did not withdraw from the Ruhr until 1925.

The Munich putsch, 1923

Weimar Germany faced political as well as economic troubles in this period. In 1923, a new nationalist leader called Adolf Hitler first came to prominence.

In November 1923, Hitler and the Nazis tried to seize control of the Bavarian Government. The plan was to capture Munich and from there march on Berlin. Hitler was convinced people would join him in overthrowing the Weimar regime.
- On 8 November, at a political meeting in a Munich beer hall, Hitler forced Kahr, the head of the Bavarian Government, at gunpoint to join him.
- The Nazi plan soon began to go wrong. On 9 November, Bavarian police opened fire on Nazi Stormtroopers in Munich and sixteen Nazis were killed.
- Ludendorff (the former First World War general who was now a Nazi supporter) and Hitler were arrested and charged with high treason.

However, it was clear that Hitler's views had some support in Germany.
- Many Nazi supporters, including Hitler, received light or minimum sentences.
- Hitler served his sentence in the comfortable Landsberg Fortress and spent his time writing his memoirs.
- The memoirs were published as *Mein Kampf* (My Struggle), in which Hitler outlined his view of German history and what Germany needed to do to recover.

The Munich Putsch became an important piece of Nazi propaganda once the Nazis gained power. The sources opposite show two differing accounts of Hitler's role in the events.

SOURCE 3

From the official biography of Hitler published by the Nazi Party in 1934.

The body of the man with whom Hitler was linked shot up into the air like a ball, tearing Hitler's arm with him, so that it sprang from the joint and fell back limp and dead ... Hitler approached the man and stopped over him ... a boy severely wounded. Blood was pouring from his mouth. Hitler picked him up and carried him on his shoulders.

SOURCE 4

Rudolf Olden, *Hitler the Pawn* (written in 1936).

At first shot Hitler had flung himself to the ground. He sprained his arm, but this did not prevent him from running. He found his car and drove into the mountains.

Exam tip Ask these questions of any source:
- What is it? (a document, diary extract, cartoon, picture, etc.)
- Who produced, wrote or drew it?
- When was it produced, written or drawn?
- Why was it produced, written or drawn?

Revision tasks

Copy and complete the table below using the information and evidence in this section. Use key words for column three 'outline of events'. Then give each threat a rating, on a scale of 1–10, in terms of its seriousness for the Weimar Republic (1 being not serious and 10 being extremely serious) and then explain your score.

Threat	Date	Outline of events	Threat rating	Explain your score
1 Spartacist revolt				
2 Kapp putsch				
3 French invasion of the Ruhr				
4 Hyperinflation				
5 Munich putsch				

7.3 German recovery in the 1920s under Stresemann

Economic recovery

From the end of 1923, the German economy began to recover.
- There was a new currency, the Rentenmark, and Ruhr industries restarted production.
- In 1924, Stresemann, now Foreign Minister, signed the Dawes Plan. This gave Germany loans from the USA and reparation payments were made easier.
- German industry benefited from new investment and unemployment fell sharply.

However, some groups, such as shopkeepers, small businessmen and farmers, continued to struggle in these years.

The Locarno treaties, 1925

During the mid-1920s, Stresemann's aim was to get Germany accepted again as a member of the international community. He had great success in this field.
- Germany signed the Locarno treaties (a set of seven agreements) in 1925 and agreed to accept the Treaty of Versailles, the terms of which set out the borders between France, Germany and Belgium.
- In 1926, Germany was admitted into the League of Nations.

Extremist groups

Despite the gradual recovery of the German economy, extreme political groups in Germany continued to grow.

- In the elections of 1924, the Nazis won only fourteen seats in the Reichstag, and in 1928, they won only twelve. Throughout the country, however, Hitler was building a small but firm base of support.
- The Communists were also organising themselves throughout the country. They created the Red Fighting League and regularly fought street battles with Nazi Stormtroopers (the SA). In 1924, the KPD (Communists) held 45 seats in the Reichstag and this grew to 54 in the 1928 election.

Cultural life during the Weimar Republic

The Weimar Republic claimed some important cultural achievements.

- German cinema developed in the 1920s and produced stars such as Marlene Dietrich.
- Artists such as George Grosz and Otto Dix led new movements in the visual arts.
- Theatre flourished, producing world-renowned writers such as Bertolt Brecht.
- Walter Gropius' Bauhaus School developed new ideas in the design of buildings and furniture, and became one of the twentieth century's most influential artistic movements.

Revision task

How had Germany changed by the end of the 1920s? Use a key words list to summarise the situation in 1921 and what changed by 1928:

	1921	1928
Economy		
Employment		
International affairs		
Politics at home		

7.4 The effects of the Depression on Germany

Effects of the Wall Street Crash, 1929

The recovery of the German economy was fragile. It depended heavily on American money. In 1929, disaster struck with the Wall Street Crash (see page 102).

- Many US banks recalled their loans. German companies were unable to pay.
- German businesses began to close. Millions lost their jobs.

Unemployment and the rise of extremism

Between 1928 and 1930, German unemployment rose from 2.5 million to 4 million. This provided an opportunity for extremist groups such as the Communists and the Nazis.

- As unemployment rose, more and more people felt let down by the Weimar Government and began to support extremist parties.

- In the 1930 election, the KPD (Communists) increased its number of seats in the Reichstag from 54 to 77.
- Nazi support increased from 12 seats in 1928 to 107 in 1930. The Nazis were now the second largest political party in the Reichstag.

How the Depression helped Hitler

The Depression helped Hitler in several ways.

Economic chaos

It caused a period of chaos in Germany. No government could take control and solve Germany's terrible economic problems.
- Unemployment was the major issue. By January 1932, it stood at 6 million. Hitler promised to get these people back to work.
- German farmers were also in crisis. They could not sell their produce and the banks were repossessing their land.

Fear of Communism

As the Depression deepened, some workers turned to the Communists and the KPD vote rose. This alarmed many wealthy and powerful industrialists as well as middle-class businessmen and farmers who feared a communist take over as had happened in Russia. They supported the Nazis for their anti-Communist stance.

Disillusionment with democracy

By 1932, Germans had lost faith in democratic political parties. They seemed unable to agree on any actions to solve the problems of the Depression. President Hindenburg was running Germany using his emergency powers. Through clever campaigning and his brilliant speaking skills, Hitler promised strong leadership. Hitler exploited all these fears and problems to win support.

7.5 How the Nazis took power: the German elections, 1932–33

The presidential election, 1932

In the 1932 election, Hitler ran for President against the ageing President Hindenburg.
- In his speeches, Hitler blamed the 'November criminals' (those who had signed the Treaty of Versailles) and Jews for the problems Germany was facing.
- He promised to build a better Germany, and many people believed him.

Hitler did not win, but he only lost to Hindenburg on a second vote. The Nazis felt they were close to success.

Elections for the Reichstag, July 1932

The 1932 general election campaign was very violent. Nazis and Communists fought each other in street battles and nearly 100 people were killed.

The Nazis became the largest party in the Reichstag and Hitler demanded to be made Chancellor. Hindenburg was suspicious of Hitler and refused, appointing Franz von Papen, a conservative politician with no Reichstag party base, as Chancellor.

> **Revision task**
>
> Which factors changed the Nazis' level of support between the beginning and end of the 1920s?
> a) List the factors.
> b) Underline the factor you think to be the most important.
> c) Write a paragraph to explain your choice.

New Reichstag elections, November 1932

Papen had little support in the Reichstag. To achieve his aims, he needed to win more support in the Reichstag and so he called another election in November 1932.

The Nazis lost seats in this election, but they still remained the largest party. Papen did not get the increased support he needed.

Hitler becomes Chancellor, January 1933

It was becoming increasingly clear that President Hindenburg could not continue to work with a Chancellor who did not have support in the Reichstag.

- Hindenburg and von Papen decided to make Hitler Chancellor.
- They believed they would be able to control him once he was in power.
- On 30 January 1933, Hitler became Chancellor and von Papen Vice-Chancellor.

When he was appointed, Hitler tried to increase the number of Nazis in government, persuading Hindenburg to dissolve the Reichstag and hold another general election.

The Reichstag fire, 1933

During the election campaign, on the night of 27 February 1933, the Reichstag was set on fire. The interior was totally destroyed. A Communist, Marinus van der Lubbe, was arrested for the crime, allowing Hitler and the Nazis to exploit the fire for their own purposes. They quickly blamed the KPD (Communists).

Hitler persuaded President Hindenburg to pass an emergency law restricting personal liberty. Under this law, thousands of Communist supporters were thrown into prison. But despite increasing their share of the vote in the election, the Nazis still did not have an overall majority in the Reichstag. They were forced to join together with the 52 nationalist members to create a government.

Election results, 1932–33

Presidential election result, 1932	
Candidate	No. of votes
Hindenburg	19 million
Hitler (Nazi)	13 million
Thaelmann (KPD)	4 million

General election results, July 1932	
	No. of seats
Moderate parties	
Social Democrats	133
Centre Party	75
Extremists	
KPD (left wing)	89
Nazis (right wing)	230
Nationalists (right wing)	40

General election results, November 1932	
	No. of seats
Moderate parties	
Social Democrats	121
Centre Party	70
Extremists	
KPD (left wing)	100
Nazis (right wing)	196
Nationalists (right wing)	51

General election results, March 1933	
	No. of seats
Moderate parties	
Social Democrats	120
Centre Party	73
Extremists	
KPD (left wing)	81
Nazis (right wing)	288
Nationalists (right wing)	52

Source evaluation: The Reichstag fire

The Reichstag fire was particularly important in the Nazis' rise to power. A key question is whether the fire was staged by the Nazis. The following sources address this possibility.

SOURCE 5

Rudolph Diels was head of the Prussian (German) military police. He explained what he found at the police office in the Reichstag.

Marinus van der Lubbe was being questioned. He was smeared in dirt and sweating. He panted as if he had completed a tremendous task. There was a wild triumphant gleam in his eyes. He had Communist pamphlets in his pockets.

SOURCE 6

William Shirer, an American writing in 1959 about the Reichstag fire, in his book *The Rise and Fall of the Third Reich*.

From Goering's palace an underground passage ran to the Reichstag building. Through this tunnel Karl Ernst, a former hotel porter who had become the leader of the Berlin SA, led his stormtroopers. They scattered petrol and quickly returned to the palace. At the same time, van der Lubbe climbed in and set some fires of his own.

SOURCE 7

Adolf Hitler, 28 February 1933.

This act of arson is the most outrageous act yet committed by the Communists in Germany. The burning of the Reichstag was to have been the signal for a bloody uprising and civil war …

These sources illustrate the problem of dealing with conflicting evidence. They suggest three possible explanations of the fire.

- Van der Lubbe acted alone.
- Van der Lubbe acted on behalf of the Communists.
- Nazi Stormtroopers (the SA) caused the fire, hoping to blame the Communists and win more support for Hitler in the general election.

The historian needs to consider each source carefully. Source 5 may be a primary source but it is evidence from a Nazi police officer. Source 6 sounds balanced and confident, but where did Shirer get his evidence? Source 7 shows Hitler quickly taking the opportunity to spread anti-Communist propaganda.

Hitler takes control: the Enabling Act, March 1933

Hitler still did not have enough support to have complete control of Germany. An Enabling Act would give him the right to pass laws for the next four years without having to obtain the support of members in the Reichstag. However, to pass an Enabling Act, Hitler needed to obtain the votes of two-thirds of Reichstag members, but he only had the support of just over half. This is what happened:

- Hitler ordered his Stormtroopers to continue intimidating the opposition.
- The 81 Communist members of the Reichstag were expelled.
- In an atmosphere heavy with violence, the Enabling Act was passed by 441 votes to 94.
- Hitler was given the power to rule for four years without consulting the Reichstag.

In July 1933, Hitler increased further his grip on power. Using the powers of the Enabling Act, he outlawed all other parties making Germany a one-party state. The democratic Weimar Republic had been destroyed and Germany had become a dictatorship.

Exam practice

1 'The main reason for the fall of the Weimar Republic was the rise of the Nazi Party.' How far do you agree with this statement? Explain your answer.

(10 marks)

Exam tip This question tests your knowledge and understanding but it goes further. A question that asks 'How far …' is also inviting you to **evaluate**. The question suggests one main reason for the collapse of the Weimar Republic but in a question like this don't make the mistake of only writing about the factor mentioned in the question. Remember to write about the other factors that lurk below the surface.
A top level answer (worth 7–10 marks) will evaluate the role of Nazis, but also the role of other parties and the impact of economic depression) in order to show a good understanding of the period.

Exam tip When using sources, always use your background knowledge to help you understand it and place it in context. Ask yourself 'How does what this source says fit in with what I know?'

The Night of the Long Knives, June 1934

Once he had gained power, Hitler's priority was to rid himself of possible rivals. Ernst Röhm, leader of the SA, had played a major role in helping Hitler achieve power. However:

- The German army saw the SA as a rival. It would not support Hitler unless the SA was disbanded.
- Some members of the SA wanted Hitler to follow a socialist programme of reform. Hitler was opposed to this as he would lose the support of wealthy industrialists.
- Röhm was a threat to Hitler's dominance of the Nazi Party.

Hitler made a deal with the generals of the German army. They promised to support him as commander-in-chief of the armed forces if the SA was disbanded, and if he started a programme of rearmament. On 30 June 1934, assassination squads from the SS (Hitler's bodyguards) murdered Hitler's potential SA rivals (including Röhm). It is estimated that up to 400 people were killed in the 'Night of the Long Knives'.

Just over one month later, President Hindenburg died. Hitler thereafter combined the posts of chancellor and president and also became commander-in-chief of the armed forces. From this point onwards, soldiers swore personal allegiance to Hitler, who became known officially as *der Führer* (the leader).

Revision task

1 Use the information and evidence on pages 72–76 to create a timeline of Hitler's steps to power. Make sure it includes the following events:
   - the Wall Street Crash
   - the Depression
   - elections of 1932
   - the Reichstag fire
   - Hitler's appointment as chancellor
   - the Enabling Act
   - the Night of the Long Knives

2 Why was the Enabling Act so important? List the changes it brought about.

7.6 Life in Nazi Germany

Nazis believed in complete loyalty and obedience. The two major tools to achieve this were propaganda and terror.

Propaganda

Hitler made Joseph Goebbels Minister of Propaganda.

Goebbels' job was to spread Nazi ideas and encourage all Germans to be loyal to Hitler. Goebbels (a former journalist) used his new powers to control all information that reached the German people in the following ways:

- All newspapers were censored by the Government and only allowed to print stories favourable to the Nazis.
- Radio was also controlled by the Government. Cheap radios (which could only receive the Government-controlled station and had a limited range) were manufactured so that most Germans could afford one.
- The Nazis took control of the German film industry. German films of the 1930s often showed great German heroes defeating their enemies.
- Goebbels organised mass rallies. At the rallies, hundreds of thousands of Nazi supporters sang songs and watched sporting events and firework displays.
- The Nazis used sporting events to spread their propaganda. The 1936 Berlin Olympics was used by the Nazis to suggest the superiority of the **Aryan race**.

Key terms

Aryan race: the Nordic blond-haired, blue-eyed physical ideal of Nazi Germany. In practice, it became used as the Nazi term for non-Jewish Germans.

Victims of propaganda

The main aim of propaganda was to give the German people a Nazi view of events. Another aim was to target certain groups inside and outside Germany, including:

- anyone who supported the terms of the Treaty of Versailles
- foreigners who criticised Hitler and the Nazis
- Communists and socialists
- democrats and liberals
- Jews.

Terror: A police state

In July 1933, Germany became a one-party state. All other political parties were banned and people who criticised the Nazis were imprisoned.

This policy was enforced ruthlessly by the SS and the Gestapo. The SS, originally Hitler's bodyguards and the police force of the Nazi Party, now controlled all Germany's police forces. The Gestapo was the secret police. It used terror tactics to intimidate, arrest and kill possible opponents.

Political enemies of the Nazis, such as liberals, socialists and Communists, were often arrested and sent without trial to concentration camps. The Nazis also persecuted people they termed 'asocials' – people who did not fit in a Nazi state. The list included Gypsies, homosexuals, alcoholics, juvenile delinquents, prostitutes, tramps and beggars and anyone who refused to work.

Such people were treated harshly. Around 500,000 tramps and beggars were sent to concentration camps in 1933. About the same number of Gypsies died in Auschwitz and other death camps.

> ### Comment
> *Other victims of the Nazis included people who were mentally ill and people who suffered from genetic diseases. In 1939, a secret policy of euthanasia (medical killing) began. By 1944, 200,000 people had been killed because of their illnesses.*

Nazi control of society

The Nazis took control of key parts of everyday life.

Education

Teachers had to belong to the German Teachers League and follow a Nazi curriculum.

- School textbooks were rewritten to support Nazi ideas and history.
- Children were taught that the Aryan race was superior to others.
- Outside school, children were encouraged to join youth groups organised by the Nazis (for example, Hitler Youth, German Girls League), where they were indoctrinated with Nazi ideas and beliefs.

The Church

In 1933, the Catholic Church in Germany signed a concordat (agreement) with Hitler. Both sides agreed not to interfere with each other's policies or actions.

The Nazis closed down a number of church organisations and set up their own 'church' called the Reich Church. It was not Christian and banned followers from using the Bible, crosses and religious symbols.

The role of women

- Hitler stated that women's role was *Kinder, Küche, Kirche* (children, kitchen, church).
- Marriage loans were given to women who gave up their jobs.
- There were restrictions on the employment of women as civil servants and in the professions.
- Women were not allowed to be members of the Reichstag.

Work

- An organisation called the German Labour Front (DAF) replaced the trade unions. Workers were not allowed to leave their jobs without government permission, and strikes were made illegal.
- Opposition was rare. By the late 1930s, pay had increased and workers accepted the long working hours and lack of rights because of the higher pay.
- From 1935, six months' work for the Reich Labour Service was made compulsory for all young men.

Leisure

- DAF's 'Strength Through Joy' organisation provided workers with sports facilities, cheap holidays and entertainments.
- It also ran a scheme for workers to save up to buy a 'people's car' (Volkswagen), although no one got a car through the scheme before production at the car plant was switched to military vehicles in 1939.

7.7 Nazi treatment of the Jews

Jewish people received the worst treatment of all those persecuted by the Nazis.

Persecution

In 1933, the Nazis organised a boycott of all Jewish businesses, doctors, dentists, etc. Jewish shops were marked with the star of David and the word 'Jude'.

Jewish children were intimidated at school and Germans were taught that Jews were unclean and responsible for Germany's defeat in the First World War.

In 1935, the Nuremberg Laws were introduced in Germany. Under these laws:
- Jews could no longer be German citizens
- marriages between Jews and Aryans were forbidden.

Kristallnacht

It is not clear how much most Germans knew about the persecution. However, in 1938 an event occurred that left nobody in any doubt.

On 7 November 1938, a Polish Jew, Herschel Grynszpan, shot a German diplomat, Ernst von Rath, in Paris. Hitler ordered an immediate attack on Jews and their property in Germany. From 9–10 November, thousands of Jewish businesses were attacked and 200 synagogues burnt down. This was called Kristallnacht ('the night of crystal' or 'the night of broken glass').

Violence against Jews in Germany increased. Himmler, head of the SS, began to expand the building of concentration camps.

Source evaluation: Kristallnacht

Below are two differing views about Kristallnacht. Which source gives the more reliable view of the events of 9 November 1938?

SOURCE 8

Nazi press statement, 10 November 1938.

It was a spontaneous wave of anger throughout Germany as a result of the cowardly murder of Third Secretary von Rath in the German Embassy in Paris.

SOURCE 9

An American observer, 1938.

The damage was done by SS men and stormtroopers not in uniform, each group having been provided with hammers, axes, crowbars and incendiary bombs.

As with other sources we have examined, the test for reliability depends particularly upon who wrote the source and why they wrote it. Source 8 gives a Nazi view of events and we have little reason to trust what it says. Source 9 is probably a more reliable view of events and it is supported by our background knowledge. However, Source 9 would be more useful (and we could be more sure about its reliability) if we knew who the observer was, and where they had observed the events described. We would then be able to cross-check this description with other evidence.

The 'Final Solution'

At the beginning of 1942, when the Second World War was at its height, the Nazis finalised their plans for the extermination of all Jews in Europe. This policy of genocide became known as the 'Final Solution'.

- New extermination camps were built and older camps updated.
- Between 1942 and 1945, 4.5 million Jews were gassed in death camps such as Auschwitz, Treblinka, Chelmno and Sobibor.
- In total, the Nazis murdered over 6 million Jews.

7.8 Opposition to the Nazis

Many Germans thought Hitler was a fine leader and genuinely supported him. Even among those who did not, many were unwilling to put their lives at risk. The Gestapo could arrest people merely on suspicion of opposing the Government. People were encouraged to inform on others. Many people were imprisoned and executed without trial. Given this use of terror and the brainwashing techniques used by Goebbels and the youth groups, it is understandable why there was so little opposition. However, there was some.

- Many people, including Jews, left Germany and fled to other countries. These included famous scientists, artists, writers and musicians who criticised the Nazi regime.
- Some Church leaders, such as Galen, the Catholic Bishop of Münster, and the Lutheran Pastor Niemöller, spoke out against Hitler. Niemöller was arrested in 1937 and spent the next eight years in concentration camps.

Young people protested in their own way. For example:

- The 'Swing' movement was made up of middle class teenagers who protested against Nazi control by listening to banned jazz music and welcoming Jews to their clubs.
- The 'Edelweiss Pirates' were mainly working class teenagers who refused to join the Hitler Youth and mocked the Hitler Youth activities.

During the Second World War youth opposition to the Nazis increased.

- Some of the 'Edelweiss Pirates' turned to active resistance – for example shielding deserters, or stealing arms, and committing acts of sabotage.
- Some students formed the 'White Rose Movement' distributed leaflets condemning Nazi policies. Their leaders Hans and Sophie Scholl were executed in 1945.

The July Bomb Plot

In the early days of Nazi rule the army had been fiercely loyal to Hitler. It was the foundation of Hitler's power. However after 1942 when it was clear that Hitler and the Nazis were going to lose the war eventually opposition grew within the army itself. The most famous opposition plot against Hitler took place on 20 July 1944, six weeks after the Allied armies landed in German-occupied France on D-Day. A group of army officers led by Colonel von Stauffenberg attempted to blow up Hitler at his Prussian headquarters. The bomb killed four people, but Hitler survived. The plotters were arrested, put on trial and executed.

> ### Revision tasks
>
> 1 Create a mind map to show the various means by which the Nazis sought to control German society. You should have two branches: control by force (coercion) and control by persuasion (consent).
>
> 2 Explain the Nazi view of the role of women in society.
>
> 3 Make a table to show opponents of the Nazi regime. Include their name and their method of opposition.

7.9 Nazi economic and foreign policy

The recovery of the German economy

In 1933, nearly 6 million people were unemployed. When Hitler came to power he promised economic prosperity to the German people. If he was to remain in power, therefore, he had to reduce unemployment.

- Thousands of Germans were employed in public works schemes created by the Nazis. New roads, houses, hospitals and schools were built.
- Businesses were paid subsidies to hire more workers.
- More jobs were created in the civil service.
- Some also took over jobs formerly held by Jews.

But rearmament was probably the key policy in getting Germany back to work.

Rearmament

- The production of arms and ammunition was significantly increased.
- The German army, air force and navy were enlarged, despite restrictions imposed by the Treaty of Versailles.
- Iron, steel and coal production rose rapidly as a result and made wealthy Nazi industrialists, such as Krupps, even richer.
- Compulsory military service was introduced in March 1935. The number of troops in the German army grew from 100,000 in 1933 to 1.4 million by 1939.

The effects of these measures were dramatic, and it is possible to see why many Germans were prepared to ignore the darker side of the Nazi regime.

- Unemployment fell from over 6 million in 1933 to about 250,000 in 1939.
- By 1938, Germany was the wealthiest country in Europe and per capita (per head) incomes of Germans equalled those of people in Britain.

Effects of rearmament on the German economy

Germany's economic recovery was fragile.

- The Nazis spent a large proportion of the country's wealth on maintaining huge numbers of people in the armed forces.
- Many of the former unemployed were in non-productive jobs (such as the army). They did not contribute to economic recovery. Administration and bureaucracy also increased significantly.
- The German balance of payments throughout the 1930s (value of imports versus exports) gave cause for concern.
- Germany's worsening relations with its neighbours caused its share of world trade to fall from 10 per cent in 1929 to 8 per cent in 1938.
- The German economy was built on preparing for war and territorial expansion.

German territorial expansion

Hitler never concealed his aims. In *Mein Kampf*, he outlined his plan for Germany's future. Hitler aimed to:

- destroy the Treaty of Versailles and make Germany great again
- unite all the German peoples under one leader – as a result of the Treaty of Versailles and the Treaty of St Germain, many Germans in the 1930s were living within the borders of Poland, Czechoslovakia and Austria
- achieve *lebensraum* for the new Germany in eastern Europe. Hitler regarded the Slav peoples of eastern Europe, particularly the USSR, as inferior. These territories were therefore ideal for conquest and occupation.

During the 1930s, Hitler began to put these plans into action. They are described in detail on pages 34–38.

Key terms

Lebensraum: the German word for living space – territory claimed by a country on the grounds that it needs more space to grow and survive (for example, Hitler's claim to land in eastern Europe).

Revision tasks

1 How do Nazi economic and foreign policies help explain the lack of opposition to the Nazis in Germany during the 1930s?

2 What evidence is there that Hitler's economic policy was based on getting ready for war? Note down some key words for your answer.

7.10 Germany and the Second World War

German victories

The war began spectacularly well for Germany.

- Within six weeks of the German invasion of Poland in September 1939, the Poles were defeated and out of the war.
- The German war machine had developed a new type of warfare – *Blitzkrieg* (lightning war). Massive air power combined with fast-moving tanks (Panzers) brought quick victories for the German armed forces.
- By June 1940, German troops had entered Paris and by the end of the year most of Europe including France, the Netherlands, Belgium, Norway and Denmark was under German occupation.
- By the end of 1941, the Germans had advanced deep into the USSR and reached the outskirts of Moscow.

The impact of the war on Germany

Germans soon felt the impact of war. Food rationing began in September 1939. From November 1939, clothes were rationed.

As the war went on, the state began to control life and work even more closely than before. The Gestapo kept a close watch for people who did not support the war effort. The SS became increasingly powerful. Germans were bombarded with propaganda. Sometimes they were told how well the war was going. Sometimes they were encouraged to support the war effort.

The conquest of Europe stretched German resources to their limits. All German industry was devoted to the war effort. From 1942 onwards, there were serious food shortages. An even bigger problem was a shortage of housing due to bombing.

- The Allies carried out massive bombing raids on German cities.
- In February 1945, 3,000 British and US bombers destroyed the German city of Dresden. It is estimated that over 100,000 people died.
- The bombing raids did not defeat Germany, but they helped to undermine German morale and disrupt industry.

By 1945, it was clear to most Germans that they were losing the war. In 1945, Goebbels was put in charge of the German Home Defence Force. He had to organise teenagers and old men to fight the invading Soviet, US and British forces. It was a hopeless situation.

The defeat of Germany

In the end, the combined forces of Britain, the USA and the USSR were too strong for Germany. There were times when it seemed that Britain might be strangled by the German U-boats attacking Atlantic supply lines. However, the enormous resources of the USA and USSR were too powerful even for Hitler's Germany.

- In January 1943, at Stalingrad, 300,000 German troops surrendered to the Soviet army.
- In July 1943, Allied troops were advancing in Italy.
- In June 1944, the Allies launched their invasion of Normandy. By March 1945, Allied troops had crossed the Rhine into the heartland of Germany.

On 30 April 1945, deep in an underground bunker under the Chancellory building, Hitler committed suicide. On 7 May 1945, Hitler's Third Reich surrendered to the Allies; the Second World War (in Europe) was over.

> ### Revision tasks
> 1 Explain the term '*Blitzkrieg*'.
> 2 What evidence is there to support the view that *Blitzkrieg* was effective?
> 3 **Chapter review** Here are ten events, terms or people you have studied in this depth study. Without checking back see if you can write a one or two sentence summary of what it was and why it was important in German history 1918–1945.
>   a) The Weimar Constitution
>   b) Hyperinflation
>   c) Gustav Stresemann
>   d) 'Mein Kamf'
>   e) The Night of the Long Knives
>   f) 'Kinder, Kuche, Kirche'
>   g) Kristallnacht
>   h) Rearmament
>   i) Lebensraum
>   j) Joseph Goebbels

Summary/revision plan

You need to have a good working knowledge of the following areas. **Tick off each item** once you are confident in your knowledge.

☐ **1 The origins of the Weimar Republic and revolution of 1918–19**
- A democratic Germany
- Problems in the new Republic
  - Spartacist Revolt, 1919
  - The Kapp putsch, 1920

☐ **2 Economic and political problems in Germany during the 1920s**
- Reparations and the invasion of the Ruhr
- Hyperinflation, 1923
- Crisis under control
- The Munich putsch, 1923

☐ **3 German recovery in the 1920s under Stresemann**
- Economic recovery
- The Locarno treaties, 1925
- Extremist groups
- Cultural life during the Weimar Republic

☐ **4 The effects of the Depression on Germany**
- Effects of the Wall Street Crash, 1929
- Unemployment
- The rise of extremism

☐ **5 How the Nazis took power: the German elections, 1932–33**
- How the Depression helped Hitler
  - Fear of Communism
  - Disillusionment with democracy
- The presidential election, 1932
- Elections for the Reichstag, July 1932

- New Reichstag elections, November 1932
- Hitler becomes Chancellor, January 1933
- The Reichstag fire, 1933
- Election results, 1932–33
- The Enabling Act, March 1933
- The Night of the Long Knives, June 1934

☐ **6 Life in Nazi Germany**
- Propaganda
- Terror: A police state
- Nazi control of society
  - Education
  - The Church
  - The role of women
  - Work
  - Leisure

☐ **7 Nazi treatment of the Jews**
- Persecution
- Kristallnacht
- The 'Final Solution'

☐ **8 Opposition to the Nazis**
- Youth movements
- The July Plot

☐ **9 Nazi economic and foreign policy**
- The recovery of the German economy
- Rearmament
- German territorial expansion

☐ **10 Germany and the Second World War**
- German victories
- The impact of the war on Germany
- The defeat of Germany.

Check your knowledge online with our Quick quizzes at www.hodderplus.co.uk/ modernworldhistory.

Chapter 8: Russia, 1905–1941

In 1917, Russia experienced war and revolutions that eventually brought the Communists to power and made Russia the USSR. In this chapter, you will consider how the Communists took control and kept it, and how this affected the people of Russia/the USSR.

Focus points

In the OCR course, each Paper 1 depth study option is divided into key questions, and each key question is divided into focus points. To do well in the examination, you need to have a well-thought-out view on each of the key questions and focus points.

Key question 1: Why did the Tsarist regime collapse in 1917?
Focus points
- How did the Tsar survive the 1905 revolution?
- How well did the Tsarist regime deal with the difficulties of ruling Russia up to 1918?
- How far was the Tsar weakened by the First World War?
- Why was the revolution of February (March) 1917 successful?

Key question 2: How did the Bolsheviks gain power, and how did they consolidate their rule?
Focus points
- How effectively did the Provisional Government rule Russia in 1917?
- Why were the Bolsheviks able to seize power in November 1917?
- Why did the Bolsheviks win the Civil War?
- How far was the New Economic Policy a success?

Key question 3: How did Stalin gain and hold onto power?
Focus points
- Why did Stalin, and not Trotsky, emerge as Lenin's successor?
- Why did Stalin launch the 'Purges'?
- What methods did Stalin use to control the Soviet Union?
- How complete was Stalin's control over the Soviet Union by 1941?

Key question 4: What was the impact of Stalin's economic policies?
Focus points
- Why did Stalin introduce the Five-Year Plans?
- Why did Stalin introduce collectivisation?
- How successful were Stalin's economic changes?
- How were the Soviet people affected by these changes?

Key content

In order to fully understand the focus points, you will need to have a good working knowledge of:

- the collapse of the Tsarist system
- the problems of the Provisional Government
- the Bolshevik revolution and dictatorship
- opposition to the Bolsheviks and the Civil War, 1918–20
- War Communism and the New Economic Policy
- the struggle to succeed Lenin
- Stalin's attempts to modernise the USSR
- Stalin's control over home and foreign policies.

8.1 The collapse of the Tsarist system

The Tsarist system of government

The Russian monarch was known as the Tsar. He ruled as an **autocrat**. He believed that God had made him Tsar and that he therefore had absolute authority to rule Russia. The Tsar ruled with the support of the aristocracy (landowners), the Church, the army and the civil service.

The 1905 revolution

In January 1905, a peaceful but very large gathering of workers came to the Tsar's palace in St Petersburg to ask for the Tsar's help in improving working conditions and pay. The crowds were attacked by troops, and the event became known as Bloody Sunday. Bloody Sunday sparked off strikes, peasant revolts and then mutinies in the armed forces.

The revolution of 1905 almost toppled the Tsar. Several factors helped him survive.

- His best troops remained loyal. This allowed him to put down most of the rebellions by force by March 1906.
- He published the 'October Manifesto', which promised the middle classes a **Duma** that would give them some say in how Russia was run.
- He gave some concessions to the peasants – for example, lower taxes and improvements in education.
- He appointed Peter Stolypin as his chief minister to bring more reforms to Russia. Stolypin punished rebellion brutally, but he also developed Russia's economy. This helped to reduce discontent until the economy took a downturn in 1912.

Opposition to the Tsar

However, opposition to the Tsar continued. There were many strikes and protests by workers in the years 1906–14. Probably the most important of these was the strike in the Lena goldfields in 1912.

There were several opposition groups.

- Some middle-class Russians wanted more say in Russia's government, but the Duma was virtually powerless before 1914.
- There were also the Socialist Revolutionaries (SRs) who mainly represented the peasant farmers and also the Bolsheviks.
- The third group was the Communists – divided into Bolsheviks and Mensheviks who disagreed with each other about the tactics for overthrowing the tsarist system.

By 1914, poor working conditions, food shortages and the opposition parties had created a very tense atmosphere in Russia.

Key terms

Autocrat: a ruler who holds absolute power in a country and does not have to explain his actions to anyone else.
Duma: a representative assembly (parliament) that the Tsar consulted but which had little power.

Exam practice

1 Describe the main events of the 1905 Russian Revolution.

(4 marks)

Exam tip This is typical of the questions you will face in questions 8 or 9.

This is a starter question. It tests your **factual knowledge**. Try to include four details about the 1905 revolution.

The impact of the First World War

It was the First World War that finished off the Tsarist system. Even with the protests, strikes and demonstrations of 1914, the Tsar could probably have used the army and police to keep order.

When war began in 1914, the Tsar had the complete support of his people. However, war began to take its toll and by 1917 the Tsar's Government was facing collapse. There were various reasons for this:

- The Russian army was not a match for the well-equipped Germans.
- Casualties were enormous (around 9 million by 1917).
- The Tsar took personal control of the army and so took personal blame for Russia's defeats.
- The Tsar's wife and her adviser Rasputin became increasingly unpopular at home.
- Food shortages began because the inadequate railway system could not get enough food to the cities.
- Prices rose and wages fell as goods became in short supply – this led to strikes.

The February (March) Revolution

This is often called the March Revolution. Confused? The explanation is simple. In 1917, Russia was using a different calendar from the West. As a result, the first Russian revolution took place in February by the Russian calendar, but March for the rest of Europe. This book uses the Russian dates.

The unrest began in January 1917 with a strike in an armaments factory in Petrograd.

- Unrest and strikes spread quickly and in February bread queues turned into riots.
- The workers began to form councils (called soviets) and the leaders of the Duma (such as Alexander Kerensky) began opposing the Tsar openly.

By the end of February, the troops had joined the rioters and the Tsar had no choice but to abdicate (give up power) on 2 March. The Tsar's regime was replaced by the Provisional Government.

8.2 The problems of the Provisional Government

The Provisional Government of 1917 was headed first by Prince Lvov. He was replaced by the Socialist Revolutionary Alexander Kerensky in July of that year. Kerensky had already served in the Provisional Government as Justice Minister and War Minister. He was also deputy chairman of the Petrograd Soviet (workers' council). Many people already believed the soviets were more effective as a means of government than the Duma.

Conditions in 1917

The Provisional Government was faced with pressures from outside as well as its own weaknesses. Continuing the war against the Germans made the Provisional Government deeply unpopular. This was made worse by heavy casualties.

- Mutinies broke out in the army.
- There was a revolt at the Kronstadt naval base in July.
- Peasants were taking over the landowners' estates by force.
- Opposition was growing from the Bolsheviks.
- The Petrograd Soviet, controlled by the Bolsheviks, became more and more hostile to the Government as it failed to solve Russia's economic problems.

Exam practice
1 Explain the reasons why there was so much opposition to the Tsar in 1917.

(6 marks)

Exam tip This tests your knowledge and understanding.
- A low level answer (worth 1–2 marks) will simply state one or two reasons.
- A better answer (worth 3–4 marks) will describe AND explain several reasons – which means giving more detail about why each factor led people to oppose the Tsar.
- A top level answer (worth 5–6 marks) will explain all the reasons AND evaluate the importance of each reason.

Lenin and the Bolsheviks

At the time of the February Revolution, Lenin, leader of the Bolsheviks, came back from exile in Germany. His aim was to overthrow the Provisional Government with a second revolution of the working classes.

Lenin published his views in April 1917 in the 'April Theses'. He said that the Bolsheviks offered 'Peace, bread and land', and 'all power to the soviets'.

Kerensky, the Kornilov revolt and the Bolsheviks

Alexander Kerensky began to get a hold on his opponents and Lenin was forced into hiding. However, Kerensky was then challenged by the new commander of the army, General Kornilov, who wanted to impose a strict regime and crush opponents, rather like the Tsar had done.

Kerensky asked the Bolsheviks to help him defeat Kornilov, which they did. But Kerensky still had problems. He had lost the support of the army and was dependent upon the Petrograd Soviet (with its strong Bolshevik influence) to run Russia.

The Bolshevik Revolution, October 1917 (also known as the November Revolution)

Support for the peasants and workers' soviets grew rapidly through 1917, especially after the defeat of Kornilov. In October, Lenin persuaded the Petrograd Soviet to take the decision to overthrow Kerensky's Government.

The Bolsheviks staged their revolution efficiently and quickly under the brilliant organisation of Leon Trotsky. Within two days, Trotsky's Red Guards had seized railway stations, telegraph offices and other targets such as the Winter Palace. Kerensky fled and the Bolshevik takeover succeeded with very little bloodshed.

> ## Revision task
> Write key point summaries of how each of the following factors helped the Bolsheviks come to power:
> - the First World War
> - Bolshevik strategies
> - Lenin's leadership
> - the Provisional Government – its policies and problems
> - the Kornilov revolt
> - the Bolshevik revolution.
>
> Explain which factors you think are more important than others.

> ## Exam practice
> 1 'The main reason for the success of the Russian Revolution in October 1917 was the quality of Lenin's leadership.' How far do you agree with this statement? Explain your answer. *(10 marks)*

Key terms

October/November revolution: They are the same thing. Russia used a different calendar from the rest of Europe.

Exam tip This question tests your knowledge and understanding but it goes further. A question that starts 'How far …' is also inviting you to **evaluate**. In your exam, question 8 or 9 will usually include an element of evaluation like this.

Don't make the mistake of only writing about the factor mentioned in the question. Remember to write about the other factors that lurk below the surface.

A top level answer (worth 7–10 marks) will evaluate the role of Lenin, but also other relevant reasons (e.g. the effect of the First World War on Russia and the failure of Kerensky's Provisional Government) in order to show a good understanding of the period.

8.3 The Bolshevik Revolution and dictatorship

The Provisional Government was replaced by the Council of the People's Commissars under Lenin. Lenin's aims were clear. He followed the theories of the political thinker Karl Marx and wanted a **dictatorship of the proletariat**.

Since the Bolsheviks saw themselves as representing the proletariat, 'dictatorship by the proletariat' came to mean dictatorship by the Bolsheviks – that is, the Communist Party.

> ### Key terms
>
> **Dictatorship of the proletariat:** the transition period between a capitalist and a Communist state where a period of dictatorship is required.

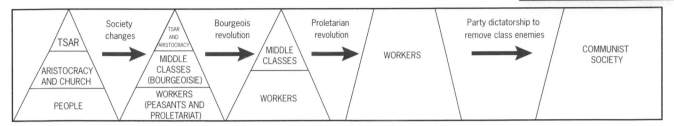

The road to Communism according to Marxist theory.

Setting up a Marxist state

Lenin was not interested in democracy. The elections held in late 1917 showed that the Bolsheviks did not have the support of most Russians.
- The Constituent Assembly, which met in January 1918, contained twice as many Socialist Revolutionaries (SRs) as Bolsheviks and the SRs opposed Lenin.
- Bolshevik Red Guards closed down the Assembly.

By July 1918, the Russian Congress of Soviets had agreed a new system of government for Russia.
- Power was concentrated in the hands of the local soviets, which then sent representatives to regional soviets.
- The soviets were dominated by Bolshevik activists loyal to Lenin.
- The result was that Lenin effectively became a dictator.

Lenin was determined to force through his plans to make Russia a Communist state. His secret police (the Cheka) began to imprison and murder political opponents.

Negotiating peace

Peace had been the first promise in Lenin's slogan, 'Peace, land and bread'. In December 1917, the Bolsheviks agreed a ceasefire. However, in March 1918 the Bolsheviks were forced to sign the Treaty of Brest-Litovsk. Under the treaty:
- Russia lost various amounts of territory, including important coal and iron resources, one-third of the land providing its grain harvest, and more than a quarter of its population.
- Russia also had to pay 300 million roubles in compensation.

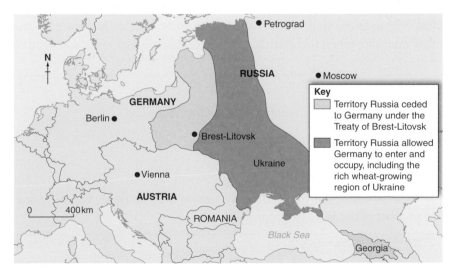

Russian losses under the Treaty of Brest-Litovsk.

State of the land and economy

The question of land and its ownership was vitally important in Russia. More than 80 per cent of the population were peasants living in the countryside on the estates of wealthy landlords. When Lenin abolished private ownership of land, this effectively allowed the peasants to take possession of the land out of the hands of the landowners and the Church. The countryside was in a state of chaos in the early days of Bolshevik rule, and beyond the Government's control. The Bolsheviks were strong in the towns and cities but not in the countryside.

- There was soon a problem of food shortages because Russian money was worthless and the peasants were not being paid for their produce.
- Peasants did not trust the Bolsheviks, who wanted to change the way farming was organised from individual to collective (or co-operative) farming.

Source evaluation: Bolshevik rule

Below are two viewpoints on Bolshevik rule during this period.

SOURCE 1

American writer, Leonard Schapiro, *The Communist Party of the Soviet Union*, 1963.

Bolshevik practice within a few days of 25th October was at variance with Lenin's repeated promises that when they were in power the Bolsheviks would guarantee to each political party … facilities for publishing a newspaper. Some socialist and liberal papers, as well as the conservative papers, were closed down in the first few days.

SOURCE 2

Eugenie Fraser, *The House by the Dvina*, a historical novel, 1984.

In the town, after six months of living under a new government, conditions remained chaotic. The minds of the authorities are too occupied with establishing their doctrine and persecuting those who have opinions contrary to their own to bother with the less important matters such as clothing and feeding hungry citizens.

> **Exam tip** Ask these questions of any source:
> - What is it? (a document, diary extract, cartoon, picture, etc.)
> - Who produced, wrote or drew it?
> - When was it produced, written or drawn?
> - Why was it produced, written or drawn?

Sources 1 and 2 do not present a very favourable picture of the Bolshevik rule. However, Source 1 was written by an American during the Cold War (see Chapter 4). Such writings from the 1960s must be used with care since they may not be very reliable, or may use events selectively in order to create a particular impression of the Bolsheviks.

Source 2 is from a historical novel. It is based on historical research and fits many things you know from your background knowledge. When looking at this kind of source the skills of the historian must be used to make a judgement – we must take care when using such a work as evidence, since it is a secondary source.

Revision tasks

1 Create a key word summary of the following topics:

- Bolshevik system of government
- Treaty of Brest-Litovsk
- Changes in land ownership

2 What evidence can you find in this section that the Bolsheviks did not enjoy the support of the Russian people?

8.4 Opposition to the Bolsheviks and the Civil War, 1918–20

Who made up the opposition?

The Bolsheviks did not have the support of all Russians when they seized power. By May 1918, they had even more enemies, especially after the losses of the Treaty of Brest-Litovsk.

By the summer of 1918, the Bolsheviks were faced with a range of opponents. The only thing uniting these opponents was their opposition to the Bolsheviks. These opponents, called the Whites (in contrast to the Bolshevik Red Guards) were made up of former tsarists, Mensheviks, Socialist Revolutionaries and foreign powers opposed to the new regime in Russia.

The Bolsheviks in danger

In the early stages of the Civil War, the Bolsheviks were facing several different threats.

- The Czech Legion (which was made up of former prisoners of war) had seized sections of the vital Trans-Siberian railway.
- Admiral Kolchak had set up a White Government in Siberia and was marching on Moscow.
- General Denikin was advancing with his army from southern Russia.
- Northern Russia, led by the White General Yudenich, was opposing the Bolsheviks.
- Foreign powers supplied the Whites with arms and weapons, and later landed troops to help the Whites as well. US, Japanese, French and British troops landed at Archangel, Murmansk and Vladivostok.

Bolshevik victory

Against what seemed to be overwhelming odds, the Bolsheviks won the Civil War. The crucial year was 1919. Under Trotsky's leadership, the Red Army defeated Kolchak and destroyed the Czech Legion. Denikin's advance on Moscow was stopped and by 1920, he was being pushed back. By late 1920, White forces were completely defeated. The Bolsheviks won because of their own ruthless, disciplined commitment and the failings of their enemies. The strengths of the Bolsheviks were:

- They had large, well-organised armies under the leadership of Trotsky and had good communications.
- They made good use of propaganda to show that the White were in league with foreigners and wanted to bring back the Tsar.
- The Red Army and the Cheka (secret police) kept a ruthless control over the Bolshevik territories, making sure that most people obeyed Lenin's rule.

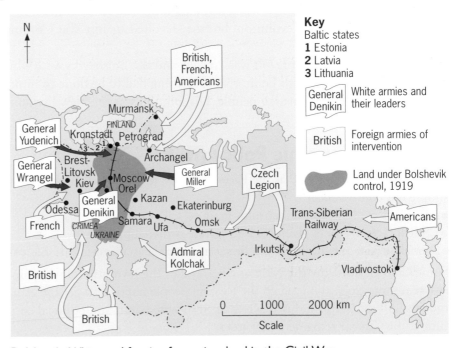

Bolshevik, White and foreign forces involved in the Civil War.

- The brutal policy of War Communism (see below) ensured that the Red Army and the population of the towns were fed and supplied.
- The Reds controlled the major towns and could use their factories and industries to support the war effort.

The failings of the Whites were as follows.

- The Whites had no aim upon which they all agreed. In some cases, they disliked each other almost as much as they opposed the Reds.
- Their forces were spread across a huge area and they could not co-ordinate their attacks – they were beaten one by one.
- Their harsh treatment of people in the lands they captured led many to support the Bolsheviks against them.

Revision tasks

1 Make your own key words summary of who the Whites were and why they opposed the Bolsheviks.

2 Explain how the Bolsheviks won the Civil War (eight to ten key words).

8.5 War Communism and the New Economic Policy

War Communism

To defeat his opponents in the Civil War, Lenin knew that he had to make sure that his armies were fed and equipped. To achieve this, he introduced the policy of **War Communism**.

- Land and industry were nationalised – taken over by the state.
- In the factories, there was severe discipline (for example, strikers could be shot) and key items, such as food and coal, were rationed.
- In the countryside, peasants were forced to hand over their surplus produce (what they did not need themselves) to the Government.
- Opposition was rooted out and destroyed by the Cheka (even the royal family was executed). This policy was known as the 'Red Terror'.

Key terms

War Communism: it had the *appearance* of Communism, but was carried out due to Bolshevik necessities during the civil war.

The cost of the Civil War and War Communism

By 1921, Lenin was facing a shattered and demoralised country.

- War Communism had made the industrial workers poor and restless.
- War Communism and war damage had led to famine in the countryside – millions died in 1921.

The Kronstadt mutiny of 1921 was a turning point. The Kronstadt sailors had been leading supporters of the revolution, but they revolted against War Communism in March 1921.

Although the Kronstadt revolt was crushed and the Bolsheviks were winning the Civil War, it was clear to Lenin that something had to be done to improve the living conditions of the Russian people. His solution was the New Economic Policy (NEP).

The New Economic Policy (NEP)

Lenin introduced the NEP at the Party Congress in March 1921. Its measures were simple but controversial.

- Peasants could keep their surplus grain to sell at a profit.
- Small factories were given back to private ownership.
- Small private businesses could be set up to trade at a profit.

Some Communists saw the NEP as a betrayal of the revolution, but Lenin saw it as a temporary measure to keep the Russian people happy and get the economy moving. All the major industries remained in state hands and political control (under the Cheka) remained very strict.

The importance of Lenin

Lenin died in January 1924. He had brought huge changes to Russia.

- He had led the Communist revolution.
- He had established the USSR (Union of Soviet Socialist Republics).
- He had created a powerful, disciplined Communist Party by using the Cheka to purge (remove) opponents of his policies.
- The USSR had become a one-party state, which was effectively a dictatorship where the Communist Party controlled industry, the army, the police, the press – in fact, almost all aspects of life.

Source evaluation: Lenin

Lenin has often had a 'good press' in history, especially when compared to Stalin. The questions that historians now ask are:

- What kind of man was Lenin?
- Was he just as ruthless as Stalin?
- Was he good or bad for Russia?

Sources 3 and 4 present two different views from British newspapers immediately after the death of Lenin.

SOURCE 3

The Times, 23 January 1924.

This extraordinary man was first and foremost a professional revolutionary … A man of iron will and inflexible ambition, he was absolutely ruthless and used human beings as mere material for his purpose.

SOURCE 4

Daily Herald, 23 January 1924.

Lenin is dead. All through Russia that news has struck as a deep personal loss. For 'Ilyitch' was loved of his own Russian people – whom he understood and loved so well – as no leader of men in our time has been loved.

For historians, these are useful sources – they show the attitudes of the day very clearly. *The Times* was a conservative newspaper opposed to Socialism and Communism. It reflects what many of its conservative readers would think of Lenin. The *Daily Herald* was also a British newspaper, but was more favourable towards Socialism and Communism. Again, its comments reflect what many of its readers probably thought about Lenin.

However, neither source is reliable for telling us what Lenin was actually like. They each only express an opinion. We cannot therefore simply accept what they say as true without question.

Revision tasks

1 Write your own summary of War Communism. Use key words under these headings:

Reasons it was needed	How it worked	Effects

2 Now write a summary of the NEP, using the same headings.

3 If you were a Russian being interviewed by a British newspaper after Lenin's death, how would you explain the importance of Lenin in the USSR?

8.6 The struggle to succeed Lenin

The candidates

Trotsky	Kamenev and Zinoviev	Bukharin	Stalin
When Lenin died, the most obvious candidate to take over the leadership was Trotsky. He was brilliant, talented and had an outstanding record as leader of the Red Army.	Kamenev and Zinoviev were both leading Bolsheviks. They believed in spreading revolution and both were unhappy about the NEP.	Bukharin was more moderate. He wanted to build up the new Russia slowly and favoured keeping the NEP in the short term.	Stalin expressed no strong views – he was a hardworking administrator and few expected him to win the leadership contest.

Stalin succeeds

The contest was eventually won by Stalin, although it took him five years to become completely established as Lenin's successor. Stalin was able to defeat his rivals for a number of reasons.

- He had taken on many important jobs including General Secretary of the Communist Party. This gave him an important power base – he had many supporters in the ranks of the party (who owed their position to him).
- Trotsky made himself unpopular. His ideas for spreading world revolution alarmed moderate Communists. He was also arrogant and offended many party members.
- The other four candidates disagreed with each other on important issues such as industrialisation and the NEP.
- They all underestimated Stalin. At first, Stalin sided with the other three against Trotsky, who was thrown out of the **Politburo** in 1927. He continued to play Bukharin, Zinoviev and Kamenev off against each other by allying with one and then another, while he strengthened his own position.

By 1929, Stalin had defeated his opponents and was the dictator of the USSR.

Key terms

Politburo: the ruling committee of the Communist Party, in charge of policy-making.

Source evaluation: Stalin

SOURCE 5

John Reed, an American Communist who lived in Russia, writing in his book *Ten Days that Shook the World*.

He's [Stalin] not the intellectual like the other people you will meet. He's not even particularly well informed, but he knows what he wants. He's got willpower and he's going to be on top of the pile some day.

SOURCE 6

Trotsky on Stalin.

I said to Smirnov: 'Stalin will become the dictator of the USSR.' 'Stalin?' he asked me with amazement. 'But he is a mediocrity, a colourless nonentity.' 'Mediocrity, yes; nonentity, no … He is needed by all of them – the tired radicals, the bureaucrats, the NEP men, the kulaks [wealthier peasant farmers], the upstarts …'

Sources 5 and 6 present some views on Stalin from the time. They provide us with some interesting and useful evidence. Both are first-hand accounts, or primary sources. Both also give clues as to how Stalin won the contest (for example, his determination, his supporters), which should agree with your own background knowledge. However, Source 6 was written by Trotsky, Stalin's bitter opponent. We must be careful about accepting what he says at face value – he might be trying to give excuses for his own defeat.

Revision task

Use a key words list to explain why Stalin succeeded Lenin as a leader. Refer to:
- Stalin's opponents
- Stalin's qualities.

8.7 Stalin's attempts to modernise the USSR

Stalin believed that the USSR was under threat from non-Communist states. He also believed that the only way for the USSR to make itself secure was to become a modern, industrial country. His aim was to force the USSR to make 50 years' progress in 10 years. There were two key aspects of Stalin's plans:

- the need to expand heavy industry (the Five-Year Plans)
- the need to improve food production (**collectivisation**).

Industry: The Five-Year Plans

Stalin seems to have had a number of reasons for industrialising the USSR:

- security so the USSR didn't depend on imports from other countries.
- to create a showpiece of communist success for the outside world
- to carry out his idea of 'socialism in one country'.

In order to achieve his aims he came up with the Five-Year Plans which were incredibly ambitious targets for industrial production. Few targets were met, but even so industries made huge advances. The first Five-Year Plan was started in 1928.

The effects of the Five-Year Plans

Historians disagree about the aims and the effects of the Five-Year Plans. One thing on which all historians do agree is that the USSR was transformed.

- The main aim was achieved – by 1940, the USSR was in the 'first division' of industrial powers, along with Britain, Germany and the USA.
- Vast projects, such as the Belomor Canal, the Dnieper Dam and the metalworks at Magnitogorsk, were completed with great speed.
- Huge towns and factories were built from nothing, deep inside the USSR to protect them from invasion.
- Foreign technicians were brought in and enormous investment was put into education and training to produce skilled workers.
- Great pressure was put on workers to meet targets and to be 'Stakhanovites'. Stakhanov was a miner who managed to produce over 100 tons of coal in one shift, and was held up as a model to inspire all workers.
- The cost was high. Safety standards came second to meeting targets, discipline was harsh and many workers ended up in labour camps (gulags). All investment went into heavy industries – there were few consumer goods (clothes, luxuries).
- In 1932 living and working conditions were reported to be worse than in 1914.

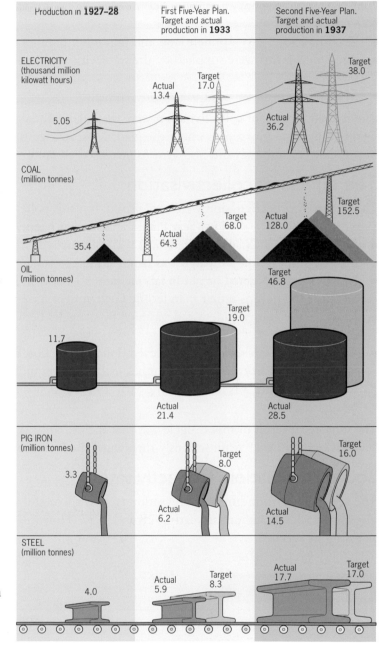

Targets and actual production under the Five-Year Plans.

Farming: the need for collectivisation

Stalin had made clear his ambitions to transform the USSR. The Five-Year Plans could only work if Soviet agriculture could significantly improve the amount of grain production. There were two main reasons:

- to feed the growing population of industrial workers
- to export any surpluses to raise cash for investment in industry.

How collectivisation worked

Most farms were smallholdings tended by peasant families. These holdings could never be efficient enough for Stalin's plans so he introduced the policy of collectivisation.

- Peasants had to give up their land and join other families on very large farms.
- These new farms were supplied by the state with seed, tools, tractors and other machinery.
- Most of the produce went to the Government.

The real opponents of collectivisation were the kulaks. Kulaks were richer peasants who had become prosperous under the NEP. Most refused to co-operate with the new policy because they did not want to give up their land.

The effects of collectivisation

The effects of collectivisation were very mixed, but this policy certainly had less claim to success than the Five-Year Plans. This is what happened.

- By 1941 almost all land in the USSR was collectivised.
- A huge propaganda campaign was launched to persuade peasants to modernise.
- Kulaks were murdered or put in labour camps – many killed their own animals or burnt their crops rather than let the Government have them.
- Much of the countryside was devastated by struggles between Stalin's agents and the kulaks.
- Although collectivisation was achieved, food production fell dramatically. Grain production fell from 73 million tonnes in 1928 to 69 million tonnes in 1933. In Ukraine, there was famine in the early 1930s and at the same time food was being exported.

The long-term result of this struggle was that the peasants were battered into submission and never again seriously threatened the Communist regime.

Source evaluation: Collectivisation

The key issue surrounding collectivisation is: how successful was it? Source 7 gives livestock figures for the years 1928 and 1933. How might these be useful in assessing its success?

SOURCE 7

Livestock	1928	1933
Pigs	26 million	12 million
Sheep/goats	147 million	50 million
Cattle	70 million	38 million

USSR livestock in 1928 and 1933.

Exam practice

1 What were the Five-Year Plans? *(4 marks)*

2 Explain why Stalin introduced collectivisation.

(6 marks)

Exam tip

These are typical of the questions you will face in questions 8 or 9.

1 This is a starter question. It tests your **factual knowledge**. Try to include four details about the Five-Year Plans.

2 This tests your knowledge and understanding.
- A low level answer (worth 1–2 marks) will simply state one or two reasons.
- A better answer (worth 3–4 marks) will describe several reasons why collectivisation was introduced and explain each one more fully.
- A top level answer (worth 5–6 marks) will do all the above, but also argue which reason was the most important.

Key terms

Collectivisation: the process in Stalin's USSR in the 1930s of bringing small farms together to create large ones, which were meant to be more efficient.

These figures suggest that Stalin's agricultural policies were disastrous, and this is supported by other evidence that you will have read. As always, however, the historian must be careful. Statistics are not always accurate or reliable, and more importantly they do not always present a complete picture. Other years may have been better or worse and this information covers livestock, not crops. You would need to refer to your own background knowledge that grain production also dropped from 73 million tonnes in 1928 to 69 million tonnes in 1933.

Revision task

Copy and complete the table below by using the information and evidence in this section.

	Five-Year Plans	Collectivisation
Aims		
Methods		
Successes/failures		
Costs		

8.8 Stalin's control over home and foreign policies

Opposition to Stalin

Radical policies such as Stalin's were bound to cause concern. Criticism within the Communist Party grew because of the human cost of Stalin's policies.

In 1934, Stalin's ally Sergei Kirov was murdered. Stalin saw this as evidence of a conspiracy and began a series of political purges (imprisonments and executions).

Historians are now fairly sure that Stalin planned Kirov's murder to give him an excuse to purge the USSR of opponents, whom Stalin saw as traitors.

The purges

From 1934 to 1938, thousands were arrested, imprisoned, murdered or simply disappeared. They came from all areas of Soviet life.

- The Communist Party: the number of party members fell from 3.5 million in 1934 to 2 million in 1935.
- Leading party members such as Zinoviev, Kamenev and Bukharin were tortured. Then, at show trials, they 'confessed' and were executed.
- Many less important opponents (or even supporters who were not enthusiastic enough) were arrested and executed or sent to labour camps.
- In 1937, around 25,000 army officers (including the Commander of the Red Army, Marshal Tukhachevsky) were purged.

The effects of the purges were mixed. Stalin was certainly secure. His new secret police (the NKVD) ruled the population with terror. Over 8 million had been killed or sent to labour camps.

However, Stalin had weakened the USSR. Many of those purged had been skilled or educated, and industrial progress slowed down. The army was seriously weakened and suffered badly against the Germans in 1941.

Exam practice

1 Stalin made changes both in industry and agriculture. Which were the more important – the industrial or agricultural changes? Explain your answer.

(10 marks)

Exam tip This question tests your knowledge and understanding but it goes further. It asks you to **evaluate** (weigh the importance of) two different developments. In your exam, question 8 or 9 will usually include an element of evaluation like this.
- A low level answer (worth 1–3 marks) will simply describe these changes.
- A better answer (worth 4–6 marks) will describe AND explain the importance of what these changes meant for the Soviet Union.
- A top level answer (worth 7–10 marks) will describe and explain the industrial and agricultural changes but also reach a considered decision, supported by evidence, as to which was more important and why.

The constitution

Stalin's hold on power became more secure in 1936 with the USSR's new constitution. At first sight, it seemed more democratic – all citizens voted for members of the **Supreme Soviet**. However, it had no real power and decisions were still made by Stalin and his closest supporters.

The culture of Stalin's USSR

- Stalin's USSR was disciplined and seemingly full of fear.
- Some real advances in industry were made, but at a high cost for many workers.
- Freedom of speech was denied to Soviet citizens.
- Basic standards of education improved, but it was heavily controlled by the NKVD.
- Artists, writers, musicians and performers had to please Stalin with their work, get out of the USSR or face being purged.
- Posters, radio broadcasts and the press all made clear the need for loyalty to the party and to Stalin.
- Lenin's ideal of a classless society did not seem to match the realities. High-ranking party officials and the military seemed to enjoy a much higher standard of living than most Soviet citizens.

Stalin's attitudes to world revolution

Stalin was too busy building socialism in one country to be concerned with Trotsky's ideas of spreading world revolution. In fact, Stalin was concerned with keeping the USSR secure, and even joined the League of Nations in 1934.

Concern about fascism

Fascism was a political idea that was totally opposed to Communism. Fascist governments were already in power in Italy (1924) and Germany (1933). Stalin supported the Communist-backed republicans in the Spanish Civil War (1936) and supplied military aid, but by 1939 Spain, too, was a fascist state. Stalin began to feel very concerned, especially when Germany and Japan signed the Anti-Comintern Pact in 1936, which placed the USSR between two powerful, hostile neighbours.

The search for security

Stalin's obvious allies were Britain and France, both of whom were concerned about Hitler. However, Britain and France were just as worried about Stalin as they were about Hitler.

The Munich crisis of 1938 (see pages 35–36) convinced Stalin that Britain and France could not be relied upon, so in 1939 the Nazi–Soviet Non-Aggression Pact was signed (also called the Molotov-Ribbentrop Pact after the ministers who arranged it).

Both Hitler and Stalin shocked their followers with the agreement, but each was buying time. Stalin kept his side of the agreement and even helped Hitler with supplies when the Second World War broke out. However, Hitler declared war on the USSR in June 1941 and the 'Great Patriotic War' began.

Key terms

Supreme Soviet: an elected body of representatives (the equivalent of the British Parliament), but which had no real power. It only met for two weeks a year. It was the Communist Party under Stalin that made the important decisions.

Fascism: a right-wing system of government generally led by a single strong leader or dictator who uses physical force and intimidation to maintain control and power.

Revision tasks

1 Why was there opposition to Stalin's policies?

2 List three major effects of the purges.

3 List three ways in which freedom was restricted in Stalin's USSR.

4 Do you agree that Stalin's main concern was protection from possible German invasion? What evidence could you use to demonstrate this?

Revision task

Chapter review

Here are ten events, terms or people you have studied in this depth study. Without checking back see if you can write a one or two sentence summary of what it was and why it was important in Russian history 1905–1941.

a) Tsar Nicholas
b) The Duma
c) The Provisional Government
d) The Treaty of Brest-Litovsk
e) The 'Whites'
f) War Communism
g) Stakhanovites
h) The Five Year Plans
i) The purges
j) The NKVD

Summary/revision plan

You need to have a good working knowledge of the following areas. **Tick off each item** once you are confident in your knowledge.

❑ 1 **The collapse of the Tsarist system**
- The Tsarist system of government
- The 1905 revolution
- Opposition to the Tsar
- The impact of the First World War
- The February (March) Revolution

❑ 2 **The problems of the Provisional Government**
- Conditions in 1917
- Lenin and the Bolsheviks
- Kerensky, the Kornilov revolt and the Bolsheviks
- The Bolshevik Revolution, October 1917 (the November Revolution)

❑ 3 **The Bolshevik Revolution and dictatorship**
- Setting up a Marxist state
- Negotiating peace
- State of the land and economy

❑ 4 **Opposition to the Bolsheviks and the Civil War, 1918–20**
- Who made up the opposition?
- The Bolsheviks in danger
- Bolshevik victory

❑ 5 **War Communism and the New Economic Policy**
- War Communism
- The cost of the Civil War and War Communism

- The New Economic Policy (NEP)
- The importance of Lenin

❑ 6 **The struggle to succeed Lenin**
- The candidates
  - Trotsky
  - Kamenev and Zinoviev
  - Bukharin
  - Stalin
- Stalin succeeds

❑ 7 **Stalin's attempts to modernise the USSR**
- Industry: The Five-Year Plans
  - The effects of the Five-Year Plans
- Farming: collectivisation
  - How collectivisation worked
  - The effects of collectivisation

❑ 8 **Stalin's control over home and foreign policies**
- Opposition to Stalin
- The purges
- The constitution
- The culture of Stalin's USSR
- Stalin's attitudes to world revolution
- Concern about fascism
- The search for security.

Check your knowledge online with our Quick quizzes at www.hodderplus.co.uk/modernworldhistory.

Chapter 9: The USA, 1919–1941

After the First World War, the USA was the world's richest and most powerful country. In this chapter, you will see that, despite its wealth, the USA also had its problems in the period 1919–41.

Focus points

In the OCR course, each Paper 1 depth study option is divided into key questions, and each key question is divided into focus points. To do well in the examination, you need to have a well-thought-out view on each of the key questions and focus points.

Key question 1: How far did the US economy boom in the 1920s?
Focus points
- On what was the economic boom based?
- Why did some industries prosper while some did not?
- Why did agriculture not share in the prosperity?
- Did all Americans benefit from the boom?

Key question 2: How far did US society change in the 1920s?
Focus points
- What were the 'Roaring Twenties'?
- How widespread was intolerance in US society?
- Why was prohibition introduced, and then later repealed?
- How far did the roles of women change during the 1920s?

Key question 3: What were the causes and consequences of the Wall Street Crash?
Focus points
- How far was speculation responsible for the Wall Street Crash?
- What impact did the Crash have on the economy?
- What were the social consequences of the Crash?
- Why did Roosevelt win the election of 1932?

Key question 4: How successful was the New Deal?
Focus points
- What was 'the New Deal' as introduced in 1933?
- How far did the character of the New Deal change after 1933?
- Why did the New Deal encounter opposition?
- Did all Americans benefit from the New Deal?
- Did the fact that the New Deal did not solve unemployment mean that it was a failure?

Key content

In order to fully understand the focus points, you will need to have good working knowledge of:

- the economic boom of the 1920s
- American society in the 1920s
- the Wall Street Crash and the Depression
- Roosevelt and the New Deal
- successes and failures of the New Deal.

9.1 The economic boom of the 1920s

Background: the USA up to 1920

America's industry and farming had grown steadily since the 1860s.

- The country had huge natural resources (coal, iron, timber, oil).
- It had a growing population, of which many were immigrants willing to work hard.
- Railways, mining and manufacturing were all strong.
- Americans believed strongly in 'self-help' or '**rugged individualism**'.

US businesses also made money from the war in Europe, supplying loans, arms and equipment. The First World War made the USA wealthy and confident. Americans felt they were doing well. It also made them **isolationist**. They did not want to be dragged into Europe's wars.

Republican policies

Throughout the 1920s, Republican presidents were in power. President Harding believed in what he called 'normalcy' – letting the USA get back to normal life as it had been before the war. Key Republican policies were:

- Isolation – the USA was not to get involved in foreign wars or disputes.
- Tariffs were placed on foreign goods to make them expensive in the USA so that people would buy American goods instead.
- Low taxes – these helped businesses to grow, and gave workers money to spend.

When Harding died suddenly in 1923, Vice-President Coolidge became President. Coolidge followed the same policies as Harding. Another Republican, Hoover, succeeded him in 1928.

The boom period

In the 1920s, the profits of many American companies rose enormously. Goods were produced quickly and cheaply because of new mass-production techniques.

The biggest **economic boom** came in the industries making consumer goods – goods for ordinary families to buy. Sales of household goods, such as vacuum cleaners and washing machines, boosted the electrical industry. Advertising credit and hire purchase made it easy to spend. Wages for many Americans rose, and there was a feeling of confidence. President Hoover summed up the feelings of many Americans at the time (see Source 1).

The single most important industry was the motor industry – by 1930, there were 30 million cars on the roads. A healthy car industry helped create further jobs in related areas, such as car parts and road construction.

The figures in Source 2 on the right seem to support this image of a boom in the USA during the 1920s.

> ### Key terms
>
> **Rugged individualism:** the notion that people should overcome problems and succeed by their own efforts and hard work, not by receiving help from the Government.
> **Isolationism:** withdrawing from international politics and policies.
> **Economic boom:** a period of time that sees individual incomes and company profits increase.

> ### SOURCE 1
>
> President Hoover in a speech in 1928.
>
> *We in America are nearer to the final victory over poverty than ever before in the history of any land.*

SOURCE 2

Production of cars	1926	4.3 million
	1929	5.3 million
Number of cars registered	1920	8.1 million
	1929	23.0 million
Values of radios sold (in US dollars)	1922	60.0 million
	1929	824.5 million

US Government statistics (1929) on economic performance in the 1920s.

As well as buying goods. Americans wanted a share of some of the profits that companies were making. To do this, they bought and sold shares in companies.

Weaknesses in the US economy

There were worrying weaknesses in the US economy during this period.

- Some major industries did not grow in the 1920s (for example, coal and textiles).
- Some industries could not export goods because of tariffs in other countries. Often these tariffs were simply a reaction to American tariffs.
- Farmers had produced too much food and prices were very low. Farm incomes fell from $22 billion in 1919 to $13 billion in 1928.
- Many ordinary Americans did not share in the boom. African Americans, in particular, suffered from discrimination and often had the worst jobs.
- Wealth in the USA was concentrated in a small number of hands. Around 5 per cent of the population owned 32 per cent of the country's wealth. Meanwhile, 42 per cent of the population lived below the poverty line.

Source 3 shows some of the differences in earnings.

The major companies worked together to keep wages down and keep prices high, to ensure the largest profits possible. However, the combination of low wages and high prices actually stopped many people from buying goods, and this stored up problems for the future.

SOURCE 3

Average wages per month of American workers (in US dollars)	
Farmers in South Carolina	129
Town workers in South Carolina	412
Town workers in New York	881
Fruit farmers in California	1246

US social survey of wages in 1929.

Revision tasks

1 Use four to six key words to explain US industrial growth in the 1920s.

2 Copy and complete the table below to show the main features of the US economy in the 1920s.

US economy in the 1920s	
Signs of 'boom' or prosperity	Signs of weakness

9.2 American society in the 1920s

Like the economy, American society was full of contrasts in the 1920s. There were very real advances for some Americans – they owned cars and electrical goods, and enjoyed themselves as never before.

Entertainment

During the 1920s, films became a national obsession. Millions of Americans went to the cinema each week to watch new stars such as Rudolph Valentino, Buster Keaton and Charlie Chaplin. Hollywood became the centre of a multi-million dollar industry. At the same time, jazz music became a craze and the USA became the centre of a world entertainment industry.

Women

After the First World War, women were given the vote in the USA. At the same time, they gained greater freedom by working and earning their own money. By 1929, 10 million American women had jobs. A symbol of this new independence was the flappers – independent young women named after their short skirts.

However, most women were housewives doing the work they had always done. Even those in work were paid less than men. Political parties had very few female members or politicians. There is also evidence that women in small towns and traditionally minded communities disapproved of **flappers** and working women.

Key terms

Flapper: a term for young women in 1920s America who wore short skirts, listened to jazz and challenged acceptable behaviour.

Intolerance and isolationism

The Red Scare

The Communist revolution in Russia (see page 87) alarmed some Americans, particularly leading industrialists. They saw the USA's trade unions as a threat that could lead to a revolution.

The radicals in the USA's immigrant communities were immediate targets. They were suspected of planning revolution. Police, soldiers and ex-servicemen disrupted meetings and raided offices, and thousands of people were arrested. The Government was involved in and supported this campaign. In one extreme case, two Italian radicals, Vanzetti and Sacco, were executed for murder. Most historians are now convinced that they were innocent of this crime.

Immigration

Most Americans were immigrants or the children of immigrants. However, after the First World War, the USA tried to slow down the flow of immigrants with the 1921 Immigration Act.

- By 1929, immigration had fallen from 850,000 people a year (before the First World War) to 150,000.
- The 1924 Amendment to the Immigration Act meant that the majority of new immigrants came from Britain, Ireland and Germany rather than from eastern Europe or Italy.

The Ku Klux Klan

The Ku Klux Klan was another example of the darker side of the 1920s in the USA. It was originally formed to terrorise African American slaves after they had been given freedom in the nineteenth century. The Klan also attacked Catholics and Jews. It was a movement of mainly poor whites concerned about their livelihoods in 1920s America – one sign that the 'Roaring Twenties' were not great times for all.

Prohibition and crime

By the end of the First World War, there was a strong temperance (anti-alcohol) movement in the USA. Temperance groups pressured the Government to pass the 18th Amendment to the US Constitution, commonly known as the Volstead Act, prohibiting the manufacture or sale of alcohol in 1919.

Prohibition was essentially a failure. Making it illegal didn't stop the alcohol trade – it simply forced it underground. **Bootleggers** made large amounts of money smuggling alcohol into the USA, or through illegal brewing. People simply did not support prohibition. The demand for alcohol was always there. Secret bars called speakeasies were easy to find if people wanted a drink.

Law enforcement was also ineffective. There were not enough agents to enforce prohibition and they were poorly paid. Agents and police officers were often bribed or intimidated. Gangs of criminals began to run bootlegging and other forms of crime (gambling, drugs, prostitution) almost like a business. These gangs would sometimes fight with each other for control of the trade.

Revision task

Copy and complete the table below by using the information on pages 100–101.

US society in the 1920s	
High points	Low points

Key terms

Prohibition: the law in the USA that made making and consuming alcohol illegal.

Bootleggers: people who carried liquor into the USA from Canada or Mexico. The name comes from the fact that they sometimes hid the bottles inside their knee-length boots.

Comment

The most notorious gang leader was Al Capone, who virtually controlled the city of Chicago by bribing the mayor and other politicians. Capone was almost certainly responsible for the St Valentine's Day Massacre in 1929 when six members of a rival gang were killed.

Exam tip When looking at this period, it is important to consider whether the 1920s were good times for all Americans. For example, were they good times for:
- women
- immigrants
- political radicals
- African Americans?
As historians, we must look at a wide range of sources to make a balanced judgement. From the information in this section, it is clear that the USA in the 1920s was good for some, but much less so for others.

9.3 The Wall Street Crash and the Depression

The causes of the Crash

Historians can identify long-term and short-term causes of the Crash.
The longer-term causes were the weaknesses in the US economy (see page 100):

- overproduction in agriculture – driving prices down
- overproduction of consumer goods – driving prices down
- inequality – the rich were very rich while the poor were very poor
- foreign competition – reducing demand for American goods.

Short-term causes related to shares. Many ordinary Americans bought shares in companies. Normally, this is good for business. However, in the USA in the 1920s, the rush to buy shares caused problems.

- Many people bought and sold shares to make quick profits instead of keeping their money invested for some time. They were speculators, not investors.
- Companies were forced by shareholders to pay out profits to shareholders rather than re-investing them.
- Americans borrowed money on credit to buy their shares.

These kinds of share dealings depended on confidence that share prices would continue to rise. Once people started worrying about the long-term weaknesses in the US economy, disaster struck. In September 1929, the prices of shares began to come down – slowly to start with – but people soon began to realise that the shares they owned were worth less than the loans they had used to buy them. Suddenly, everyone tried to get rid of their shares. The worst day was 'Black Tuesday', 29 October 1929. As a result, share prices collapsed, as shown in Source 4 below.

SOURCE 4

Company	Share values in cents		
	3 Sept 1928	3 Sept 1929	13 Nov 1929
New York Central	256	256	160
Union Carbide and Carbon	413	137	59
Electric Bond and Share	203	186	50

Share prices, 1928–29 (from the *Wall Street Journal*).

The effects of the Crash

The effects of the Crash were disastrous.

- Many individuals were bankrupt – they could not pay back the loans they used to buy their (now worthless) shares.
- Some homeowners lost their homes because they could not pay their mortgages.
- Even some who had savings lost their money when banks collapsed.
- Many farmers suffered a similar fate as banks tried to get back their loans.

The confidence of individuals was shattered. Many faced unemployment, and those in work faced reduced hours and wages. People stopped spending.
   Big institutions also suffered.

- About 11,000 banks stopped trading between 1929 and 1933.
- At the same time, demand for goods of all types fell.
- As a result, production fell and so did wages and jobs.

Unemployment rose dramatically as shown in the graph below.

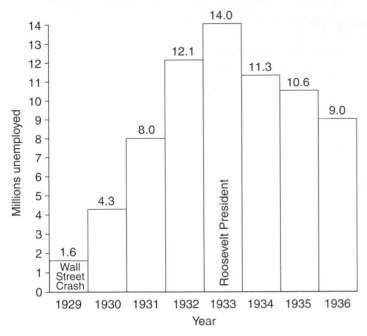

US unemployment, 1929–36.

President Hoover's response to the Crash

Most Americans blamed President Hoover for the Crash. This was not wholly fair since there were larger forces at work than Hoover's policies. However, people blamed Hoover partly because of his government's inaction in tackling the problem. Hoover insisted that the situation was not too serious, and that 'prosperity is just around the corner'. This upset many Americans.

In some ways, Hoover was unfairly criticised. He did take action between 1929 and 1933.

- He set up the Reconstruction Finance Corporation (RFC), which lent money to banks, industries and agriculture.
- He tried to encourage US exports (without much success).

Overall, however, Hoover still believed in 'rugged individualism' and showed little sympathy for the poor, starving Americans living in shanty towns called 'Hoovervilles'.

The Bonus March

Among the most serious events of this troubled time was the 'Bonus Army' march of 1932. The 'Bonus Army' was made up of ex-servicemen who had fought in the First World War. They were due to be paid a bonus by 1945, but because of massive unemployment they were asking for it early. The marchers moved on Washington but were dispersed by troopers on Hoover's orders.

Revision tasks

1 What were the causes of the Crash? Copy and complete the summary table below.

Short-term causes	Long-term causes

2 How did the Crash affect Americans? Find four to six key words for your answer.

3 'Hoover deserved all of the criticism and blame he got.' How far do you agree with this statement? Make a list of key words to summarise arguments 'for' and 'against'.

9.4 Roosevelt and the New Deal

The presidential election, November 1932

Hoover was decisively beaten by Franklin D. Roosevelt in the 1932 presidential election. Roosevelt was well educated and a talented, passionate politician. He had complete faith in his ideas for bringing the USA out of the Depression. During the election campaign, his key phrase was his offer of a 'New Deal' for Americans.

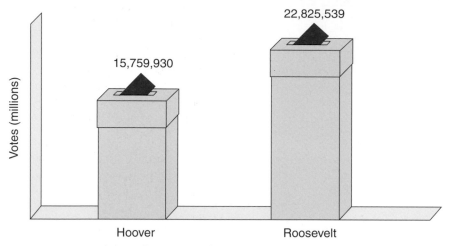

US presidential election result, November 1932.

Roosevelt's first 'Hundred Days'—the First New Deal

When Roosevelt took office in March 1933, the USA was facing a deep economic crisis. Many of the country's banks were closed. Industrial production was down to 56 per cent of the 1929 level. Over 13 million people were unemployed. Roosevelt was determined to act quickly. From 9 March to 16 June 1933 (the 'Hundred Days'), he managed to get the US **Congress** to pass many new laws. This first New Deal legislation is summarised in the table opposite.

The Second New Deal

In later years, Roosevelt updated some laws and created further legislation where it was needed. The Hundred Days, or First New Deal, was about economic recovery. The Second New Deal was more about making the USA a fairer society for all.

- In 1935, the Works Progress Administration replaced the Public Works Administration (PWA). It extended the range of work provided, from building work to the Federal Theatre Project that gave work to unemployed artists and writers.
- The National Labor Relations Act, or Wagner Act (1935), forced employers to recognise trade unions after the National Recovery Administration (NRA) was declared illegal by American courts. This law meant that workers kept the protection that the NRA had given them.
- The Social Security Act (1935) provided federal aid for the elderly and set up an unemployment insurance scheme. However, the provisions were still far less comprehensive than in Germany or Britain.

Key terms

Congress: the American representative assemblies (the equivalent of Parliament in Britain). There are two houses, the Senate and the House of Representatives. Roosevelt had majority Democrate support in both houses.

Hundred Days Legislation, 9 March–16 June 1933

Legislation	Problem	Action
Emergency Banking Act Securities Exchange Act	Americans had little confidence in the banks and might withdraw all their savings – this would lead to collapse.	The Government declared a bank holiday and closed all banks. When the banks were reopened eight days later, the Government restored confidence in the banking system by officially backing 5,000 banks to reassure Americans that their money was safe. The Securities Exchange Act set up a commission to regulate the stock market to make sure that the speculation that caused the 1929 crash would not happen again.
Federal Emergency Relief Administration (FERA)	Poverty and unemployment	500 million dollars allocated to help relieve suffering of poor (food, clothing, etc.). Seed and equipment for farmers, schemes to create jobs.
Civilian Conservation Corps (CCC)	Unemployment among young men	Men aged 18–25 given six months' work. Had to send most of their pay home to parents/wives. About 300,000 joined in 1933; by 1940 there were 2 million.
Public Works Administration (PWA) (became Works Progress Administration in 1935)	Unemployment	Paid for public works projects (e.g. schools, roads, hospitals) and used unemployed workers.
Agricultural Adjustment Administration (AAA)	Rural poverty, unemployment and low crop prices	Advised farmers on marketing and farming techniques and helped solve problem of overproduction. Farmers became more organised but wealthy farmers gained most.
National Industrial Recovery Act (NIRA)	General economic condition of USA	Set up NRA (National Recovery Administration), which set standards on working practices (hours, child labour). This helped create more jobs. Employers in the scheme displayed the eagle symbol of Government approval, and the Government encouraged people to use these firms. Over 2 million employers were members.
Tennessee Valley Authority (TVA)	Agricultural overproduction and regular flooding had ruined livelihoods of farm workers in Tennessee Valley. No alternative jobs in industry. Area covered parts of six states and was too big for any one state to deal with.	Huge public works projects: dams, irrigation, canals and water transport. Hydro-electric power created thousands of jobs. Farmers given loans and training in soil conservation. New housing built.

Opposition to Roosevelt

To people at the time, the New Deal was extraordinary. No US Government had ever played such a role in the lives of ordinary Americans. It was bound to attract opposition. Opponents of the New Deal included:

Business leaders

They were unhappy about various aspects of the New Deal including:

- regulations on working conditions which prevented them running the business now they wished.
- trade unions allowed to bargain collectively with employers on behalf of their members
- the huge cost of the welfare programmes (which came from taxes paid by Americans).

The states

They were concerned about the New Deal because:

- measures such as the TVA cut right across the rights of individual states
- some states feared that the Federal Government was becoming too powerful.

Politicians

- Republicans (not surprisingly) bitterly opposed the Democrat Roosevelt. They thought he was making the Government too powerful and quashing the traditional reliance on self-help.
- Even some conservative Democrats opposed him for the same reasons.
- However some radicals in the USA, such as Huey Long, believed the New Deal did not go far enough.

The Supreme Court

The Supreme Court clashed with Roosevelt.

- Its judges (mainly old and Republican) ruled that several of the New Deal measures were illegal.
- Matters came to a head in 1937 when Roosevelt wanted to make some of his own supporters into Supreme Court judges. This plan failed, but afterwards Supreme Court opposition lessened.

Revision tasks

1 Produce your own profiles of Hoover and Roosevelt.

2 Write a key words list to summarise
   a) the features of the First New Deal, and
   b) the different features of the Second New Deal.

3 Find three examples from this section that you could use to argue that the New Deal was 'revolutionary'.

Source evaluation: The cost of the New Deal

The New Deal and its measures caused huge divisions in American public opinion. This is reflected in evidence from that time, such as Sources 5 and 6 opposite, which were published in American newspapers in election year, 1936. We can use our background knowledge of 1936, the election, Roosevelt's policies and his opponents to work out the message and purpose of both these cartoons.

The cartoon in Source 5 pokes fun at the industrialists. The 'poor' (but well-fed and well-dressed) industrialists are complaining about Roosevelt's New Deal. However, all around are newspaper headlines that show prosperity. This is a pro-New Deal cartoon.

The cartoon in Source 6 is anti-Roosevelt. We see him pumping away billions of dollars on a leaky pump, and the water is supplied by the poor taxpayer. The clear message is that Roosevelt is wasting money on stupid schemes. This source comes from opponents of Roosevelt.

SOURCE 5

A cartoon poking fun at industrialists who complained about Roosevelt's New Deal.

SOURCE 6

A cartoon showing the 'New Deal pump' leaking away.

9.5 Successes and failures of the New Deal

Roosevelt and the voters

The most obvious of Roosevelt's successes in this period was that he won re-election in 1936, 1940 and 1944 – the only President ever to serve four terms in office. Roosevelt was the first President to talk regularly to the people. His weekly 'fireside chats' on the radio were listened to by 60 million Americans. However, most historians agree that the New Deal had mixed results.

Assessing the New Deal

Weaknesses

When Roosevelt cut back his programmes in 1937, unemployment rose dramatically.

- He reduced, but did not conquer, unemployment in the 1930s; unemployment was only solved by the USA's entry into the Second World War in 1941.
- The USA's trade (and the world's trade) did not recover.
- African Americans gained relatively little from the New Deal.

Successes

- In the USA, the Depression did not lead to the collapse of government or extreme movements taking hold.
- Many millions of jobs were created and vital relief (food, shelter, clothing) was supplied to the poor.
- Agriculture and industry benefited from improved infrastructure (roads, services).

Exam practice

1 Study Source 6. 'The New Deal was an unnecessary experiment that wasted millions of dollars.' How far do you agree with this interpretation? Use the source and your own knowledge to explain your answer. *(7 marks)*

Exam tip This is typical of the questions you will face in question 7.

It tests your knowledge and your ability to interpret sources.
- A low level answer (worth 1–3 marks) will give a basic understanding of the source and of the period.
- A better answer (worth 4–7 marks) will give a more detailed understanding of the period and show that the source provides one interpretation only.

Source evaluation: The achievements of the New Deal

Historians and others at the time argued about the success or failure of the New Deal. Here are two contrasting views expressed in the 1930s.

SOURCE 7

R. Shaw, *The New Deal – Its Unsound Theories and Irreconcilable Policies*, 1935.

The New Deal is nothing more or less than an effort to take away from the thrifty what the thrifty and their ancestors have accumulated, and give to others who have not earned it, or whose ancestors haven't earned it for them, and would never have earned it and never will earn it.

SOURCE 8

Letter sent to President Roosevelt in the 1930s.

Dear Mr President,
This is just to tell you everything is alright now. The man you sent found our house alright and we went down to the bank with him and the mortgage can go on for a while longer. Well, your man got it back for us. I never heard of a President like you, Mr Roosevelt. Mrs — and I are old folks and don't amount to much, but we are joined with millions of others in praying for you every night. God bless you Mr Roosevelt.

Exam tip Ask these questions of any source:
- What is it? (a document, diary extract, cartoon, picture, etc.)
- Who produced, wrote or drew it?
- When was it produced, written or drawn?
- Why was it produced, written or drawn?

As historians, we have to take care in using these sources, for several reasons.

- Neither source is attempting to balance the successes and failures of the New Deal – each represents a single view.
- Each source could be a 'one-off'. We do not know how many letters like Source 8 Roosevelt received, and we are not sure how many people agreed with the views expressed in it. However, our knowledge of the period does help, because we know millions did vote for Roosevelt.
- As for Source 7, the title of the book from which this source has been taken is in itself an attack on the New Deal. It indicates the bias of the writer.

Revision task

Copy and complete the following table to show the extent to which the features of the New Deal restored prosperity in the USA. You will need to add more rows for other New Deal legislation.

Feature of New Deal	Restored prosperity	Did not restore prosperity
Emergency Banking Act		
Tennessee Valley Authority		

Exam practice

1 Study Source 7. How far did the Roosevelt Government win support for the New Deal? Use the source and your own knowledge to explain your answer.

(7 marks)

2 Study Source 8. Why would the American Government want to publish this letter to the President? Use the source and your own knowledge to explain your answer.

(6 marks)

Summary/revision plan

You need to have a good working knowledge of the following areas.
Tick off each item once you are confident in your knowledge.

❑ **1 The economic boom of the 1920s**
- Background: the USA up to 1920
- Republican policies
- The boom period
- Weaknesses in the US economy

❑ **2 American society in the 1920s**
- Entertainment
- Women
- Intolerance and isolationism
  - The Red Scare
  - Immigration
  - The Ku Klux Klan
- Prohibition and crime

❑ **3 The Wall Street Crash and the Depression**
- The causes of the Crash
- The effects of the Crash
- President Hoover's response to the Crash

❑ **4 Roosevelt and the New Deal**
- The presidential election, November 1932
- Roosevelt's first 'Hundred Days'
- The Second New Deal
- Opposition to Roosevelt
  - Business leaders
  - The states
  - Politicians
  - The Supreme Court

❑ **5 Successes and failures of the New Deal**
- Roosevelt and the voters
- Assessing the New Deal
  - Weaknesses
  - Successes.

Check your knowledge online with our Quick quizzes at
www.hodderplus.co.uk/modernworldhistory.

Revision tasks

Chapter review
Here are ten events, terms or people you have studied in this depth study. Without checking back see if you can write a one or two sentence summary of what it was and why it was important in US history 1919–1941.
a) Isolationism
b) Motor industry
c) Republican policies
d) The Red Scare
e) Al Capone
f) Speculation
g) Franklin Roosevelt
h) The Hundred Days
i) The Tennessee Valley Authority
j) The Supreme Court

Chapter 10: The causes and events of the First World War, 1890–1918

Between 1914 and 1918, the Great Powers fought each other to dominate Europe. But after four years of horrific slaughter, Europe was in ruins, millions of people had been killed, and many former European rulers gone for ever. In this chapter, you will look at why and how the war started, the main events on the Western and other fronts, and how technology and tactics changed as the conflict developed.

Focus points

In the OCR course, each Paper 1 depth study option is divided into key questions, and each key question is divided into focus points. To do well in the examination, you need to have a well-thought-out view on each of the key questions and focus points.

Key question 1: Why was there increasing tension between the Great Powers, 1890–1914?

Focus points

- Did the alliance system make war more likely?
- How far did colonial problems create tensions between the Great Powers?
- Why were problems in the Balkans so difficult for the Great Powers to solve?
- How important was the Kaiser in causing the worsening international situation?
- Why did the arms race escalate, 1900–1914?

Key Question 2: Why did the First World War break out in 1914?

Focus points

- Why was Franz Ferdinand assassinated?
- How did the assassination of Franz Ferdinand lead to the outbreak of war?
- How far were the actions of Austria–Hungary, Britain, Germany and Russia responsible for the outbreak of war?
- How far did the Schlieffen Plan contribute to the outbreak of war?

Key Question 3: What happened on the Western Front?

Focus points

- Why did the war get bogged down in the trenches?
- What was living and fighting in the trenches like?
- How far did General Haig mismanage the Battle of the Somme?

- How important were new developments such as tanks, machine guns, aircraft and gas?
- What was the importance of America's entry into the war?
- Why did Germany agree to an armistice in 1918?

Key Question 4: How important were the other fronts?
Focus points
- Who won the war at sea?
- What happened in the Gallipoli campaign of 1915?
- Why was Russia defeated in 1918?

Key content

In order to fully understand the focus points, you will need to have a good working knowledge of:

- the alliance system and the arms race between the Great Powers
- events leading to the outbreak of war in 1914
- war on the Western Front, 1914–18
- living and fighting in the trenches
- the changing technology of war
- war on the Eastern Front, 1914–18
- the war in Africa, the Pacific and the Middle East
- the war at sea.

10.1 The alliance system and the arms race between the Great Powers

In 1914, the most powerful countries in Europe were members of two opposing alliances: the Triple Alliance (Germany, Austria–Hungary and Italy) formed in 1882 and the Triple Entente (France, Russia and Britain) formed in 1907.

The Central Powers, or Triple Alliance

Germany

The German **Kaiser**, Wilhelm II, wanted Germany to become a great power. His father, Frederick III, and **Chancellor** Bismarck had created Germany in 1870 from a collection of small German states. They had followed a cautious policy but this changed when Wilhelm II came to power. Kaiser Wilhelm II:

- created German colonies in Africa to rival France and Britain
- ordered the building of a large German navy to compete with Britain
- built up the Triple Alliance from fear of being 'surrounded' by France and Russia
- expanded the German army to compete with Russia.

Austria–Hungary

The Austro-Hungarian empire was made up of many different ethnic groups: Germans, Slovaks, Czechs, Serbs and others. Many of these groups wanted independence. The Austro-Hungarian emperor, Franz Joseph, faced many problems so joined the Triple Alliance to increase Austria's influence and power. He believed this alliance would help solve Austria's problems because:

- the Serbs in the Austrian empire wanted to join with Serbia
- the Czechs and Slovaks wanted their own state
- Serbia was becoming much stronger and was supported by Russia.

> ## Key terms
> **Kaiser:** emperor.
> **Chancellor:** chief minister (equivalent of Prime Minister in Britain).

Italy

Italy had been created in 1860 from a collection of smaller states. By 1882, the Italian Government was also looking to create new colonies and extend its influence so became part of the Triple Alliance.

Entente Cordiale, 1904 and Triple Entente, 1907

Britain

For much of the nineteenth century, Britain had been the most powerful country in the world. Its large navy spread British influence worldwide, and helped defend its huge empire in India, Africa and the Far East. Britain was said to exist in 'splendid isolation' and regarded France and Russia as dangerous rivals. By 1900, however, British policy began to change.

- Britain and France had reached several agreements about trade and colonies in Africa. There was a growing friendship between the two countries and this became the Entente Cordiale in 1904.
- Britain was very concerned about Germany's military growth, the threat to its colonies and to peace in Europe.

France

France had been defeated in 1871 in the Franco-Prussian War. The French Government:

- was becoming increasingly worried by Germany's military strength
- formed an alliance with Russia in 1894
- wanted to regain Alsace–Lorraine
- wanted Britain to become more involved in preserving peace in Europe.

Russia

Russia was the largest of the Great Powers, but also the most under-developed. In 1905, Russia lost a war with Japan and revolution broke out. The Russian emperor, Tsar Nicholas II, managed to defeat the revolutionaries but Russia remained vulnerable. The emperor's priorities were to:

- build up the Russian army
- keep close links with Serbia and other Slav groups
- maintain close ties with France and Britain. The three countries created the Triple Entente in 1907.

The arms race

From 1900 onwards, all the Great Powers increased the size of their armed forces. The table below shows the size of armies at the time war broke out.

Country	Number of soldiers in 1914
Germany	4,500,000
Britain	750,000
France	3,750,000
Austria	750,000
Russia	1,250,000
Italy	750,000

Britain and Germany were also involved in a naval arms race. As an island, Britain had always had a large navy. Kaiser Wilhelm II, however, also wanted to build up the German navy.

Exam practice

1 Describe the main features of Kaiser Wilhelm II's foreign policy. *(4 marks)*

Exam tip This is typical of the questions you will face in questions 8 or 9.

This is a starter question. It tests your **factual knowledge**. Try to include four details showing what Kaiser Wilhelm was trying to achieve.

In 1906, the British launched a new type of battleship, HMS *Dreadnought*. It was larger and more heavily armed than any other ship and made other battleships **obsolete**.

Key term

Obsolete: out of date.

The old battleships were no match in size, speed or firepower for the Dreadnought. HMS *Dreadnought* represented such a marked advance in naval technology that the name became associated with an entire generation of battleships, known as 'Dreadnoughts'. The German Kaiser decided that he also needed to build Dreadnoughts to keep up with Britain. A naval arms race began as the table below shows.

Year	Britain	Germany
1906	🚢	
1907	🚢🚢🚢	
1908	🚢🚢	🚢🚢🚢🚢
1909	🚢🚢	🚢🚢🚢
1910	🚢🚢	🚢
1911	🚢🚢🚢🚢🚢	🚢🚢🚢
1912	🚢🚢🚢	🚢🚢
1913	🚢🚢🚢🚢🚢🚢	🚢🚢🚢
1914	🚢🚢🚢	🚢

Britain 🚢 Total built by 1914: 29   Germany 🚢 Total built by 1914: 17

Number of Dreadnoughts built by Britain and Germany, 1906–14.

Plans for war

All the Great Powers had war plans and these had been created to take into account the complicated alliance system.

1. Germany

Germany's plan of attack was called the Schlieffen Plan. It needed the German army to quickly sweep through Belgium and defeat France in the first few weeks of war. This would then allow the German army to move to the Eastern Front to defeat the Russians. The Schlieffen Plan had been designed to overcome the problem that Germany would have to fight on two fronts. It became vital therefore that France was defeated as quickly as possible. In 1914, Germany had approximately 2.3 million well-trained troops. Its navy had seventeen Dreadnought-type battleships and battle cruisers.

2. France

The French plan of attack was called Plan 17. In a war, French troops would invade Germany through the territories of Alsace and Lorraine. These territories had been lost to Germany in 1871. The French had approximately 2 million well-trained troops.

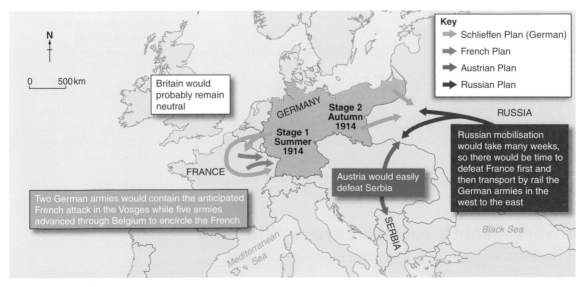

The Schlieffen Plan.

3. Britain

British preparations for war were based on supporting the French army with a small but highly trained and mobile expeditionary force. Britain would rely on its powerful navy to blockade German ports and use its forces overseas to harass the Germans. Britain had approximately 600,000 well-trained troops. Its navy included 29 Dreadnought-type battleships and battle cruisers.

4. Austria

The Austrian plan of attack was called Plan R. In a war, Austria would invade Russia with thousands of troops and, at the same time, attack Serbia in the south. The Austrians had approximately 1.25 million troops.

5. Russia

The Russian plan of attack relied upon using its huge army to defeat the enemy. It had approximately 3 million poorly trained and poorly equipped troops.

10.2 Events leading to the outbreak of war in 1914

Moroccan crises, 1905 and 1911

In 1905 and 1911, two crises in Morocco increased the tension between the Great Powers.

- Kaiser Wilhelm had begun creating an African empire to compete with Britain and France. He also wanted to show his interest in north Africa, so in 1905 he visited Morocco and made a speech encouraging it to seek independence.
- The French, most of whose African colonies were in north Africa, were looking to take control of Morocco and were furious with the Kaiser's intervention.
- A conference was held at Algeciras in 1906 to reduce tensions, but the Kaiser found himself humiliated as Britain and France supported each other against Germany's views on north Africa.

A year later, in 1907, the Entente Cordiale between Britain and France was extended into the Triple Entente to include Russia. After his public humiliation at the Algeciras conference, the Kaiser saw the Triple Entente as a further example of Britain and France trying to encircle and undermine Germany.

In 1911, there was another Moroccan crisis.

- France tried to take over Morocco and said that it would compensate Germany for any loss of trade.
- The Kaiser responded by sending a gunboat to the Moroccan port of Agadir to indicate opposition to the French plans.
- Another conference was held with Britain and France supporting each other against Germany again. France took over Morocco and Germany was given land in central Africa as compensation.

Tensions between Britain and France on the one side and Germany on the other continued to increase.

The Balkan wars – south-eastern Europe 1910–1914

The Balkans is an area in south-east Europe which had been politically unstable.

- The area had many different nationalities.
- Turkey had ruled the area for many centuries, but Turkey's power was in decline.

Revision task

Copy and complete the table below. Use the information in the previous sections to make a summary of the war plans of the Great Powers.

Country	Plan	How was it meant to work
Germany		
France		
Britain		
Austria		
Russia		

Exam practice

1 Explain why problems in the Balkans were difficult to solve by 1914.

(6 marks)

Exam tip This tests your knowledge *and* **understanding**.

- A low level answer (worth 1–2 marks) will simply state one or two problems.
- A better answer (worth 3–4 marks) will describe several problems and explain each one more fully.
- A top level answer (worth 5–6 marks) will do all the above but also show connections between problems and show why these caused tensions between the Great Powers.

- The new countries of the Balkans were often in conflict with each other. There were two Balkan wars between 1910 and 1914.
- Russia and Austria both wanted to control the Balkans as Turkey weakened.

The assassination of Archduke Franz Ferdinand

Then in the summer of 1914, an event occurred that triggered the outbreak of war. The heir to the Austrian throne, Franz Ferdinand, and his wife were murdered by the Serbian-supported Black Hand terrorist group. Although there was no direct evidence to suggest that the Serbian Government ordered the assassination, the Austrian Government decided to blame Serbia. It issued the Serbian Government an **ultimatum** that Serbia would never have been able to agree to. When Serbia did not accept the Austrian demands, the Austrians declared war on Serbia on 28 July.

The road to war June–August 1914

28 June	Heir to the Austrian throne Archduke Franz Ferdinand and his wife are shot in Sarajevo.
23 July	The Austrian Government delivers an ultimatum to the Serbian Government, which they hold responsible for the death of the Archduke and his wife. In reality, it appears that the Austrians were looking for an excuse to crush Serbia.
24 July	The Serbian Government accepts most of the Austrian demands and suggests that the Court of Arbitration in the Hague in Holland should decide upon the rest of the demands.
25 July	Austria rejects the Serbian proposals and begins to mobilise its troops. Russia (Serbia's ally) tells the Austrians that it will also begin to mobilise its troops.
28 July	Austria declares war on Serbia.
30 July	Russia orders mobilisation of its armed forces. Germany warns Russia that continued mobilisation will mean war with Germany. Russia continues the mobilisation.
1 August	Germany declares war on Russia. Italy declares that it will remain neutral despite its membership of the Triple Alliance with Germany and Austria.
3 August	Germany declares war on France.
4 August	Germany invades Belgium as part of the Schlieffen Plan. Later that day, Britain declares war on Germany.

Mobilisation

The different plans for war all required a very quick **mobilisation**. Speed was vital if victory was to be won. Once one country began to mobilise and transport its troops to the front line, then the enemy had to do the same or risk immediate defeat. Therefore, once mobilisation began, it was very difficult to stop.

Key terms

Ultimatum: a final demand – or else!
Mobilisation: to get armed forces ready for battle.

Exam practice

1 'The system of Alliances made war more likely.' How far do you agree with this statement? Explain your answer.

(10 marks)

Exam tip This question tests your knowledge and understanding but it goes further. A question that starts 'How far …' is also inviting you to **evaluate**. In your exam, question 8 or 9 will usually include an element of evaluation like this.

- A low level answer (worth 1–4 marks) will give a limited and basic response simply describing the Alliance system or describing the outbreak of the First World War.
- A better answer (worth 5–6 marks) will describe AND explain the reasons the Alliances were set up and link them to other developments of the time, such as the plans for war.
- A top level answer (worth 7–10 marks) will describe and explain the role of Alliances in leading to war, such as fuelling the arms race, or increasing the impact of local problems like the assassination in Sarajevo in order to show a good understanding of the issue.

10.3 The main events

The failure of the war plans, 1914

The Schlieffen Plan was designed to give Germany a quick and decisive victory against France. German troops were to move through Belgium and encircle Paris from the west. This would cut off the French army and France would be forced to surrender. Before the war began, however, the German commander von Moltke altered the Schlieffen Plan. When war began, the plan failed for several reasons.

- The Belgian army fought very bravely and delayed the German advance at Liège.
- The British Expeditionary Force (BEF) slowed the German advance at the Battle of Mons. According to reports, British rifle fire was so rapid that the Germans thought the British were using machine guns.
- Some German troops were transferred from the Western Front to the Eastern Front because the Russians had mobilised their forces more quickly than expected.
- The German commander Kluck decided to head straight for Paris instead of encircling it from the south.
- At the Battle of the Marne, 5–11 September, Joffre, commander of the French army, was able to halt the German advance and push it back to the River Aisne. The French even transported fresh troops to the front in taxis in order to face the exhausted Germans.

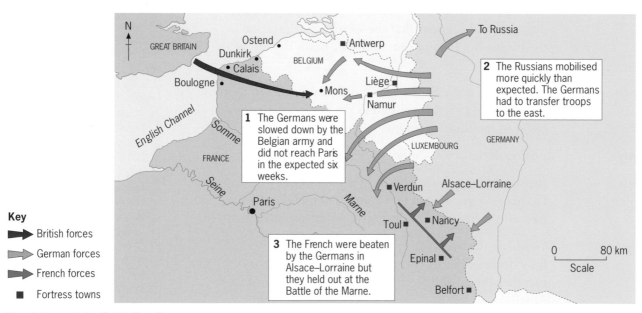

The failure of the Schlieffen Plan.

The Schlieffen Plan had failed. Both the British and German forces now abandoned their original plans and tried to cut each other off from fresh supplies and equipment. This led to a race to the English Channel between the BEF and the German army. At the First Battle of Ypres, the British managed to stop the German advance, but at a terrible cost. It is estimated that one British division lost nearly 11,000 of its 12,000 men.

The French forces launched Plan 17 against the Germans, but their advance was also halted. It has been estimated that French casualties were 300,000.

Stalemate

By December 1914, the war of movement had come to a halt. From the English Channel in the north to the Swiss border in the south, troops on both sides dug trenches in order to prevent the enemy from advancing further. Instead of soldiers being home by Christmas as leaders had promised, the war had reached stalemate with no side making the vital breakthrough.

10.4 Living and fighting in the trenches

Trench warfare

Living and fighting in the trenches of the First World War was similar for soldiers on both sides.

- New and more deadly weapons such as shells, mines and mortars completely changed the tactics used by both sides.
- Cavalry charges were replaced with infantry charges.
- Trenches were constructed as the best means of protecting a military position and soldiers against enemy shells, mortars and snipers.
- Generals on both sides tried different ways to make the infantry charge more effective. The evidence does not support the view that lives were thrown away in meaningless charges. Troops were given gas masks and better steel helmets, and camouflage was introduced.
- Trench warfare had a routine. New trenches had to be dug and old ones repaired.

The evidence in Sources 1 and 2 gives us a graphic reminder of the horrors of trench warfare as experienced by troops during the First World War.

SOURCE 1

Robert Graves, *Goodbye to All That*, an autobiography published in 1929.

Going along whistling, I saw a group of men bending over a man lying in the bottom of a trench. He was making a snoring noise mixed with animal groans. At my feet lay his cap slashed with his brains. One can joke with a wounded man, one can disregard a dead man, but no one can joke over a man who takes three hours to die after the top of his head has been taken off by a bullet fired at twenty yards' range.

SOURCE 2

E. M. Remarque, *All Quiet on the Western Front*, a novel by a German veteran of the First World War.

We were able to bring in the wounded who did not lie too far off. But many had to wait and we listen to them dying. For one we search for two days in vain. Kat thinks he is hurt in the spine or pelvis … his chest cannot be injured otherwise he would not cry out. We crawl out at night but cannot find him. The first day he cries for help, the next day he is delirious and cries for his family. In the morning we suppose he has gone to his rest. The dead lie unburied. We cannot bring them all in. If we did we should not know what to do with them.

Exam tip Ask these questions of any source:
- What is it? (a document, diary extract, cartoon, picture, etc.)
- Who produced, wrote or drew it?
- When was it produced, written or drawn?
- Why was it produced, written or drawn?

Revision task

Look at **Sources 1** and **2** above.

a) What does each source tell us about life in the trenches?

b) How reliable is each source as a description of life in the trenches?

The Western Front, 1915

Some generals on the side of the Allies (Britain and France) were convinced that the Germans could be defeated if large numbers of troops were used in battle. During 1915 therefore, hundreds of thousands of Allied soldiers attacked the heavily defended German trenches. At Neuve Chapelle, the British suffered 11,000 casualties in only three days. The French had nearly 50,000 casualties near Compiegne.

At the Second Battle of Ypres in April 1915, the Germans used chlorine gas against French troops, but still did not make the breakthrough needed.

Verdun and the Somme, 1916

The history of 1916 on the Western Front is about two battles: Verdun and the Somme.

The Battle of Verdun

Verdun was a heavily fortified French city. Falkenhayn, the German commander, believed he could defeat the French army by concentrating his troops in one small area. He also believed that since Verdun was such a vital fortress, its loss would destroy French morale and lead to France's defeat.

On 21 February 1916, the Germans launched their bombardment of Verdun. Within three days, it looked as if the city was about to be captured. At this point, the problem of saving Verdun was given to General Petain. He moved food, ammunition and equipment into the city and after five months the Germans stopped their attack. Petain became a national hero. The cost to the French and Germans had been high. The Germans lost 281,000 men and the French lost 315,000 men.

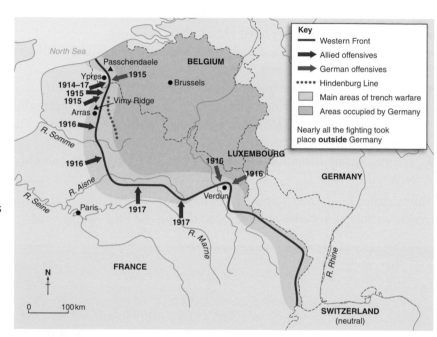

The Battle of Verdun.

The Battle of the Somme

General Haig, the British commander, decided to launch a major attack against the Germans along the River Somme. He hoped that by using artillery he would weaken the German front line and allow British troops to advance. The battle began with a five-day bombardment of the German positions along an eighteen-mile front.

The German troops, aware that the attack was coming, had prepared dugouts deep underground in order to survive the bombardment. On 1 July, 200,000 Allied soldiers attacked the German trenches along the Somme. British troops were ordered to walk rather than run towards enemy trenches since they were carrying up to 66 pounds of equipment.

In the ten minutes between the end of the bombardment and the British attack, the Germans were able to return to their trenches and machine guns. As a result, on the first day of the battle, 20,000 British were killed and 40,000 wounded. The Battle of the Somme ended in the middle of November 1916. Only 15 kilometres of land had been gained by the Allies at a cost of 600,000 casualties. At the end of 1916, there was no breakthrough on the Western Front.

Source evaluation: Artillery at the Battle of the Somme

How effective were the tactics used at the Battle of the Somme in 1916? These two sources present differing views about the effectiveness of the artillery bombardment on enemy defences.

SOURCE 3

Sir Douglas Haig speaking about the Battle of the Somme.

The work of our artillery was wholly admirable, though the strain on the personnel was enormous. The excellence of the results attained was the more remarkable, in view of the shortness of the training of most of the junior officers and the NCOs.

SOURCE 4

George Coppard, a British machine gunner at the Somme.

How did the planners imagine that Tommies, having survived all other hazards and there were plenty in crossing No Man's Land – would get through the German wire? Had they studied the black density of it through their powerful binoculars? Who told them that artillery fire would pound each wire to pieces, making it possible to get through? Any Tommy could have told them that shell fire lifts wire up and drops it down again, often in a worse tangle than before.

The fact that one source is written by the general in charge of the offensive and one written by an ordinary soldier is very important. Source 3 claims that the artillery performed very well whilst Source 4 insists that the bombardment was pointless. It is important to remember that the historian must look at all the available evidence and then make a judgement.

The changing technology of war

Artillery

The use of artillery caused the greatest number of deaths amongst troops during the First World War. It is estimated that 75 per cent of all casualties resulted from the use of high explosive or shrapnel shells.

By 1914, there had been important developments in the use of artillery. Guns were now organised into artillery batteries, were more sophisticated and more accurate. During the war, for example, the French introduced the 75mm gun and it soon became the best of its type. It was easy to aim, could fire rapidly and cut down advancing soldiers with ease.

Machine guns

The first modern-type machine gun was developed by Hiram Maxim in the USA in 1883. By 1914, however, many military commanders still thought that the machine gun was an unreliable and untested invention. Lloyd George, however, was so impressed with these new weapons that by the end of the war nearly 250,000 had been manufactured for the British army.

The effect of the machine gun on the battlefield was remarkable. The water-cooled machine guns used by both sides could fire up to 600 rounds a minute. The guns frequently cut down hundreds of troops before they were able to advance more than a few yards. The machine gun was one of the most devastating weapons used in the First World War.

Revision tasks

Read **Sources 3** and **4**.

1 What different views do these sources have on the effectiveness of artillery?

2 What factors might affect the reliability of each source?

3 Do you believe one source more than the other? Compare your views with your friends'.

Gas

The use of gas in war had been banned by international agreements signed at the Hague in 1899 and 1907. Nonetheless, gas was used for the first time by the Germans at the Second Battle of Ypres in April 1915. Gas did not have a major impact on the outcome of the First World War. It was unpredictable in battle and, by 1917, effective gas masks had been produced to protect soldiers on the battlefield.

Tanks

The British used tanks for the first time at the Battle of the Somme in July 1916. They were successful in battle, but there were not enough of them to break the deadlock on the Western Front.

The first tanks were armour-plated with cannon and machine guns and moved at three miles per hour. The first models were often unreliable and liable to break down. Those that were successful often advanced too quickly for supporting troops and were captured or destroyed. At the Battle of Cambrai, however, the 400 British tanks were used to great effect, although much of the land captured by the tank crews was later recaptured by the Germans.

Aeroplanes

One of the most important new weapons to be introduced in the First World War was the aeroplane. The British had 63 aircraft at the beginning of the war and commanders used them to report on enemy troop movements.

In 1915, the Germans produced an aircraft (Fokker EI) that was capable of firing a machine gun safely through a rotating propeller. The British and French soon copied the idea and 'dogfights' between rival aircraft became more common. By 1917, the Germans had developed a twin-engine bomber and when war ended both the Allies and Central Powers had developed four-engine bombers. The range and power of these early aircraft was very limited, however, and they had little impact on the outcome of the war.

Balloons and Zeppelins

Small balloons were frequently used on the battlefield for observation purposes before the widespread use of aircraft. Hydrogen-filled Zeppelins were also used by the Germans for reconnaissance and bombing purposes. A small number of Zeppelins bombed London and the east coast of England in April 1915. Although the actual damage caused was minimal, the effect upon civilian morale in Britain was alarming.

> ### Comment
>
> *There were different kinds of gas: chlorine and phosgene gas worked by destroying the lungs. Mustard gas was particularly horrible and destroyed flesh.*

Revision tasks

1 Copy and complete the table below.

	Impact on the war	How it was used by each side	Importance to the eventual outcome of the war
Artillery			
Machine guns			
Gas			
Tanks			
Aeroplanes			
Balloons and Zeppelins			

2 Which wartime technology was most important to the Allied victory? Explain the reasons for your answer.

Exam practice

1 What was the Zimmermann Telegram? *(4 marks)*

2 The following have been suggested as reasons why the USA entered the First World War in 1917:
   i   the sinking of the *Lusitania*
   ii   Germany's use of U-boats
   iii the Zimmermann Telegram.
   Which do you think was the most important reason for US entry into the First World War? Explain your answer referring only to i, ii and iii. *(10 marks)*

Exam tip

This is typical of the questions you will face in questions 2 or 3.

1 This is a starter question. It tests your **factual knowledge**. Include four relevant facts about the Zimmerman Telegram.

2 This question tests your knowledge and understanding but it goes further. You need to show you understand each of the events listed but to get the highest marks you need to evaluate which was the most significant reason and why

1917

The USA joins the war

In April 1917, the USA joined the Allies in the war against the Central Powers. For some time, German U-boats had been sinking American ships. In 1915, the passenger liner *Lusitania* was sunk in the Atlantic and 128 Americans died. Then, two years later, in January 1917, the German Foreign Minister Arthur Zimmermann sent a telegram (the Zimmermann Telegram, which was decoded by British intelligence) to the Mexican Government encouraging them to become a German ally and to declare war on the USA. It was intercepted and decoded by British Intelligence and handed to Woodrow Wilson who published it on 28 February 1917. This finally triggered the USA to join the Allies and declare war on Germany. With the USA in the war, the Germans needed a swift victory before the full impact of the American army was felt on the Western Front.

Mixed fortunes for the Allies

The Allies had another mixed year on the Western Front in 1917. The new French commander, General Nivelle, launched his troops against what he thought was the weakest section of the German front line. The French advanced straight into a trap, the Germans having earlier discovered the French plans and prepared for their advance. The French suffered nearly 125,000 casualties and made no breakthrough.

One effect of the French setback was on the morale of the troops. In early 1917, thousands of French troops mutinied. General Petain was called upon to restore discipline to the French army. He did this by having hundreds of mutineers shot, improving food rations and extending leave for his soldiers.

The British had a major victory in June 1917 at Messines when they blew up a hillside occupied by German troops by placing TNT in tunnels dug out by engineers. In the summer, however, at the Third Battle of Ypres (Passchendaele), 400,000 British troops were killed or wounded in a sea of mud created by weeks of heavy rain. At Cambrai in November, the British successfully used tanks against the Germans. However, the British advance was so swift that the soldiers were unable to keep up and in a counter-attack the Germans regained lost ground.

Source evaluation: Military tactics on the Western Front

How successful were the military tactics used on the Western Front between 1914 and 1918? Sources 5 and 6 give different views on the achievements in 1917.

SOURCE 5

Extract from the diary of a New Zealand officer whose men fought at Passchendaele.

My opinion is that the generals who direct these battles do not know of the conditions, mud, cold, rain, and lack of shelter for the men. The Germans are not so played out as our high command think. Exhausted men struggling through mud cannot compete against dry men with machine guns.

SOURCE 6

Telegram sent by Prime Minister Lloyd George to Field Marshal Haig, 16 October 1917.

The war cabinet desires to congratulate you upon the achievements of the British armies in the great battle which has been raging since 31st July. Starting from positions from which the enemy had every advantage and despite being hampered by most unfavourable weather, you and your men have nevertheless driven the enemy back with skill and courage and filled the enemy with alarm. I am personally glad to pass this message to you and to your gallant troops and to state again my confidence in your leadership.

In Source 5 we are told about the weariness of the troops and the determination of the enemy. In Source 6, however, Prime Minister Lloyd George is congratulating his commander-in-chief for success on the battlefield. Clearly the nature of the sources is different. One is a personal diary the other an official telegram. You would expect the diary to be more honest than a telegram of congratulation from the Prime Minister. However you could also argue that Source 6 takes a much wider view of events whilst Source 5 only sees events in a specific area.

> ### Revision task
> Read **Sources 5** and **6**. Explain the different views expressed about military tactics used on the Western Front.

The Western Front, 1918

In March 1918, the Germans and Russians signed the Treaty of Brest-Litovsk. The Russian army had been defeated and the Germans were now able to transfer a million men from the Eastern to the Western Front. Ludendorf, the German commander, decided that since he now had many more men than the Allies, he must make an all-out attack on the Western Front before large numbers of American troops arrived in Europe.

On 21 March 1918, the Ludendorf offensive began. The Germans advanced rapidly and had soon moved forward 40 miles along an 80-mile front. The Germans reached the River Marne in July and, once again, the French capital looked as if it might fall to the Germans.

The Allied commander, General Foch, began his counterattack on 18 July. With the help of newly arrived American troops, he was able to reverse the German advance. In August, with the help of tanks, the British defeated the Germans at Amiens. More victories followed in Flanders and at Ypres. On 4 October, with the Hindenburg Line (Germany's line of defence) broken and the German army in retreat, Ludendorf asked for a truce. On 11 November, an armistice was signed and the First World War was over. Germany had been defeated.

10.5 War on the Eastern Front, 1914–18

1914

At the beginning of the war, the Russians invaded East Prussia and won a number of small victories against the Germans, including Gumbinnen on 19 August.

The Germans, however, soon recovered and heavily defeated the Russian second army led by General Samsonov at Tannenberg. In the battle, the Russians lost 125,000 men, many of whom drowned in the swamps around the Masurian Lakes.

At the beginning of September, the Russian first army was defeated at the Battle of the Masurian Lakes in which the Russians lost a further 100,000 men.

Against the Austrian army, however, the Russians were much more successful. After initially advancing into Russian territory, the Austrians were driven back over 100 miles into Galicia.

1915

In August, the retreating Russian army was forced to abandon Warsaw. By the end of the year, the Russians had been driven out of Poland completely.

1916

In June, the Russian General Brusilov launched an offensive against the Austrian army and won some early successes. The Romanians also joined the war on the Russian side. Hindenburg moved German forces to help the Austrians and soon the Russians were in retreat. Altogether, 500,000 Russians were killed, wounded or taken prisoner. The Germans also moved into Romania and captured the capital city, Bucharest.

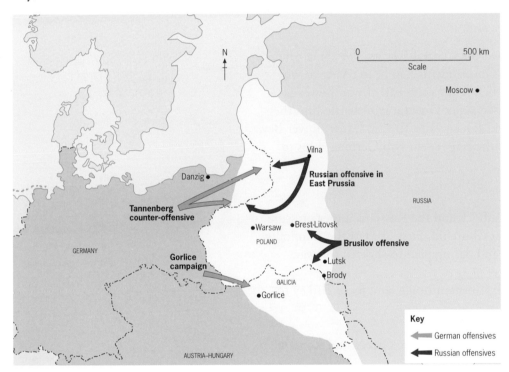

Map showing the Eastern Front.

1917

Russian defeats on the Eastern Front forced the Tsar, who had made himself army commander, to abdicate in February 1917. The new Provisional Government led by Kerensky continued the war and hoped for a victory to help its cause. In the summer of 1917, however, the Russian army began to fall apart, and in October Kerensky's Government was overthrown by the Bolsheviks, led by Lenin. The Bolsheviks wanted to take Russia out of the war and they signed an armistice with Germany in December.

1918

The Russians and Germans signed the Treaty of Brest-Litovsk. Russia had been heavily defeated and had to pay a heavy price. In the peace treaty with Germany and Austria, Russia lost Poland, Latvia, Lithuania, Finland, Estonia and the Ukraine. It also gave up one-third of Russian land and most of its coal and iron industries.

10.6 The war in Africa, the Pacific and the Middle East

Africa

German colonies were attacked in the early stages of the war. In Africa, there was little resistance. In 1915, the German colonies of Togoland, Cameroon and South-West Africa fell to the Allies.

The Pacific

In the Pacific, Australian and New Zealand forces took possession of Samoa and New Guinea. Japan had made an alliance with Britain in 1902 and joined the war against Germany in August 1914. The Japanese captured the German colony of Kiachow in China and the Caroline and Marshall Islands in the Pacific.

The Middle East

Turkey

In October 1914, Turkey joined the Central Powers. For some time, both the British and German Governments had been trying to win the support of the Turks. Just before the outbreak of war, however, the British refused to deliver two super Dreadnought battleships they had been building for the Turkish navy. The Turkish leader, Enver Bey, joined the German side when the Kaiser sent two German ships to help the Turkish navy.

Gallipoli

With the Western Front in deadlock and the Russians under pressure on the Eastern Front, Winston Churchill, First Lord of the Admiralty, came up with an imaginative and daring plan to shorten the war.

Churchill's plan aimed to:

- capture the Turkish capital, Constantinople, and force Turkey to surrender
- reopen a supply route to Russia
- encourage the neutral countries of Bulgaria, Greece and Romania to join the war on the side of the Allies
- surround Germany and Austria–Hungary.

In February 1915, the British navy failed to open the stretch of water known as the Dardenelles. The fleet retreated and in April a force of British and ANZAC (Australian and New Zealand) troops landed on the Gallipoli peninsula. They were soon pinned down by Turkish machine guns. In August, the Allies attacked again, this time landing a force at Suvla Bay. By delaying their advance, however, the Allies gave the Turks the chance to regroup and no further advance was made. Many Allied troops died of disease, dysentery and hunger.

At home in Britain, the commanders of the Gallipoli campaign were heavily criticised. Sir Ian Hamilton was sacked and replaced by Sir Charles Munroe. He decided to evacuate the Gallipoli peninsula. By the end of 1915, the Allies withdrew having suffered 200,000 casualties.

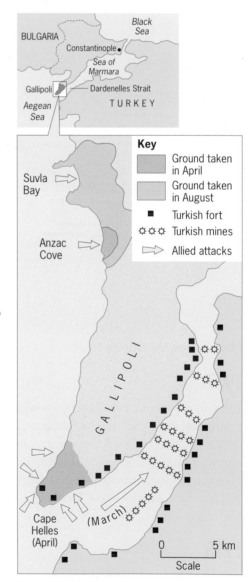

The Gallipoli campaign.

Mesopotamia

The Turks defeated a combined British and Indian army at Kut el Amara in 1916. The Allies recovered, however, and in March 1917 went on to capture Baghdad.

Palestine

At the beginning of the war, Turkish-controlled Palestine was seen as a threat to British-controlled Egypt. In Arabia, local tribes rose in revolt against the Turks and were assisted by army officers sent by the British. One of these officers, Colonel T.E. Lawrence, organised guerrilla attacks on the important Hejaz railway. By December 1917, the British (under the leadership of General Allenby) had captured Jerusalem from the Turks, and in September 1918 Damascus was also taken.

10.7 The war at sea

Background

The British and German navies were the most powerful in the world and control of the high seas would be an important factor in the final outcome of the war. The aim of the Royal navy was to keep shipping lanes free from German attack, blockade German ports, and resupply British troops in the colonies. The German navy aimed to disrupt Britain's food and munitions supplies and protect German colonies.

Minor clashes

Before 1916, there were only a few clashes between the Allies and the Central Powers at sea. In 1914, German raiders bombarded Scarborough. In 1915, another group of German vessels clashed with the British near Dogger Bank in the North Sea. In the Pacific region, German ships were sunk at the Battle of Coronel in November 1914 and in the Falkland Islands in December 1916.

Map showing clashes at sea.

The Battle of Jutland, May–June 1916

At the end of May 1916, Admirals Hipper and von Scheer led the German High Seas Fleet into the North Sea. In a carefully worked-out plan, they aimed to destroy the British Grand Fleet by tempting the British ships into a trap. Unknown to the Germans, however, the British had discovered the German radio codes and were able to decode all German messages.

On the evening of 31 May 1916, the two fleets had a running battle off the coast of Jutland in Denmark. The outcome of the battle was indecisive, although both sides claimed victory. The losses are shown in the table. German casualties were much lighter than the British, but the German fleet never set sail into the North Sea again. The British Grand Fleet had not proved its superiority, but Admiral Jellicoe claimed it had been the Germans who had fled and headed for home.

	German losses	British losses
Ships	11	14
Men (killed)	2,500	6,000

Source evaluation: The Battle of Jutland

Understanding the origin of a piece of evidence is vital for a historian to assess its reliability. Below are two sources about the Battle of Jutland.

SOURCE 7

The Kaiser speaking to the sailors of the German fleet, 5 June 1916.

A brave leader led our fleet. The superior English armada appeared. What happened? The English were beaten. The spell of Trafalgar has been broken.

SOURCE 8

An extract from a British history of the Great War published in 1988.

After Jutland, despite losing more ships and more men, the British navy kept control over the North Sea. The blockade of Germany continued. The Germans had to turn to submarine warfare and the morale of the surface fleet was damaged.

Sources 7 and 8 above give a different view of the outcome of the Battle of Jutland. Source 7 is a primary source whilst Source 8 is secondary evidence written by a British historian over 70 years after the battle. In terms of reliability, it is understandable that the Kaiser in Source 7 speaks of a British defeat. Whatever the outcome of Jutland for the Germans, we would expect the Kaiser to use it for propaganda purposes. Source 8, on the other hand, appears more balanced. We would hope that 70 years after the event, a British historian would be able to provide an unprejudiced view of this major episode of the war.

War against the submarine

For supplies, Britain depended heavily on keeping the shipping lanes free from attack. In 1915, the German Government announced it would attack any ship from any country suspected of carrying supplies to Britain.

The most famous victim of the German U-boat war was the large British passenger line, *Lusitania*. On 7 May 1915, en route from New York to Liverpool with over 1,900 passengers and crew, the *Lusitania* was hit by torpedoes from U-boat 20. The liner sank eight miles off the Irish coast in under twenty minutes with the loss of approximately 1,200 lives, including over 120 Americans.

Despite American protests, German U-boats continued to sink ships in the Atlantic. By 1917, the Germans had over 300 submarines and began 'unrestricted submarine warfare'. This tactic was so effective that at one stage Britain was reduced to a mere six weeks' supply of grain. The German submarine campaign, however, had severe consequences. On 6 April 1917, the USA entered the war on the Allied side. US President Woodrow Wilson said the German policy of unrestricted submarine warfare was a major factor in the USA's decision to declare war on Germany.

By 1917, new technology was helping in the fight against the U-boat.

- The British developed the convoy system to protect merchant ships.
- Nets and mines were used, particularly in the English Channel.
- Some Allied ships were equipped with depth charges.
- Q-boats (disguised merchant ships) were developed to trick U-boats into attack.

By 1918, Germany had been unable to isolate Britain by using its navy or submarines. On the other hand, Germany was successfully blockaded by the Allies and this contributed to the German surrender in November 1918.

Revision tasks

1 In your view, which side won the Battle of Jutland? Give reasons for your answer.

2 In what ways was the U-boat campaign a major threat to Britain in the First World War? Give evidence to support your answer.

3 **Chapter review**
   Here are ten events, terms or people you have studied in this depth study. Without checking back see if you can write a one or two sentence summary of what it was and why it was important in the history of the First World War.
   a) Kaiser Wilhelm II
   b) The Triple Entente
   c) Dreadnoughts
   d) Sarajevo
   e) The Schlieffen Plan
   f) The Battle of Verdun
   g) General Haig
   h) The Zimmerman Telegram
   i) The Battle of Jutland
   j) The Eastern Front

Summary/revision plan

You need to have a good working knowledge of the following areas. **Tick off each item** once you are confident in your knowledge.

❑ **1 The alliance system and the arms race between the Great Powers**
- The Central Powers, or Triple Alliance
- Entente Cordiale, 1904 and Triple Entente, 1907
- The arms race
- Plans for war – Germany, France, Britain, Austria, Russia

❑ **2 Immediate events leading to the outbreak of war in 1914**
- Moroccan crises, 1905 and 1911
- The Balkan wars
- The road to war
- Mobilisation

❑ **3 The main events on the Western Front, 1914–18**
- The failure of the war plans, 1914
- The Western Front, 1915
- Trench warfare
- Verdun and the Somme, 1916
- Trench warfare
- The changing technology of war
  - Artillery
  - Machine guns
  - Gas
  - Tanks
  - Aeroplanes
  - Balloons and Zeppelins
- 1917–1918

❑ **4 War on the Eastern Front, 1914–18**
- 1914
- 1915
- 1916
- 1917: revolution in Russia
- 1918: Russia is defeated

❑ **5 The war in Africa, the Pacific and the Middle East**
- Africa
- The Pacific
- The Middle East
  - Turkey
  - Gallipoli
  - Mesopotamia
  - Palestine

❑ **6 The war at sea**
- Background
- Minor clashes
- The Battle of Jutland, May–June 1916
- War against the submarine.

Check your knowledge online with our Quick quizzes at www.hodderplus.co.uk/modernworldhistory.

Chapter 11: The USA, 1945–1975: land of freedom?

In this chapter, you will study the changes that took place in American society between 1945 and 1975. In particular, you will look at the fear of Communism and how this affected American society in the 1950s. You will also look at the civil rights movement after 1945 and the experiences of groups such as Native Americans, Hispanics and women.

Focus points

In the OCR course, each Paper 1 depth study option is divided into key questions, and each key question is divided into focus points. To do well in the examination, you need to have a well-thought-out view on each of the key questions and focus points.

Key Question 1: Why was there a 'Red Scare' in the USA?
Focus points
- How did the international situation make Americans more fearful of Communism?
- What was McCarthyism?
- Why did people support McCarthyism?
- Why did McCarthyism decline?

Key Question 2: How successful was the struggle for civil rights in the 1950s?
Focus points
- What was the state of civil rights in America c.1950?
- Did the Second World War have an impact on the position of African Americans?
- Why was the struggle over desegregated education in the 1950s important?
- What was the importance of the Montgomery Bus Boycott?

Key Question 3: Who improved civil rights the most in the 1960s and 1970s?
Focus points
- How were Martin Luther King's ideas and methods different from those of Malcolm X?
- Who did more for civil rights in America, Martin Luther King or Malcolm X?
- Who was more important in improving civil rights, President Kennedy or President Johnson?
- Did the Black Power groups harm the struggle for civil rights?
- How far did civil rights progress under Nixon?

Key Question 4: How far did other groups achieve civil rights in America?
Focus points
- Why did immigration of Hispanic Americans increase after the Second World War?
- What did the Hispanic Americans achieve in their campaign for better rights and conditions?
- What were the issues faced by Native Americans in the 1970s?
- What methods did American women use to achieve equality?

Key content

In order to fully understand the focus points, you will need to have a good working knowledge of:

- the Red Scare in the USA
- the struggle for civil rights in the 1950s
- the improvement of civil rights in the 1960s and 1970s
- civil rights for American Hispanics, Native Americans and women.

11.1 The Red Scare in the USA

How did the international situation make Americans more fearful of Communism?

In the early 1950s, many people in the USA were caught in the grip of extreme anti-Communism. This happened for a number of reasons.

- The **Cold War** significantly worsened relations between the USA and the USSR.
- It seemed that the USSR was determined to spread **Communism** throughout Europe and the rest of the world.
- Communists seized control of Czechoslovakia in 1948 and were also trying to take over the government of Greece.
- The Soviets cut the supply routes to West Berlin in June 1948, which only survived following a fifteen-month airlift by the western powers.
- In 1949, there was a Communist takeover of China by Mao Zedong and further advances by Communist groups in other parts of South-East Asia.
- In 1949, the US monopoly of atomic warfare ended when the Soviet Union created its own atomic bomb.
- In 1950, the USA became involved in the Korean War and supported South Korea against the Communist North. This further increased anti-Communism in the USA.

The fear of Communism spreading to the USA encouraged American politicians and institutions to look for any sign of Communist infiltration. Ordinary US citizens and celebrities who were thought to be Communists were immediately blacklisted and many lost their jobs.

- The FBI (Federal Bureau of Investigation) had a strongly anti-Communist director, J. Edgar Hoover. Between 1947 and 1950, about 3 million American citizens were investigated by the FBI. Nobody was charged with spying.
- Investigation of suspected anti-Communists was nothing new. In the 1930s, the **House Un-American Activities Committee (HUAC)** interviewed people who were suspected of being Communists. In 1947, ten Hollywood producers, writers and directors were interviewed by the HUAC. Although they had done nothing illegal, they were imprisoned for one year for contempt of court since they refused to answer the committee's questions.

Key terms

Cold War: political hostility between countries that stops short of actual armed conflict.
Communism: a system of government in which the state plans and controls the economy and a single party governs the country. Communism aims to ensure that all land and services are owned by the state and that all goods are equally shared by the people.
House Un-American Activities Committee (HUAC): a committee of the US House of Representatives, created to investigate people and organisations suspected of being disloyal to the USA.

- In 1950, Alger Hiss, a high-ranking member of the US State Department was imprisoned for five years, suspected of being Communist.
- In 1951, Julius and Ethel Rosenberg were found guilty of spying for the USSR and passing atomic secrets. Two years later, they were executed.
- In 1950, fear of Communism led the US Congress, against the wishes of President Eisenhower, to pass the McCarran Act. This Act forced all Communist organisations to register with the US Government, outlawed any Communist from owning a US passport or working in the defence industry, and created detention camps to be used in an emergency.

What was McCarthyism?

The wave of anti-Communist hysteria that swept across the USA was fuelled by key individuals, the most prominent of whom was Joseph McCarthy, a Senator from Wisconsin. McCarthy used the protection of the Senate to make public accusations against hundreds of US citizens, including fellow Senators and other politicians. McCarthy used TV effectively to give his allegations widespread publicity.

- McCarthy said that the State Department (Foreign Office) contained over 200 Communists. When these claims were investigated by the Senate, they were found to be a hoax.
- McCarthy accused Democratic Senator Millard Tydings of being a Communist. In the next set of elections for Congress, Tydings was defeated by a McCarthy supporter.
- Throughout 1952 and 1953, McCarthy used his position as chair of a Senate committee to continue his personal anti-Communist crusade. He targeted high profile politicians, such as George Marshall who was responsible for the Marshall Plan. McCarthy accused Marshall of being at the centre of a major Communist conspiracy against the USA.
- McCarthy ruined the lives of thousands of innocent people. Many of these, including university lecturers, were blacklisted and unable to find work again. Between 1953 and 1954, nearly 7,000 government workers lost their jobs, although none were put on trial.
- In August 1954, the Communist Control Act was introduced. This outlawed the Communist Party of the USA and made membership illegal.

The end of McCarthyism

The influence of McCarthyism ended in 1954 for several reasons.
- Many politicians, Hollywood stars and newspapers began criticising McCarthy.
- Several prominent court cases during the 1950s put an end to the type of 'blacklisting' that McCarthy encouraged. In 1956, the Supreme Court supported the case of Professor Slochower who had been sacked from Brooklyn College because he refused to deny past membership of the Communist Party. A year later, the Supreme Court ruled on the case of *Watkins v. the United States*, stopping Congress from punishing unco-operative witnesses who in previous years would have been blacklisted as suspected Communists.
- In 1954, McCarthy accused 45 army officers of being Communist agents. In the televised hearings that followed, the public was shocked at McCarthy's bullying, aggressive and confrontational manner. In contrast, the army's chief counsel, Joseph Welch, was calm, reasonable and polite, and effectively showed the weaknesses of McCarthy's case. A new Senate committee was established and it condemned McCarthy's behaviour. McCarthy's influence and power fell dramatically and he died three years later.

Exam practice

1 Describe the main features of McCarthyism.
(4 marks)
2 Explain the reasons why there was a 'Red Scare' in the USA during the 1950s.
(6 marks)

Exam tip

These are typical of the questions you will face in questions 8 or 9.

1 This is a starter question. It tests your **factual knowledge**. Try to include four details about McCarthyism.

2 This tests your knowledge and understanding.
- A low level answer (worth 1–2 marks) will simply state one or two reasons.
- A better answer (worth 3–4 marks) will describe several reasons why Americans were scared about the spread of Communism and explain each one more fully.
- A top level answer (worth 5–6 marks) will do all the above but also compare the importance of each reason.

SOURCE 1

An extract from the commentary to a TV documentary made in 1984 called '*A Walk Through the Twentieth Century with Bill Moyers*'. Bill Moyers is an American journalist.

Looking for an issue that would get him re-elected, he [McCarthy] seized on the fears of millions, and launched the squalid campaign that became known as McCarthyism. Its tactic: reckless and undocumented accusations against government employees. McCarthy soon had the celebrity he sought. The stage was his alone to command.

Source 1 above shows one view of McCarthy's tactics almost 30 years after his death. During the 1950s, however, McCarthy had a major influence on American politics.

The importance of McCarthyism

McCarthyism was important for several reasons.
- McCarthy's tactics showed how easy it was to create fear and hysteria about the threat of Communism.
- McCarthyism showed the extent of anti-Communist feeling in the USA.
- It made it difficult for ordinary citizens to criticise the Government without being labelled as Communists.
- Many US citizens were financially ruined and their reputations destroyed.
- It suggested that many Americans were unhappy with the changes taking place in their society. This attitude made it more difficult in later years to gain greater equality for women and improved rights for African Americans.
- McCarthyism showed that despite the freedoms outlined in the US Constitution, people in the USA were not, in reality, allowed complete freedom of political choice for fear of being hounded from their job or having their reputation destroyed.

Revision tasks

1 How would you describe the tone of **Source 1**? Does this affect its reliability?

2 Copy and complete the table below, using your knowledge of the Red Scare.

Causes of the Red Scare	Effects of the Red Scare on the USA

11.2 How successful was the struggle for civil rights in the 1950s?

The state of civil rights in the 1950s

There had been little progress in the development of **civil rights** since the Second World War. Throughout the 1950s, racism was an everyday part of life for African Americans, particularly in the southern states. Although the armed forces had been desegregated, plans to outlaw **lynching** and improve voting rights for poor African Americans, which were introduced in 1948, had little impact.
- Most US southern states enforced the '**Jim Crow**' laws, which **segregated** everyday facilities such as parks, buses and schools.
- African Americans had been given the vote in the early years of the twentieth century but intimidation and violence often prevented them from using it.
- African Americans faced legal and official discrimination in employment and education.
- Top universities were closed to African Americans.

Exam practice

1 'The main reason for the end of McCarthyism was because many Hollywood stars criticised Senator Joseph McCarthy.' How far do you agree with this statement? Explain your answer.

(10 marks)

Exam tip The question above tests your knowledge and understanding but it goes further. A question that starts 'How far …' is also inviting you to **evaluate**. The question mentions one reason, but for top marks you have to evaluate the importance of that reason and the other possible reasons too.

Key terms

Civil rights: legal rights, such as freedom of speech and the right to a fair trial. Most African Americans lacked these basic rights in the 1950s.

Lynching: Murder usually carried out by a mob.

Jim Crow: the name Jim Crow was made popular by a white American comedian who made fun of African Americans. Originally, Jim Crow was a character in an old song. This name became linked to the southern states who ensured that African American people remained inferior.

Segregation: keeping a group separate from the rest of society, usually on the basis of race or religion. Segregation was seen in separate schools, transport and housing.

The struggle to desegregate education

For decades it had been legal in the USA for states to have separate schools for African American and white children. The National Association for the Advancement of Colored People (NAACP) and the African American civil rights lawyer, Thurgood Marshall, had brought a series of complaints about segregated schools in the 1940s. Judge Julius Waring ruled that the states had to provide equal education for African American and white students but said nothing about integration.

The *Brown v. Topeka Board of Education* case of 1954 showed further progress in education.

- In 1951, the NAACP brought a court case against the Board of Education of Topeka in Kansas on behalf of an African American student, Linda Brown. She had to walk a considerable distance to get to school because she was not allowed to attend the whites-only school near her home.
- In May 1954, Chief Justice Earl Warren ruled in favour of Brown and stated that segregated education could not be equal because African American students had inferior facilities. He ordered the southern states to set up integrated schools 'with all deliberate speed'. The NAACP favoured using the legal system to challenge inequality and took individual cases all the way to the Supreme Court. This method was also used at Little Rock in Arkansas.
- By 1957, Arkansas had not introduced integrated education.
- In the same year, the Supreme Court ordered Arkansas governor, Orval Faubus, to allow nine African American students to attend a white school in Little Rock.
- Faubus brought out the National Guard to stop the nine students attending, insisting he was using the troops to protect them.
- Faubus only backed down when President Eisenhower sent federal troops to enforce the law that entitled the African American students to attend.

The Montgomery Bus Boycott, 1955 – the beginning of non-violent mass protest

The 1955 Montgomery Bus Boycott is usually seen as the official start of the civil rights movement.

In Montgomery, Alabama, a local law stated that African Americans were only allowed to sit or stand at the back of a bus and had to give up their seats if they were needed by white people. Rosa Parks, a NAACP activist, refused to give up her seat and was arrested and convicted of breaking the bus laws. In response, local civil rights activists set up the Montgomery Improvement Association (MIA) led by Martin Luther King. Its members boycotted the buses and organised private transport for people. This was a great success and the first example of non-violent direct action. It showed how powerful African American people could be if they worked together. Civil rights lawyers fought Rosa Parks' case in court. In December 1956, the Supreme Court declared Montgomery's bus laws illegal.

African Americans had won an important victory in the struggle for civil rights, but the pace of school integration in the south was painfully slow.

- Eisenhower's 1957 Civil Rights Act, for example, proved to be ineffective. Southern Democrats claimed that the Federal Government in Washington was interfering with the independence of each state, so in order for it to become law, key features of the Act designed to increase the number of African American voters were removed.
- Better progress was made with the 1960 Civil Rights Act following serious rioting in the southern states. This Act introduced penalties against anybody who obstructed someone's attempt to register to vote or actually vote. A Civil Rights Commission was also created.

Non-violent mass protest gathers pace

During 1959 and 1960, civil rights groups stepped up their campaign. Demonstrations, organised marches and boycotts were arranged to end segregation in public places.

In February 1960 in Nashville, Tennessee, 500 students organised sit-ins in restaurants, libraries and churches. Their college expelled them but then backed down when 400 teachers threatened to resign. By May 1960, Nashville had been desegregated.

In May 1961, both white and African American members of the Congress of Racial Equality (CORE) began a form of protest in the southern states known as 'freedom rides'. They deliberately rode on buses run by companies that were ignoring laws banning segregation. They faced much violence and opposition. By September, 70,000 students had taken part and 3,600 had been arrested. Over 100 cities in 20 states were affected.

By 1961, the civil rights movement had become a national movement. Many Americans were becoming aware of the unfair treatment of African American people, especially in the southern states.

11.3 Who improved civil rights the most in the 1960s and 1970s?

Martin Luther King

King became the leading figure in the civil rights movement until his assassination in 1968. He believed passionately in non-violent protest and favoured actions such as the bus boycott and sit-ins. He won increased support for the civil rights movement by appealing to students. In April 1960, the Student Non-violent Co-ordinating Committee (SNCC) was set up and many SNCC workers dropped out of their studies to work full-time in assisting desegregation.

- In the summer of 1961, the main civil rights groups – SNCC, CORE and NAACP – met with the Attorney-General, Robert Kennedy, and devised the Voter Education Project, which aimed to get more African American people registered to vote.
- In April 1963, King organised a march on Birmingham, Alabama, as the city had still not been desegregated. The aim of the march was to turn attention on Birmingham and expose its policies to national attention. Police Chief Bull Connor ordered police and fire officers to turn dogs and fire hoses on the peaceful protesters. The police arrested over 1,000 protesters, including King. King's tactics worked, as President Kennedy forced Governor George Wallace to release the protesters and desegregate Birmingham.
- In August 1963, King staged his most high-profile event. Over 200,000 African American and 50,000 white Americans marched together to Washington to pressure Kennedy to introduce a civil rights bill. There was no trouble and King gave his famous 'I have a dream' speech.

Comment

The march was also known as the 'children's crusade' because of the large number of children who took part.

President Kennedy and the 'new frontier'

John F. Kennedy narrowly defeated Richard Nixon in the presidential election of 1960. He was the youngest-ever US President. He talked about the USA being at the edge of a 'new frontier'. This was at first a slogan but then became a series of reforms. He urged Americans to 'Ask not what your country can do for you, but what you can do for your country'. Young Americans were invited to volunteer for the 'Peace Corps' to help attack 'tyranny, poverty, disease and war itself'. The new frontier included social reforms to help poor Americans. It also included extending the frontier into space by sending men to the moon.

In the early 1960s, President Kennedy was also keen to make progress in the area of civil rights and was determined to achieve equality for African Americans.

- In September 1962, Kennedy made a speech committing himself to the cause of civil rights.
- He made a high-level appointment of Thurgood Marshall as the first African American US circuit judge.
- He confronted the governors of the southern states who opposed civil rights.
- In October 1962, he sent 2,300 troops to ensure that one African American student, James Meredith, could stay at the University of Mississippi without being intimidated by racists.

Civil rights tactics – King versus Malcolm X

Dr Martin Luther King and Malcolm X had very different views about how African Americans should go about achieving civil rights.

- King believed in non-violent direct action. This took the form of peaceful demonstrations, legal challenges, boycotts of businesses, and rallies and meetings with influential politicians.
- King himself was a gifted speaker who was admired worldwide and whose speeches inspired his followers and challenged his opponents. He was awarded the Nobel Peace Prize in 1964.
- Malcolm Little, or Malcolm X as he became known, and most African American nationalists rejected the non-violence of the civil rights movement. Malcolm X and his followers believed in violence to achieve their goals.
- Malcolm X supported the movement known as the Nation of Islam, which wanted African Americans to rise up and create their own separate African American nation within the USA.
- Between 1967 and 1969, a group known as the Black Panthers, which claimed 2,000 members, often clashed violently with the police, with nine police officers being killed.

Comment

Martin Luther King did not invent the tactic of direct action. This had developed as a result of the key education and transport cases of the 1950s and early 1960s. He did, however, provide national leadership for such action and ensured massive publicity for the cause of civil rights within and beyond the USA.

Source Evaluation: the nature of the Civil Rights movement

Martin Luther King and Malcolm X had similar aims: to ensure that African Americans enjoyed similar rights and privileges to white Americans. However their views on how these objectives could be achieved differed. Martin Luther King believed in passive resistance and non-violence. Malcolm X was prepared to justify the use of violence as you can see from the two sources below.

Because of this fundamental difference the two leaders have often been presented as opposites. Nowadays however historians are much interested in what they had in common; and how the two aspects of the movement fed off each other. Historians also emphasise that the Civil Rights movement was a very diverse movement with many strands. Its supporters used many different approaches, and held different beliefs. It is wrong to see the movement as being about either Martin Luther King or Malcolm X. It is much more complicated than that.

These two sources are very useful for showing the beliefs of the two leaders and some of the arguments they used to justify their tactics. However they are even more useful taken together. To understand such a complex and diverse movement it is important that you use as wide a range of sources as possible.

SOURCE 2

Martin Luther King's Acceptance Speech, on the occasion of the award of the Nobel Peace Prize in Oslo, December 10, 1964.

Nonviolence is the answer to the crucial political and moral questions of our time: the need for man to overcome oppression and violence. Man must evolve for all human conflict a method which rejects revenge, aggression and retaliation. The foundation for such method is love.

SOURCE 3

Malcolm X, November 1963, New York

If violence is wrong in America, violence is wrong abroad. If it is wrong to be violent defending black women and black children and black babies and black men, then it is wrong for America to draft us, and make us violent abroad in defence of her. And if it is right for America to draft us, and teach us how to be violent in defence of her, then it is right for you and me to do whatever is necessary to defend our own people right here in this country.

The achievements of Kennedy's 'new frontier'

Whilst Kennedy's government wanted to make progress in the area of civil rights, the position of some African Americans worsened during the Kennedy years.

- The rate of unemployment for African Americans remained at twice the level that it was for whites.
- Many African Americans moved north but endured poverty and racial tension.
- Some southern states blocked the implementation of Kennedy's civil rights reforms.
- Many of Kennedy's supporters during his election campaign were from the south and did not support his civil rights policy.

The Civil Rights Act and events, 1964–65

In November 1963, Kennedy was assassinated. His successor, Lyndon Johnson, was just as committed to civil rights. On 2 July 1964, he signed the Civil Rights Act which made it illegal for local government to discriminate in areas such as housing and employment. The summer of 1964 was known as the 'freedom summer'. King and SNCC continued to encourage African Americans to register to vote, and by 1966 there were 430,000 more African Americans on the electoral roll.

King continued to target areas where discrimination was worst. In 1965, he organised a march through Selma, Alabama, which had a notoriously racist sheriff called Jim Clark, to protest against the violence being used to stop African American voters from registering. The authorities banned the march, but 600 people went ahead and were brutally attacked. The media called it 'Bloody Sunday'. King organised a second march but compromised with the authorities by turning back after a certain distance. This lost King the support of the more radical African American activists, but nevertheless helped President Johnson to push through a Voting Rights Bill in 1965, which finally became law in 1968. The Act allowed government agents to inspect voting procedures to make sure that they were taking place properly. It also ended the literacy tests that voters had previously had to complete before they voted. After 1965, five major cities had African American mayors.

In April 1968, King was assassinated, probably by a hired killer, although it has never been proved which of King's enemies hired the assassin.

Johnson and the 'Great Society'

Vice-President Lyndon Johnson became President when Kennedy was assassinated in 1963. He talked of a 'Great Society' and of taking Kennedy's reforms further with an 'unconditional war on poverty' and an immediate end to racial injustice. He was very good at politics and much more successful than Kennedy in getting measures passed by Congress. Johnson tackled areas more effectively than Kennedy. For example, he introduced Medicare which provided free medical care for the poor. There are several reasons, however, why Johnson does not get the credit that he deserves for his domestic achievements:

- He did not have Kennedy's charisma and did not work well with the advisers used by Kennedy.
- Conservatives in Congress attacked him for spending too much on welfare.
- Liberals criticised him for increasing American involvement in Vietnam.

Johnson's achievements in civil rights included:

- the 1964 Civil Rights Act
- the appointment of the first-ever African American to the White House cabinet and the Supreme Court: Thurgood Marshall became US Solicitor General in 1965 and a Supreme Court judge in 1967
- the Immigration Act of 1965, which ended the system of racial quotas for immigrants into the USA.

Exam practice

1 What was meant by 'new frontier'?
(4 marks)

2 Explain why President Kennedy faced problems in his attempt to improve civil rights between 1961 and 1963.
(6 marks)

3 How successful was President Johnson in improving civil rights between 1963 and 1968? *(10 marks)*

Exam tip

These are typical of the questions you will face in questions 2 or 3.

1 This is a starter question. It tests your **factual knowledge**. Include four relevant facts about the 'new frontier'.

2 This tests your knowledge and **understanding**.
- A low level answer (worth 1–3 marks) will simply state one or two problems facing President Kennedy.
- A better answer (worth 4–6 marks) will explain several problems facing President Kennedy and show how they are connected.

3 This question tests your knowledge and understanding but it goes further. You need to show you understand Johnson's challenges and weigh his achievements against his failures.

Despite these reforms, there was racial tension and rioting in several cities in the summer of 1968.

Johnson's war on poverty involved a range of measures.

- In 1965, two government-funded health-care programmes, Medicare and Medicaid, were set up for elderly people and families on low incomes.
- The minimum wage was increased from $1.25 to $1.40 per hour.
- The funding of the Aid to Families with Dependent Children (AFDC) scheme was increased. This gave financial help to 745,000 families on low incomes.
- The VISTA programme tried to create work in poor inner-city areas.
- The Elementary and Secondary Education Act of 1965 for the first time put federal funding into improving education in poorer areas.
- The Model Cities Act (1966) linked to the other inner-city employment programmes by clearing slums and providing parks and sports facilities.

Civil rights under Presidents Nixon and Ford

In March 1968, President Johnson surprised the American public by withdrawing from the presidential race. In November, Republican candidate and former Vice-President Richard Nixon was elected president. The further extension of civil rights for African Americans was not one of his priorities.

- In March 1970, Nixon supported southern conservatives by stopping the compulsory bussing of students in order to achieve a racial balance in schools.
- In 1971, the US Supreme Court insisted that bussing students was a reasonable method of ensuring a racial balance in schools.
- In addition, the Justice Department opposed the extension of the 1965 Voting Act and delayed desegregation of schools in Mississippi.

In August 1974, President Nixon resigned after the scandal of the Watergate break-in and cover-up. He was succeeded by Vice-President Gerald Ford. Ford faced significant economic problems and, like his predecessor, did not have civil rights high on his list of priorities. In fact, as the economic situation worsened under Ford, unemployment amongst African American youths rose to 40 per cent.

11.4 Civil rights for Hispanics, Native Americans and women

The campaigns for African American civil rights encouraged other protest movements.

Hispanics

In the early twentieth century Americans of Spanish descent were mostly confined to the south-western states of California, Arizona and Texas as well as the Gulf states and Florida. They were mainly employed in agriculture or as servants and maids.

In the same way as African Americans, **Hispanics** suffered significant discrimination.

- During the 1930s, the US Government introduced the Mexican Repatriation Programme, which encouraged Mexican immigrants to voluntarily return to Mexico. However, approximately 1 million people were forcibly deported even though 60 per cent of them were American citizens.
- In 1943, rioting broke out between US naval servicemen and Hispanic residents in Los Angeles. The Zoot riots, as they became known, continued for three days and the naval personnel were even assisted by the local police.

Hispanic children were segregated in the school system and Hispanic adults were discriminated against in housing and employment.

> ### Comment
> *The post-war era saw significant developments in the area of civil rights. Whilst the US federal government had generally encouraged greater equality at a local level, particularly in the southern states throughout the 1960s, racism and inequality were still clearly evident. It would take many more years to see the sort of integration that was originally hoped for.*

> ### Revision task
> Use the information in this chapter to list the achievements of the civil rights movement by the end of the 1960s.

> ### Key term
> **Hispanic:** a term created in the 1970s to describe US citizens who could trace their ancestry to Spain or former Spanish territories, or those who were born in the Spanish-speaking countries of Central and South America. Most Hispanics identify with specific groups such as Mexican American, Puerto Rican or Cuban rather than the more general term Latino or Hispanic.

Hispanic Migration

Despite this discrimination after the Second World War, large numbers of Hispanic workers migrated to the USA from different countries for different reasons.

An agreement between the United States and Mexico called the Bracero Program allowed Mexico to supply contract workers to the USA.

- Hispanic immigrants from Cuba began to arrive in the USA at the time of Fidel Castro's Communist takeover of Cuba in 1959. Thirty years later, Castro removed the travel restriction on his own people and allowed anyone to leave Cuba if they wanted. As a consequence, hundreds of thousands of Cubans, including 5,000 criminals who Castro had freed, left for the USA.
- In 1965, the US Congress passed an Immigration Act that removed some of the restrictions put in place in 1924. After 1965, there was a surge in immigration, which significantly increased the proportion of Hispanics and Asians in the USA.

From 1940 to 1980, the proportion of people in the USA of Hispanic origin had grown from 1.8 million to 14.6 million (1.4 per cent to 6.4 per cent of the total US population). The post-1945 immigrants were more likely to be refugees with higher order skills than earlier immigrants.

Hispanic campaigns for civil rights

- During the 1960s, Hispanics joined the civil rights cause and launched the Chicano movement. The Chicano movement had three aims: restoration of land, education reforms and rights for farm workers.
- Hispanic influence in politics increased with the election of President Kennedy who had had the support of the Mexican American Political Association.
- In 1965, Hispanic grape pickers went on strike in Delano, California, demanding union recognition for Hispanics. This was finally achieved in 1970.
- In 1966, Hispanics held a three-day march from Albuquerque, New Mexico, to the state capital in Santa Fe, demanding that land taken by the USA at the end of the 1848 Mexican-American War be returned to local Mexicans.
- In 1974, Congress passed the Equal Opportunity Act, which resulted in the implementation of more bilingual education programmes in public schools.

In the nineteenth century, the US Government's policy was to force Native American tribes to take specific plots of land called reservations. Some tribes fought in vain with the Government and US army to keep their historic land. Most tribes moved onto reservation land, which was generally of poor quality.

A policy of **Americanisation** was also introduced, which was designed to merge Native American culture with white culture. The Dawes Act of 1887 gave plots of land to Native Americans in order to undermine their nomadic lifestyle and turn them into homesteaders and farmers. The 1924 Indian Citizenship Act gave citizenship to 125,000 of the 300,000 indigenous people in the USA. Despite the Act, many Native Americans were not granted full voting rights until 1948 because of the opposition of some states.

By the twentieth century, most Native Americans depended on government assistance. Poverty and unemployment remained much higher than amongst white Americans. During the 1940s, the Bureau of Indian Affairs based in Washington DC ordered Native American children to be removed from reservations and sent to boarding schools in order to reduce the influence of their native culture.

Native Americans since 1945

During the Second World War, approximately 44,000 Native Americans served in the US armed forces. When the war ended in 1945, many of the young men who served did not return to the poverty of the reservation. They obtained better paid jobs in large US cities, and the Native American population in urban areas doubled from 24,000 to 56,000 between 1941 and 1950.

> **Key term**
>
> **Americanisation:** Policy of the US Government to set a standard of cultural values to be held by all US citizens. For example, in the nineteenth century Native American religious ceremonies were outlawed and children had to attend English-speaking schools.

Native American campaigns for civil rights

- In 1968, members of the Minneapolis Native American community founded the American Indian Movement (AIM). Its aim was to highlight issues concerning Native Americans, including poverty, housing, land, and alleged police harassment.

- In 1972, a group of approximately 500 members of AIM occupied the Bureau of Indian Affairs in Washington DC in order to publicise the poor living standards of Native Americans. The occupation lasted for seven days and $700,000 worth of damage was done to the building.

- In 1973, a further group of AIM members took part in a 71-day siege at Wounded Knee in South Dakota. Wounded Knee had been the site of the massacre of 150 Native Americans by the US seventh cavalry in 1890. During the siege, the Native Americans occupied a small church and trading post, but shooting broke out and two AIM members were killed and many others wounded.

- During the course of the siege, the Hollywood actor, Marlon Brando, asked a famous Native American, Sacheeen Littlefeather, to speak on his behalf at the Oscar ceremony. Brando refused to accept his Oscar for his performance in the film *The Godfather* as a protest at the poor treatment of Native Americans.

- Even after the peaceful end to the Wounded Knee siege, unrest continued on the Pine Ridge Reservation. In 1975, two FBI agents were killed in the course of a shootout at Wounded Knee.

The women's movement

This was not one single organisation but thousands of different groups all with similar aims – to raise the status of women and end discrimination against women in all areas of life. This movement emerged for several reasons.

- Many women were involved in the struggle for black civil rights which made them more aware of how, as well as racist, US society was also sexist. It empowered them to fight for their own civil rights.

- Inequality in employment: the number of women in employment had continued to increase in the years after the Second World War, but work for women was overwhelmingly low paid, with many earning only 50 per cent of the wages of men for doing the same job.

- In 1963, Betty Friedan wrote a bestseller called *The Feminine Mystique*. This was her term for a set of ideas that said that women's happiness came from being wives and mothers. Friedan challenged this notion, insisting that married women needed employment to avoid frustration and boredom. She wrote of hundreds of college-educated women who felt little better than domestic servants.

- Women's attitudes also changed because of the introduction of the contraceptive pill in 1960. This changed women's attitudes to sexual relations and gave them much greater independence.

SOURCE 4

From '*The Feminine Mystique*', by Betty Friedan, 1963.

As the American woman made beds, shopped for groceries, matched slipcover material, ate peanut butter sandwiches with her children, chauffeured Cub Scouts and Brownies, lay beside her husband at night, she was afraid to ask even of herself the question: 'Is this all?'

SOURCE 5

Bella Abzug, US Congresswoman and Feminist Leader.

We are coming down from our pedestal and up from the laundry room. We want an equal share in government and we mean to get it.

Exam practice

1 Read sources 4 and 5.
   'American women faced discrimination in everyday life.'
   How far do you agree with this interpretation? Use the sources and your own knowledge to explain your answer.
   (7 marks)

Women's rights received a boost from the federal government, which passed a number of important measures, and from the Supreme Court. In 1963, the Equal Pay Act required employers to pay women the same as men for the same work. This, however, did not stop discrimination against female employment. The following year, the Civil Rights Act made it illegal to discriminate on grounds of gender. In 1972, the Educational Amendment Act outlawed sex discrimination in education, and courses had to be rewritten to ensure that gender stereotyping did not occur in the curriculum. In 1973, the Supreme Court's ruling in the *Roe v. Wade* case made abortion legal.

Women's organisations campaign for civil rights

Various organisations emerged in the 1960s.

- In 1966, Betty Friedan set up the National Organisation for Women (NOW), which had 40,000 members by the early 1970s. It co-operated with a wide range of women's movements, such as the National Women's Caucus and the Women's Campaign Fund. It used similar tactics to the civil rights movement and challenged discrimination in court. NOW, however, was not an extreme organisation and still believed in traditional families and marriage.
- In contrast, there were younger feminists with more radical aims and different methods. They became known as the Women's Liberation movement (Women's Lib). They used more extreme methods. In 1968, radical women picketed the Miss World beauty contest in Atlantic City. They said that the contest treated women like objects. To make their point, they crowned a sheep as Miss World.

The women's movement achieved much publicity and support, with several important laws passed. However, there were limitations.

- Support was lost because of the extreme methods of the Women's Lib Movement, which some believed ridiculed the position of women.
- Anti-feminist organisations were set up, with the most famous, STOP ERA, led by Phyllis Schafly. ERA stood for Equal Rights Amendment, which was a proposal to amend the US constitution to outlaw sex discrimination. Schlafly led a successful campaign to prevent it becoming law as late as the 1980s.
- Despite legislation, few women had achieved top posts in Congress, business or industry by the end of the 1970s.

Comment

Whilst women saw important changes to their position in American society and achieved greater equality under the law, the same could not be said for other minority groups. Native Americans and Hispanics remained poorer members of American society and measures to improve their living standards had, at most, limited effects.

Chapter review

Here are ten events, terms or people you have studied in this depth study. Without checking back see if you can write a one or two sentence summary of what it was and why it was important in post war American history 1945–1975.

a) The Cold War
b) HUAC
c) 'Jim Crow' laws
d) Brown v Topeka Board of Education
e) Freedom rides
f) 'I have a dream'
g) Malcolm X
h) The Great Society
i) Wounded Knee
j) Betty Friedan

Revision tasks

1 Copy and complete the table below to compare Native Americans, Hispanics and women in their struggle for justice and equal rights in the USA.

	Nature of discrimination	Method of campaigning	Achievements
Native Americans			
Hispanics			
Women			

2 How similar are they? Pick one big difference and one big similarity and write some notes about how they were similar or different.

Summary/revision plan

You need to have a good working knowledge of the following areas. **Tick off each item** once you are confident in your knowledge.

- ❑ **1 The Red Scare in the USA**
  - How did the international situation make Americans more fearful of Communism?
  - What was McCarthyism?
  - The end of McCarthyism
  - The importance of McCarthyism
- ❑ **2 How successful was the struggle for civil rights in the 1950s?**
  - The state of civil rights in the 1950s
  - The struggle to desegregate education
  - The Montgomery Bus Boycott, 1955 – the beginning of non-violent mass protest
  - Non-violent mass protest gathers pace
- ❑ **3 Who improved civil rights the most in the 1960s and 1970s?**
  - Martin Luther King
  - President Kennedy and the 'new frontier'
  - Civil rights tactics – King versus Malcolm X
  - The achievements of Kennedy's new frontier
  - The Civil Rights Act and events, 1964–65
  - Johnson and the 'Great Society'
  - Civil rights under Presidents Nixon and Ford
- ❑ **4 Civil rights for Hispanics, Native Americans and women**
  - Hispanics
    - Discrimination
    - Reasons for increased migration
    - Hispanics and the civil rights movement
  - Native Americans
    - Discrimination in the 19th and 20th centuries
    - Native American campaigns for civil rights
  - Women
    - The women's movement
    - Women's organisations campaign for civil rights

Check your knowledge online with our Quick quizzes at www.hodderplus.co.uk/modernworldhistory.

In this chapter, you will study the changes that took place in British society between 1890 and 1918. In particular, you will look at the problems of poverty in the 1890s and early 1900s and how the Liberal Government tried to tackle these from 1906 onwards. You will also look at the campaign to win women the right to vote and how the First World War affected people's lives.

Focus points

Each key question in the OCR course is divided into focus points. To do well in the examination, you will need a good understanding of each focus point.

- What were working and living conditions like for the poor in the 1890s?
- How were social reformers reacting to the social problems of the 1890s?
- Why did the Liberal Government introduce reforms to help the young, old and unemployed?
- How effective were these reforms?
- What was the social, political and legal position of women in the 1890s?
- What were the arguments for and against female suffrage?
- How effective were the activities of the suffragists and the suffragettes?
- How did women contribute to the war effort?
- How were civilians affected by the war?
- How effective was government propaganda during the war?
- Why were some women given the vote in 1918?
- What was the attitude of the British people at the end of the war towards Germany and the Paris Peace Conference?

Key content

In order to fully understand the focus points, you will need to have a good working knowledge of:

- poverty and living conditions in the 1890s
- the work and impact of Charles Booth and Seebohm Rowntree
- the introduction and effectiveness of Liberal reform
- the arguments for and against female suffrage
- the activities of the suffragists and suffragettes
- women's contributions to the War effort
- voting rights for women, 1918
- the life of British civilians during the War.

12.1 Poverty in the 1890s

As Britain developed as an industrial nation, millions of people moved from the countryside to cities in order to work in the new factories. Often, however, living conditions for workers were terrible. Although wages increased at the end of the nineteenth century, many people lived in desperate poverty.

The poor faced problems of:

- poor housing
- low wages
- unemployment
- illness (if a worker fell ill he or she could not earn money)
- irregular work
- little help for the elderly, sick or unemployed.

12.2 Why did the Liberal Government introduce reforms in 1906?

The simple answer to this question is that these groups needed help. There was terrible poverty in Britain. However, it was such a major shift in policy that it needs some explaining. There were four main factors.

1 Changing attitudes

In the nineteenth century, attitudes to poverty were as follows:

- Poverty was often blamed on the individual. People were poor because they were lazy (idle) and would not work, or they wasted their money.
- Many politicians believed that each individual was responsible for his or her own welfare so people should work hard and save for their old age.
- The only way to get help if you were poor was to enter the **workhouse**. Conditions in the workhouse were deliberately harsh in order to discourage people from seeking help.
- Charities existed to help the poor, but most people relied on family for assistance.

> **Key term**
>
> **Workhouse:** an institution financed by the state where the poor did unpaid work in return for food and accommodation.

By 1900, public opinion was changing.

- People realised that poverty could be caused by many factors.
- They also felt that the government should give some help to the poor instead of leaving it all to charity.

2 Social reformers

This change in attitude was partly because of the work of social reformers. They produced undeniable proof of the scale of poverty in Britain and its causes. The most important reformers were:

- Charles Booth – he carried out research into poverty in London and published *Life and Labour of the People in London* in seventeen volumes from 1889 to 1902.
- Seebohm Rowntree – he studied poverty and its causes in York and published a report called *Poverty: A Study of Town Life* in 1901.

Both researchers found that 28 to 31 per cent of the population lived around the poverty line. The poverty line meant being unable to afford decent housing, food, clothing, health care or even an occasional luxury such as a newspaper.

3 The Boer War

In 1899, Britain went to war in South Africa. Half of those who volunteered to fight were actually unfit for service. The percentage of unfit recruits also varied according to where they lived. Many had been so badly fed as children that they had not grown properly. This was extremely worrying for the Government. Unless something was done, Britain would not have a strong army to defend its interests.

4 Political factors

Political factors help explain why the Liberals introduced reforms.

Dynamic individuals

Two leading Liberal politicians, David Lloyd George and Winston Churchill, believed strongly in reform. They believed social reform would make the people better off and the country stronger as a result.

Rivalry with the Labour Party

In 1906, the newly formed Labour Party did well in the general election, gaining 29 seats. The Liberals wanted to win over ordinary people with their reforms so that they would vote Liberal rather than Labour.

Source evaluation: The motives for liberal reforms

It is very difficult to say what factors had the biggest influence on the Liberals when they introduced their reforms. Look at Source 1. You can see that the number of Labour MPs increased between 1906 and 1910. This could be used as evidence that the main reason the Liberals brought in reforms was their concerns about Labour. On the other hand, the actual number of Labour MPs is so small that you could argue that the Liberals were not really worried about Labour.

Source 2 provides evidence of changing attitudes in the 1900s. You can see that the Government accepts that most unemployed workers were not scroungers. You can also see that one of the problems for unemployed workers was finding out where there were jobs available.

SOURCE 1

The number of Liberal and Labour MPs elected to Parliament in elections 1900–10. The main Liberal reforms were passed in the period 1906–11.

Election year	Labour MPs	Liberal MPs
1900	2	183
1906	29	399
Jan 1910	40	274
Dec 1910	42	272

SOURCE 2

Extract from a report on labour exchanges, where men could go to find a job, written for the British cabinet in 1908.

No one but a rascal is permanently without employment. But large numbers are either constantly under-employed or periodically unemployed ... At the base of many great and thriving trades there spreads a broad fringe of casual and underpaid labour. Vague, scanty and imperfect information about where workmen are wanted, what localities are congested or what trades are declining impedes existing relief agencies ...

Revision task

Look at the diagram on the right:
It shows the relative importance of the factors that influenced the Liberals in bringing in reforms. This diagram suggests that all the factors were equally important.

a) Redraw the diagram, but imagine that the only knowledge you had of the topic was from **Sources 1** and **2**.

b) Now redraw it again using all your knowledge of this topic.

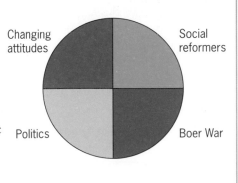

Changing attitudes

Social reformers

Politics

Boer War

12.3 What were the reforms and how effective were they?

Over the years 1906–1911 the liberal government passed a series of laws to help children, the old, the working and the unemployed. They are summarised in the table below.

Revision task

The third and fourth columns in the table are blank. Make your own copy of the table and complete it using the facts and figures in the bullet list below. You will have to decide where everything goes.

Groups the Liberals were trying to help	Actions taken	This was a good measure because …	This was not a good measure because …
Children	Free school meals, 1906		
	School medical inspections, 1907		
	School clinics, 1912		
	Children and Young Persons Act, 1908		
The old	Old Age Pensions Act, 1908		
Working people	Labour exchanges, 1909		
	National Insurance Act Part 1, 1911		
	National Insurance Act Part 2, 1911		

- All people aged over 70 received 5s a week, or 7s 6d for a couple. It was paid for by the Government.
- By 1914, over 150,000 children received one good meal a day from local councils.
- Children became protected persons; parents who neglected or abused their children in any way could be prosecuted.
- Children convicted of crimes were sent to special prisons called Borstals.
- Children got free, compulsory medical checks.
- If a worker became ill, the worker could get 10s a week sick pay for thirteen weeks. It was paid for by contributions from workers, government and employers.
- If a worker was unemployed, the worker received 7s 6d per week. It was funded by worker, employer and government contributions.
- Measures protecting children were difficult to enforce. Borstals were not always better places for children than prisons.
- Medical treatment for children did not become free until 1912.
- School meals were the responsibility of local councils. They did not have to provide them.
- The average working family could not survive on 7s 6d per week. Unemployment pay ran out after fifteen weeks.
- The pension was not a generous measure and could be refused to those who had failed to work to the best of their abilities in their working life.
- The poorest workers resented having to pay 4d per week from their wages.
- Unemployed workers could go to government labour exchanges to find out what jobs were available in their area. By 1913, exchanges were finding 3,000 jobs a day for workers.
- Many of the jobs in the exchanges were short-term and casual. The Government did nothing to make jobs more secure.

Source evaluation: Reactions to the liberal reforms

For historians, one of the problems is assessing whether or not these reforms had much effect. The big arguments at the time centred on whether the reforms were doing enough or whether they were doing too much. You can see from Source 3 below what Lloyd George thought. His main point is that he was making a start. He realised the reforms would not end all the problems of the poor.

SOURCE 3

Extract from a speech by David Lloyd George. He was Chancellor of the Exchequer and one of the most important figures in persuading the Liberal Party to pass welfare measures.

I never said that the National Insurance Bill was the final solution. I am not putting it forward as a complete remedy. It is one of a series. We are advancing on the road, and it is an essential part of the journey.

An examination question might focus on how people felt about the reforms. It might focus on what historians have said about the reforms. For example, look at Source 4. The historian in this source is even more positive about the reforms than Lloyd George himself. If these two sources appeared in an examination paper you could make use of one of them to support the other one in a question on reliability.

SOURCE 4

Historian Eric Hopkins, *A Social History of the English Working Classes*, published as a university level textbook in 1979.

There can be no doubt that taken as a whole the Liberal reforms constitute an impressive body of social legislation, the greatest ever passed by one government up to that time.

Whatever the focus of the exam paper, you need to develop a balanced view of the reforms. For each reform, you need to be able to say how it did have an effect and also be aware of how it was limited. The revision task on page 144 will help you do this.

12.4 What were the arguments for and against female suffrage?

The arguments for female suffrage

- Votes for women would improve life for all women. It would mean equal working conditions, better access to education and other benefits.
- Australia and New Zealand had given women the right to vote in national elections. In the USA, women had the right to vote in some states.
- Many women were already involved in politics at the local level, especially on boards of education and poor law boards.
- Women paid the same rates and taxes as men, so they should be able to vote for the politicians who spent those taxes.
- By the early 1900s, the vast majority of men could vote. Britain was not a democracy if 50 per cent of the adult population was denied the vote.

Exam tip In the examination, you need to look at each of the Liberal reforms and, using the evidence and your own knowledge, explain how well the reforms worked.

Key term

Female suffrage: the right of women to vote.

The arguments against female suffrage

- Women and men had different responsibilities or 'spheres'. Men were suited to work and politics while women were suited to the home and caring roles.
- Most women either did not want the vote or were not interested in it.
- Women were irrational and would not vote wisely.
- Giving the vote to some women would mean giving the vote to all men, some of whom were not worthy of it.
- Women did not fight in wars, so they should not be able to vote for governments that might have to declare war.

Sources 5 and 6 provide examples of the kind of arguments used by either side.

Exam tip The key to understanding sources is to increase your background knowledge. The more you know the easier source evaluation will be.

SOURCE 5

A poster produced by the WSPU 1912.

SOURCE 6

Comment by Prime Minister Herbert Asquith, 1906.

They [women] are for the most part hopelessly ignorant of politics, credulous [easily fooled] to the last degree, and flickering with gusts of sentiment like a candle in the wind.

Exam practice

1 Study Sources 5 and 6. How are these sources different? Use the sources and your own knowledge to explain your answer. *(9 marks)*

Exam tip This question tests your **factual knowledge** and your ability to **interpret and evaluate sources**. Try to show your knowledge and understanding of the period when the source was produced.

Questions which ask you to compare sources are usually asking you to compare the content of the source (its message and how that is conveyed) and its origin (or provenance).
The more you compare the detail of the source, and its context, and the more you use your (relevant) background knowledge the better your marks should be.

Revision tasks

1 Find a key word to sum up each of the arguments in favour of women's suffrage. For example, the first argument could use the key word 'improvements'.

2 Do the same for arguments against women's suffrage.

3 Try to create mnemonics of the arguments for and against the vote for women.

12.5 How effective were the activities of the suffragists and suffragettes?

The suffragists

There were many societies campaigning for the vote for women in Britain during the nineteenth century. In 1897, the various societies came together to form the **NUWSS**, often called the suffragists. The NUWSS was led by Millicent Fawcett.

- They built up an impressive organisation and membership. By 1914, the NUWSS had over 400 branches in all parts of the country and over 100,000 members.
- The membership was mainly made up of middle-class women. However, there were branches in some of the northern textile towns. There were also quite a few male members of the organisation.
- They were very good at propaganda. They produced newsletters and posters.
- They ran political campaigns, organised petitions and wrote letters to MPs. They held large rallies, such as the Hyde Park demonstration in 1908 and the Women's Pilgrimage in June 1913.

Were the suffragists an effective movement?

- Arguably, the NUWSS was not effective because it failed to get the vote for women by 1914.
- However, the suffragists did manage to get women's suffrage bills proposed to Parliament several times between 1900 and 1914. The closest was the Conciliation Bill, put forward in 1910 but then abandoned by the Liberals. They also managed to keep the issue of women's suffrage in the public eye, at a time when Prime Minister Asquith and many other MPs did not want to even consider the issue.

The suffragettes

The suffragettes was the name often given to the **WSPU**. It was founded in 1903 by Emmeline Pankhurst and her daughters, Sylvia and Christabel. It was more radical than the NUWSS who were frustrated by the lack of progress in the campaign to win women the right to vote.

Direct action

The WSPU decided that the way to achieve female suffrage was by direct action. It believed that this would make female suffrage such a major issue and attract such publicity that the Government would end its opposition. Direct action began in 1908 with suffragettes breaking windows in Downing Street and chaining themselves to railings. The police and the Government treated suffragettes very harshly. They were often assaulted in demonstrations. The Government responded with force-feeding, which was painful, degrading and potentially harmful. The Liberals then introduced the 'Cat and Mouse' Act in 1913 – hunger strikers were released in order to recover and then returned to prison to finish their sentence.

The WSPU called off violent protest in 1910, but then began again in 1912 with a campaign of arson and vandalism after the failure of the Conciliation Bill. The most famous incident came on 4 June 1913 when the suffragette Emily Wilding Davison threw herself in front of King George V's horse at the Epsom Derby and was severely injured, dying four days later. Davison had previously committed violent acts for the suffragette cause, including a bomb attack on the house of David Lloyd George, the Chancellor of the Exchequer, earlier the same year.

Hunger strikes

Some suffragettes deliberately got themselves arrested to draw attention to their cause. Once in prison some went on hunger strike demanding to be treated as political prisoners.

> **Key terms**
> **NUWSS:** the National Union of Women's Suffrage Societies.
> **WSPU:** the Women's Social and Political Union.

Were the suffragettes an effective movement?

- The suffragettes didn't achieve the vote by 1914.
- They divided the women's movement. From 1909 onwards, the suffragists distanced themselves from the suffragettes.
- Suffragette violence turned some MPs against female suffrage. It also turned sections of public opinion against female suffrage.
- However, the suffragette's actions meant that the issue of female suffrage was never forgotten.
- WSPU members were effective campaigners, publishing posters and leaflets. Their newspaper, *Votes for Women*, had a circulation of 40,000 by 1914.
- Many women (and men) admired the willingness of the suffragettes to suffer for their cause. The hunger strikes gained the suffragettes a lot of sympathy and support.

SOURCE 7

Exam practice

1 Study Source 7. Why was this poster published in 1909? Use the details of the source and your own knowledge to explain your answer. *(8 marks)*

Exam tip This question tests your **factual knowledge** and your ability to **interpret and evaluate sources**. A question that asks why this was published at particular time requires you to show your knowledge and understanding of the period when the source was produced.

A top level answer (worth 6–8 marks) will show a good understanding of the source, the purpose of its publication and a good knowledge of the Suffragette movement.

Revision tasks

1 Make two copies of the diagram on the right. Label one 'Suffragists' and the other 'Suffragettes'.

2 Choose at least two key points to go on each pan for each movement.

3 Do the successes outweigh the failures?

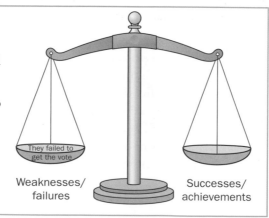

12.6 How did women contribute to the war effort?

When Britain went to war in August 1914, women seemed no nearer to getting the vote. Despite this, the suffrage movement threw itself behind the war effort. Of course, even more women who had not been part of the suffrage movement, also threw themselves into the war effort.

Women on the front line

Women did not fight in the trenches, but they were close to the front-line action.

- The British army soon copied the French system of hospital units in France and Belgium, which were staffed mainly by female nurses.
- Thousands of women worked for voluntary organisations. In France and Belgium, the Salvation Army provided soup kitchens for convalescing soldiers and front-line troops, many of which were run by women.
- The Women's Auxiliary Army Corps (WAAC) was formed in 1918. These women worked mainly as drivers, secretaries and officials on the Western Front.

Key term

Munitions factories: places where war materials, in particular weapons and ammunition, are made.

Women and recruitment

- Female members of the Active Service League encouraged young men to enlist.
- The Mothers' Union published posters criticising mothers who stopped their sons joining up.

Women and war work

- Government departments took on 200,000 women during the war.
- There was a bit more resistance to women workers in industry. Trade unions feared women would work for less and wages for male workers would drop. However, by the end of the war hundreds of thousands of women were working in industry – for example, 800,000 women worked in engineering.
- Around 260,000 women worked on Britain's farms in the Women's Land Army, helping farmers to produce as much food as possible.
- Women even kept some of the works football teams going during the war!

Women and munitions

The best known work done by women was in the **munitions factories**. Thousands of women worked in private and government-owned munitions factories. On the one hand, munitions work gave women status and money. On the other hand, it was dangerous work because of the possibility of explosions and also the adverse health effects of dangerous chemicals in the munitions.

Roles women played in the First World War.

Revision task

1 Read through this section on women's work and then try to list, from memory, at least five examples of women contributing to the war effort.

12.7 Why were some women given the vote in 1918?

The campaign to win women the vote continued during the First World War although the protests and violence stopped.

- All men over the age of 21 could vote.
- Women over the age of 30 could vote.

Around 9 million women gained the vote, usually older, better-off women.

1914–15

When war began, most of the differences between suffragists and suffragettes disappeared. They raised money for the women who were left behind when their men went off to fight. The Pankhursts concentrated on encouraging young men to volunteer for the army.

1916

Because so many men were fighting for their country, the Government decided on a new Representation of the People Act to give all men the vote. Since the Government was bringing in a law giving the vote to *all men*, the suffragettes and suffragists argued that they should give votes to *women* in the same law. They publicised the massive contribution of women to the war effort. Their case was also helped when David Lloyd George became Prime Minister in December 1916. He supported female suffrage.

1917–18

By June 1917, most members of the Government seemed to accept that some women would get the vote in the new Act. Suffragist leader Millicent Fawcett decided to accept the restriction that only women over 30 would get the vote. The Act was approved by the House of Commons in 1917 and then by the House of Lords in January 1918. Women voted in their first general election in December 1918. All women over 21 finally got the vote in 1928.

How important was the War in securing votes for women?

The biggest area of debate over women and the vote is how war work contributed to women winning the vote in 1918. Some historians believe that it was the decisive factor. Others believe that war work simply gave MPs an excuse to drop their opposition to female suffrage without looking as though they had given in to the suffragettes. Many historians argue that women would not have got the vote in 1918 without the combination of war work and suffragist/suffragette pressure.

> ### Revision tasks
>
> 1 Write short explanations of how the following key words or phrases are connected to women getting the vote in 1918.
>
> - Representation of the People Act
> - War work
> - Suffragist and suffragette actions during the war
> - David Lloyd George
> - Restrictions
> - January 1918
> - December 1918.
>
> 2 The Comment box on the right to lists the reasons why women were given the vote in 1918.
>
> - Divide these into long-term and short-term causes.
> - Rank these reasons in order of importance and decide which, if any, were key factors which led to political change in 1918.

> ### Comment
>
> *There were a number of reasons why women were given the vote in 1918:*
>
> - *the work of the suffragists and suffragettes*
> - *changing attitudes towards women's rights*
> - *international changes to women's suffrage in the USA, Canada, Australia and New Zealand*
> - *Lloyd George's Liberal political views*
> - *women's contribution to the First World War effort*
> - *changes in policies as a result of the First World War.*

SOURCE 8

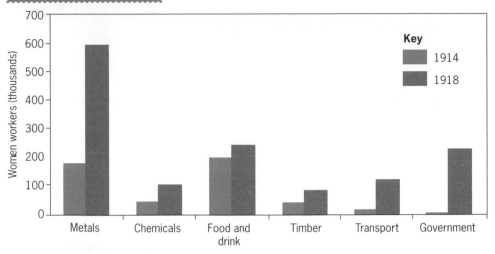

Women workers in various industries, 1914 and 1918.

SOURCE 9

A First World War postcard of female munitions workers in Cammell Laird munitions factory, Birkenhead, by artist E. F. Skinner.

SOURCE 10

A photo of women working in a munitions factory in London during the First World War.

SOURCE 11

AT LAST

A cartoon from *Punch* magazine in 1918 celebrating women being given the vote.

Exam practice

1 Study Source 8. What does this source tell us about women's work during the war? Use the details of the source and your own knowledge to explain your answer. *(8 marks)*

2 Study Sources 9 and 10. Is Source 9 a more accurate image of women's war work than Source 10? Use the details of the sources and your own knowledge to explain your answer. *(9 marks)*

3 Study Sources 5–10. 'Women's work in industry was the most important reason they won the vote in 1918.' How far do you agree with this interpretation? Use your knowledge of British Society 1890–1918 **and** the sources to explain your answer. *(16 marks)*

12.8 How were civilians in Britain affected by the war?

The First World War was a 'Total War', which meant that the entire population was involved and affected – not just the front-line troops. The Government took control of many aspects of life, which would never have happened in peacetime.

Recruitment

The recruitment campaign launched by the Government in 1914 worked far better than was predicted. Around 750,000 men joined up during the first few weeks of the campaign alone. Sometimes, whole groups of friends from one area joined up together as a 'Pals Battalion'. Between August 1914 and March 1916, 2.5 million men volunteered for the British army.

However, despite the steady flow of volunteers, there was a high casualty rate at the front, so more troops were needed. By late 1915, the British Government was considering **conscription**.

This was highly controversial and a debate raged through the winter of 1915–16. However, by May 1916 the needs of war and unrest in Ireland meant that the Government was given the power to conscript all men aged 18–41 under the Military Services Act. According to the Act, only men involved in 'reserved occupations', such as munitions work or mining, were exempt from military service.

Conscientious objectors (often known as 'conchies') had to appear before local tribunals to explain why they refused to fight. Most conchies joined up to do war work in the medical or support services. About 1,500 conchies were imprisoned.

> ### Key terms
> **Conscription:** compulsory military service.
> **Conscientious objector:** someone who refuses to join the army or fight for their country.

Government control – DORA

In August 1914, the Government passed the Defence of the Realm Act, usually known as DORA. The Act gave the Government wide-ranging powers over the media, food production, industry and many other areas.

- The Government took over the coal mines. Miners were not conscripted into the army and the Government fixed prices and wages.
- Similar action was taken with the railways and shipping.
- Early in 1915, it was clear that private enterprise was unable to supply the munitions the army needed. David Lloyd George became Minister of Munitions. He reorganised production and set up new state-run factories. By the end of the war, the Government controlled about 20,000 factories.

Food and rationing

- DORA also allowed the Government to take control of food supplies. Britain did not suffer serious shortages before 1916, but food prices did rise dramatically (about 60 per cent). Britain imported a lot of food, particularly from North America. When the German U-boats began to attack shipping on a large scale the situation became serious.
- The Government tried to increase food production by bringing all available land into production (3 million extra acres of land by 1918).
- Voluntary rationing schemes began in 1916 but did not work and so the Government introduced compulsory rationing in 1918.
- Sugar, meat, butter, jam and margarine were all rationed. As a general rule, most people supported rationing because it was fair and kept prices under control.
- There was a black market in goods, but under DORA penalties for illegal trading were very severe.

Civilian casualties

Civilian casualties were very light in Britain compared to military casualties. Nevertheless, about 1,500 civilians were killed by enemy actions.

- In December 1914, German warships shelled towns in north-east England.
- In January 1915, giant Zeppelin airships began bombing raids on England. They made a total of 57 raids.
- In May 1917, German Gotha bombers began the first of 27 raids on British towns.

Propaganda

DORA allowed the Government to control newspapers and other media during the war. There was censorship, particularly of the national press. The pacifist newspaper *The Tribunal* was shut down and the Socialist paper the *Daily Herald* was closely monitored. However, the general impression of historians is that British people and publishers largely supported the war effort.

- After the war, twelve newspaper owners were given knighthoods for their wartime services. Circulation of patriotic newspapers such as the *Daily Express* went up dramatically during the war.
- Leading authors – Rudyard Kipling, Thomas Hardy and H. G. Wells – all produced patriotic materials for no fee. They were bought in their thousands.
- Propaganda was aimed directly at children through books, games and toys. This seems to have been the most effective type.
- Patriotic films such as *For the Empire* and *The Battle of the Somme* reached huge audiences at the cinema (possibly 20 million for *The Battle of the Somme*). These films were not produced by the Government but were distributed by the War Department. It is also worth noting that *The Battle of the Somme* was a more realistic view of warfare compared to some of the earlier films made during the war, even though many of the scenes were faked.

Revision tasks

1 Read through section 12.8 on how civilians were affected by the First World War. Come up with five questions to test one of your friends or a member of your family on this topic.

2 List the main ways in which the civilians were affected by the War.

3 Use your list to create a mind map which shows in more detail how different aspects of civilian life were affected by the War.

Summary/revision plan

You need to have a good working knowledge of the following areas. **Tick off each item** once you are confident in your knowledge.

- ❑ **1 Poverty and living conditions in the 1890s**
- ❑ **2 Why did the Liberal Government introduce reforms to help the young, old and unemployed?**
  - Changing attitudes
  - Social reformers
  - The Boer War
  - Political factors
- ❑ **3 How effective were the Liberal reforms?**
- ❑ **4 What were the arguments for and against female suffrage?**
  - The arguments for female suffrage
  - The arguments against female suffrage
- ❑ **5 How effective were the activities of the suffragists and suffragettes?**
  - The suffragists
  - The suffragettes
- ❑ **6 How did women contribute to the war effort?**
  - Women on the front line
  - Women and recruitment
  - Women and war works
  - Women and munitions
- ❑ **7 Why were some women given the vote in 1918?**
- ❑ **8 How were civilians in Britain affected by the war?**
  - Recruitment
  - Government control – DORA
  - Food and rationing
  - Civilian casualties
  - Propaganda.

Check your knowledge online with our Quick quizzes at www.hodderplus.co.uk/modernworldhistory.

Chapter 13: How far did British society change, 1939–1975?

In this chapter, you will study the changes that took place in British society between 1939 and 1975. In particular, you will look at the impact of the Second World War on people's lives. You will also look at the National Health Service, the experiences of immigrants in Britain, and the role of women and young people.

Focus points

Each key question in the OCR course is divided into focus points. To do well in the examination, you will need a good understanding of each focus point.

- What impact did the Second World War have on the British people?
- What immigrants were living in Britain in 1945?
- Why did different groups migrate to Britain between 1948 and 1972?
- What were the experiences of immigrants in Britain?
- What contribution had immigrants made to British society by the early 1970s?
- What was the impact of the National Health Service on people's lives?
- What was life like for most women in the 1950s?
- How were women discriminated against in the 1960s and early 1970s?
- What factors led to changes in the roles of women?
- How much change had taken place for women by 1975?
- What was it like growing up in the 1950s?
- Why were there changes in the lives of teenagers in the 1960s?
- How did teenagers and students behave in the 1960s and early 1970s?
- How far did the lives of all teenagers change in the 1960s and early 1970s?

Key content

In order to fully understand the focus points, you will need to have a good working knowledge of:

- the impact of the Second World War on people's lives, particularly women and young people
- the Beveridge Report, National Health Service and the Welfare State
- immigration into Britain, 1945–75
- the changing role of women, 1950–75
- growing up in the 1950s, 1960s and 1970s.

13.1 The impact of the Second World War on people's lives, particularly women and young people

The Second World War changed the lives of many people in Britain in different ways.

The presence of foreign troops

Throughout the war, soldiers, sailors and airmen of different countries were based in Britain, particularly in the final stages of the war as the Allies prepared for the D-Day landings.

American soldiers

American troops, often known as GIs, began to arrive in Britain from 1942 onwards and they had a big impact on people's lives.

- The Americans were easygoing and not class conscious like the British. They were much better paid than British troops and were very popular with girls.
- In general, American GIs mixed well in British society, but sometimes there were tensions because of the cultural differences between the USA and Britain.
- Many of the US troops were African American soldiers who had come from separated and **segregated** communities in the USA. The British treated African American GIs very well and for these soldiers it was often their first experience of being treated normally by white people.

Other Allied soldiers

- Commonwealth soldiers fought with the Allies in the Second World War, including large numbers of Australians, Canadians, New Zealanders and Indians.
- There were 40,000 marriages between Canadian servicemen and British women.
- After the war, 120,000 Poles settled in Britain. Poland had been invaded by Germany in 1939 and many Poles fought on the Allied side. At the end of the war, Poland was occupied by the USSR and many Poles decided to stay in Britain rather than live in a Communist state.

Prisoners of war

The German and Italian prisoners of war held in Britain grew as the number of Allied victories increased. By 1945, there were 402,000 German and 157,000 Italian prisoners of war in Britain. Most were treated well and worked in agriculture. Surprisingly, at the end of the war, 25,000 German prisoners of war decided to make a new home in Britain despite the fact they had fought against the British.

Women's experience of war work

Many more women were involved in war work during the Second World War than in the First World War.

- In 1941, all women aged twenty or older had to register for war work. Most were sent to work in industry or the auxiliary armed forces.
- By 1945, 80 per cent of married women and 90 per cent of single women were working in industry or the forces.
- By 1943, over 443,000 women worked in the armed forces.
- Trade unions accepted female workers much more readily than they had done in the First World War.
- Millions of women still had to juggle working in factories and looking after their families. Often, flexible working arrangements and nurseries were introduced to help women cope.

Key term

Segregation: keeping a group separate from the rest of society, usually on the basis of race or religion. Segregation was seen in separate schools, transport and housing.

SOURCE 1

Extracts from interviews with two women in 1944, gathered by the Mass Observation project which monitored the lives of British people. The women were asked about their attitude to their war time work.

[A] When you get up in the morning you feel you go out with something in your bag, and something coming in at the end of the week, and it's nice. It's a taste of independence, and you feel a lot happier for it … I have everything to do at home, and so all I want is to get on part-time.
It's just what you can imagine nicely when you are middle-age.

[B] Of course when we get married I shan't want to work; I shall want to stay at home and have some children. You can't look on anything you do during the war as what you really mean to do; it's just filling in time till you can live your own life again.

Attitudes towards women workers during and after the war

Despite the new opportunities that war work provided, many women found that male attitudes had not really changed.

- Much of the work was only available during war time and stopped in 1945.
- Many of the tasks undertaken by women were simplified since some men believed that women could only do simple work.
- Although women worked in the armed forces, these were mostly supportive rather than front-line roles.

After the war:

- Many younger married women stopped working to have children. This was encouraged by the media and certain sections of society. In 1945, there was a sudden increase in the number of marriages.
- Many older women managed to continue working to help British industry recover from the war.
- In 1947, 18 per cent of married women had paid jobs compared to 10 per cent in 1939.

Young people's experience of war

Evacuation

One of the most significant ways that the Second World War affected young people was the evacuation of children from cities and industrial areas. The first evacuation was made as soon as war was declared. However for the first six months of the war, there were no air raids so many evacuees returned home. But, in September 1940, the Luftwaffe launched the Blitz on London and a second wave of evacuation began.

About half of all children in cities were moved to safer rural communities at some point during the war.

- Many evacuees were separated from their families for up to six years; many were treated well but some were treated badly.
- Most evacuees were not used to rural life and often found themselves in much wealthier households than their own.
- Meeting evacuees from the cities was often the first time middle-class families had the opportunity to experience what life was really like for the working class.
- Approximately 50 per cent of children from urban areas were never evacuated at all, and many children were brought back home because they were homesick.
- Many of the children who were never evacuated or who returned home were killed or injured alongside their parents in air raids.

Exam practice

1 Study Sources 1A and 1B. How are these sources similar? Use the sources and your own knowledge to explain your answer. *(9 marks)*

Exam tip This question tests your **factual knowledge** and your ability to **interpret and evaluate sources**. Try to show your knowledge and understanding of the period when the source was produced. But use that to help you use the sources. Good knowledge + good use of sources = better marks.

Comment

The war had a significant impact on the role of women. Although after the war, many women returned to their traditional role as wives and mothers, others continued in work. Women's confidence had grown and some were not prepared to accept the same limitations as before the war. War had changed their expectations. Marriages tended to become more equal partnerships.

School

Schooling was badly affected by the war

- Most schools in towns closed. There was a shortage of teachers since many served in the armed forces.
- Many poor children who were not evacuated from cities therefore had little education. In some areas this led to increases in vandalism and petty crime.
- Children who were evacuated to the countryside only went to school on a part-time basis for half of each day.

Health

The health of young people improved.

- Rationing reduced the quantity of food eaten, but it provided a balanced diet for children.
- Evacuees tended to have a better diet in the countryside than in the city.
- Like adults, many children suffered emotionally during the Second World War. Families were often split because of war service and thousands lost fathers, mothers and other family members from air raids or combat duties. Evacuees lived away from their parents.

> ### Exam practice
>
> 1 Study Source 2. Why was this source published in 1942? Use the details of the source and your own knowledge to explain your answer. *(8 marks)*

> ### Revision task
>
> Using **Source 1** on page 157 and the information in this section, copy and complete the table below. For each heading list the ways the war affected this group. Then highlight the two most important impacts.
>
> | Impact of Second World War | | |
> |---|---|---|
> | Soldiers | Women | Young people |
> | | | |

SOURCE 2

TAKE THEM BACK! TAKE THEM BACK! TAKE THEM BACK!..

DON'T do it, Mother—

LEAVE THE CHILDREN WHERE THEY ARE

ISSUED BY THE MINISTRY OF HEALTH

SOURCE 3

Number of evacuees, September 1939

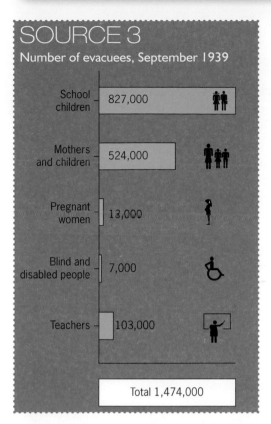

School children — 827,000

Mothers and children — 524,000

Pregnant women — 13,000

Blind and disabled people — 7,000

Teachers — 103,000

Total 1,474,000

SOURCE 4

Extract from the BBC's *British History in depth* website describing the varied experiences of evacuees during the Second World War.

Others, however, were beaten, mistreated and abused by families who didn't want them and didn't care about them.

The painful experience of John Abbot, evacuated from Bristol, reflects the darker side. His rations were stolen by his host family, who enjoyed good food whilst John was given a diet of nothing more than mashed potatoes. He was horsewhipped for speaking out and, with a bruised and bleeding body, was eventually taken in by the police.

Then there was Terri McNeil who was locked in a birdcage and left with a chunk of bread and a bowl of water.

SOURCE 5

Rene Wingwood, an evacuee from London.

The most difficult part of being evacuated is coming home again. It was the worst day of my whole life. When the time came I had completely forgotten my family and London. I was ten years old and suddenly I was taken away by the strange lady called Mother, from all these wonderful people I had grown up with and not only from them but the whole village that I knew and love. I knew every path, track and lane for miles around, every house and cottage, every man, woman and child, every cat, dog, cow and chicken. It was a beautiful world and I had to leave it all behind.

Exam practice

2 Study Source 3. How useful is Source 3 for investigating the impact of evacuation? Use the details of the source and your own knowledge to explain your answer. *(8 marks)*

3 Study Sources 4 and 5. Is Source 4 more typical of children's experience of evacuation than Source 5? Use the details of the source and your own knowledge to explain your answer. *(9 marks)*

4 Study Sources 1–5. "The Second World War had a significant effect on the lives of women and young people." How far do you agree with this interpretation? Use your knowledge of British Society 1939–1975 **and** the sources to explain your answer. *(16 marks)*

13.2 The Welfare State

The Beveridge Report

In the middle of the Second World War, Sir William Beveridge was asked to research how the quality of life for the British people could be improved in post-war Britain. He identified five giant social evils that plagued Britain: want (poverty), disease, ignorance (poor education), squalor (bad housing) and idleness (unemployment). In order to deal with these problems, Beveridge recommended a complete shake up of how the government looked after its citizens. The old idea of 'self-help' was replaced with a commitment to help the old, sick, unemployed and poor. He put forward the principle of 'universality' – everyone would be eligible for benefits whatever their situation. All workers would also contribute to a National Insurance scheme which helped fund these benefits. It was very radical but it was widely supported by the British people.

In July 1945, a Labour government was swept to power and began to implement Beveridge's recommendations which formed the basis for today's 'welfare state'. These included:

- Family Allowances Act, 1945 – an allowance of five shillings per week per child in any family
- National Insurance Act, 1946 – benefits for any worker who was unemployed, injured or sick
- National Health Service Act, 1946 (implemented July 1948) – free health care
- Town and Country Planning Act and New Towns Act, 1947 – clearance of slums and bomb-damaged housing, and relocation of many of the poorest in Britain's cities to new towns
- Children Act, 1948 – local authorities forced to set up services to protect children
- Housing Act, 1949 – massive programme of building new housing to the latest specifications.

> **Exam tip** In this section, examiners will be looking for you to show that you understand the impact of the war on people's lives and how it affected them on a day-to-day basis.

The National Health Service (NHS)

The most important and significant part of the welfare state was the creation of the National Health Service, which came into being on 5 July 1948. Labour Health Minister, Aneurin Bevan, had to overcome a lot of opposition in order to create the NHS, mostly from the conservative opposition and even the doctors' representatives from the British Medical Association (BMA).

The impact of the NHS on people's lives

Immediate impact:

- The British public welcomed free medical and dental care and demand exceeded all expectations.
- Between 1948 and 1973, the number of doctors doubled.
- High quality maternity care became available to women for the first time.
- As well as doctors and dentists, the NHS provided other healthcare professionals such as midwives and health visitors.
- Medical inspections carried out by school nurses improved the health of children.
- Free child vaccinations significantly reduced death from common diseases.

Over the next 30 years:

- Infant mortality fell from 60,000 deaths of children under five in 1945 to 20,000 deaths by 1975.
- Between 1870 and 1910, the average life expectancy of women in Britain was 45. By 1970, it had risen to 76.

> **Revision tasks**
> Draw your own mind map to show the key features of the Beveridge Report and the measures introduced from 1945–1949. You could use the 'social evils' (the five giants) as your branches and show on your mind map how the measures introduced tackle each of these 'social evils'.

13.3 Immigration into Britain, 1945–75

Britain has always been a nation of immigrants. After 1945, many different nationalities came to Britain in a new wave of immigration. These post-war immigrants came mostly from:

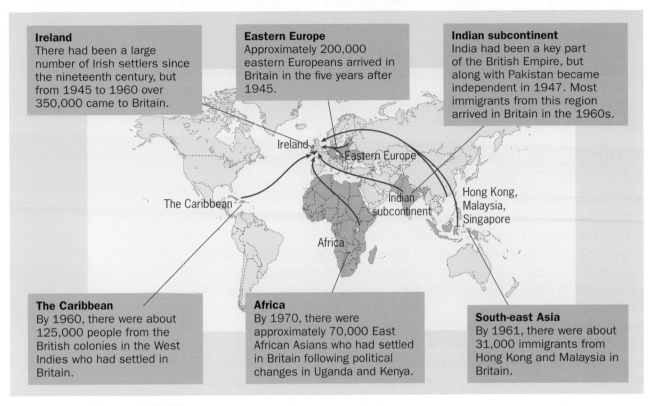

Ireland
There had been a large number of Irish settlers since the nineteenth century, but from 1945 to 1960 over 350,000 came to Britain.

Eastern Europe
Approximately 200,000 eastern Europeans arrived in Britain in the five years after 1945.

Indian subcontinent
India had been a key part of the British Empire, but along with Pakistan became independent in 1947. Most immigrants from this region arrived in Britain in the 1960s.

The Caribbean
By 1960, there were about 125,000 people from the British colonies in the West Indies who had settled in Britain.

Africa
By 1970, there were approximately 70,000 East African Asians who had settled in Britain following political changes in Uganda and Kenya.

South-east Asia
By 1961, there were about 31,000 immigrants from Hong Kong and Malaysia in Britain.

Immigration to Britain, 1945–75.

Immigration case studies: Why did immigrants come to Britain?

Case study 1: Immigration from the Caribbean

Most Caribbean immigrants came to Britain for economic reasons. At the end of the Second World War, Britain was facing a labour shortage. So:

- About 10,000 West Indian troops served successfully in the British armed forces during the Second World War and stayed in Britain to work.

Some British companies such as the NHS, London Transport, and the Hotels and Restaurant Association advertised for workers to come over from the Caribbean. These recruitment campaigns were successful because:

- Unemployment in Jamaica and the other islands was a major problem. Hurricanes devastated Jamaica in 1944 and in 1951. Then, tourism was not a major industry, and most earned a poor living from fishing and growing food.
- There had been a long history of West Indian immigration to the USA, but in 1952 this was cut back. Whereas in 1949, the British Nationality Act came into force giving all citizens of the former empire unrestricted access to Britain.
- Caribbean workers were also attracted to Britain because of the success of previous immigrants. Workers earned significantly more than those who stayed in Jamaica and the other West Indian islands.
- Individuals who were interviewed later explained that whilst most were looking for work, many were also looking for adventure.
- British culture and history was also appealing. The British education system was widely respected and West Indians were impressed by the British empire and success of British industry and commerce.

Revision tasks

- A push factor is something that is driving people away from where they currently live
- A pull factor is something that attracts them to where they are moving to.

Draw up a table to list the different push factors and pull factors that motivated immigrants to settle in Britain after the second world war. Do a separate row for each case study on pages 161–162.

In one year alone, 1954, 24,000 West Indians arrived in Britain. By 1960, there were 125,000 immigrants from the Caribbean in Britain.

Case study 2: Asian immigration from East Africa

There was a very large population of Asians (mostly from India) who had settled in East Africa during the time of British Empire. In the 1960s and 1970s many came to Britain because of persecution:

- In Kenya, many Asians had become successful businessmen, but in the 1960s lots of Kenyan Asians immigrants felt persecuted by new laws. About 20,000 of them came to Britain.
- In Uganda in 1972 President Idi Amin simply expelled 50,000 Asians, most of whom came to Britain.

Case study 3: Immigration from India and Pakistan

The first wave of immigration from India and Pakistan followed Indian independence in 1947–48.

- The first groups of settlers were Eurasians – educated, middle-class professionals who had intermarried during British rule in India.
- Many Sikhs from the Punjab region had served in the British Army in India. Employment opportunities in Britain appealed to them. Many also left because of unrest and violence between different groups after Indian independence in 1947.
- Through the late 1950s and 60s Pakistani and Indian immigrants came to Britain for economic reasons.
- Many came from poor rural communities.
- Many of these new immigrants worked in the metal, food and clothing industries, mainly located in the Midlands and north of England.

Experiences of immigrants in Britain

Whilst there were some examples to show that immigrants were welcomed in Britain, most immigrants experienced hostility and discrimination. And as immigration increased hostility increased.

Immigrants faced limitations, or worse still, active discrimination in **housing**, **working life** and **daily life**. For example:

- Local authorities required immigrants to live in Britain for five years before they could apply for council housing.
- Banks and building societies often refused to give immigrants loans or mortgages.
- Some boarding houses displayed notices saying 'No blacks' (it was legal to discriminate in this way at that time).
- Immigrants had to find whatever accommodation they could and many were exploited by landlords such as Peter Rachman who owned over a hundred properties in West London packed with immigrants paying high rents for poor accommodation.
- Immigrants also found a 'colour bar' in place at pubs and bars who refused to serve them.
- At work trade unions claimed that immigrants were taking British jobs. In the West Midlands in 1955, transport workers even went on strike complaining about the increasing number of immigrant workers.
- Immigrants found it hard to get promoted and mostly worked in low paid jobs
- In the 1959 General Election some right-wing politicians began a campaign to 'keep Britain white'

> ## Revision task
> Use key words to sum up the experience of immigrants in the 1950s under the following headings
> - Housing
> - Work
> - Daily life

Unsurprisingly, the hostility shown towards many immigrants encouraged them to live in close-knit communities. Areas such as Handsworth in Birmingham, Toxteth in Liverpool and Moss Side in Manchester became overwhelmingly Caribbean communities.

- These areas became the focus of violence against immigration in the late 1950s.
- Violence erupted in Notting Hill, London, in 1958 between white teddy boys and local immigrants.
- In 1959, the violence became extreme when six white youths murdered Kelso Cochrane a carpenter from Antigua. The police never arrested the killers.

Revision tasks

1 How do **Sources 6** and **7** show the different experiences of immigrants arriving in Britain? In what ways are their experiences similar?
2 Draw two mind maps to show:
   - the different experiences of immigrants in Britain
   - the different reactions to immigration in Britain.
   Make sure you can explain each diagram without looking at the book or any notes.

The political response

As the numbers of immigrants into Britain rose and the level of hostility towards them increased, immigration became a major political issue. Governments introduced a series of measures and laws designed to both control immigration and to challenge racial discrimination.

1962	The Conservative Government passed the Commonwealth Immigration Act. This meant that only skilled workers in shortage areas were allowed into Britain.
1964	Although the new Labour Government criticised the Commonwealth Immigration Act, immigration had become such a sensitive issue with voters that Labour restricted immigration to 8,500 per year.
1965–66	The Labour Government passed the Race Relations Act, which made it illegal to discriminate on the grounds of race or colour. The Race Relations Board was also set up in 1966 to handle complaints about discrimination, but it had few powers and was limited in its impact.
1967	The National Front Party was formed. It called for an end to immigration and for immigrants to be sent back to their country of origin. It also called for a separation of white and immigrant communities.
1968	The Labour Government passed the Commonwealth Immigrants Act, which limited immigration vouchers to 1,500 per year. It also introduced a 'close connection' clause that restricted entry to those who were born in Britain or whose parents or grandparents were born in Britain. The effect was to restrict immigration from the new Commonwealth countries whilst allowing entry to those from former white Commonwealth nations, such as Canada and New Zealand.

SOURCE 6

Sybil Phoenix, a nurse from British Guiana commenting on her arrival in Britain in 1956.

When I arrived at Paddington train station I was astonished to see a white woman sweeping up dust and rubbish on the platform with a broom. I was only accustomed to seeing white women who were painted devils who did nothing. They never even swept their own homes. They had six of us to do it for them.

SOURCE 7

A Pakistani immigrant interviewed in the late 1980s about his experiences in the 1960s.

In 1962 I left Pakistan and went to Nottingham. I knew I wasn't going to get any better job than being a British Railway cleaner. I had seen qualified people from my country who had been teachers and barristers and none of them got proper work. They were labourers, bus conductors and railway cleaners like me. Many times we could read and write much better than the people who were in charge of us. They knew I had been a Customs Inspector in Pakistan, but that didn't matter.

In April 1968, Enoch Powell, the Conservative MP for Wolverhampton, made a speech warning that many in Britain felt overwhelmed by the numbers of immigrants. His 'rivers of blood' speech, as it came to be known, was very controversial. Some people agreed with Powell and there were demonstrations of support for him in London and other areas. His speech was also heavily criticised because some said it encouraged racial tension. Powell was sacked by Conservative leader, Edward Heath, and the Labour Government passed a new Race Relations Act, which made it illegal to discriminate on the basis of race or colour in employment and housing.

1976   The Labour Government passed the Race Equality Act. This made it illegal to make racially offensive comments or publish racially offensive material. The Act set up the Commission for Racial Equality to investigate claims of racism. The need for this commission showed that earlier measures had not successfully dealt with racism.

The contribution of immigrants to British society

Despite the problems experienced by immigrants, there are also many positive aspects to immigration, particularly related to cultural and economic issues.

- *Individuals*: Many immigrants have made significant individual contributions to British society. Sybil Phoenix, for example (see Source 7 on page 163), arrived from the Caribbean in 1956. Initially, she lived in desperate poverty but in later years set up a youth group called Moonshot in Lewisham, London. She was awarded an MBE for her community work and, in 1973, became Mayor of Lewisham.
- *Public services*: Many of Britain's major public services would not have developed without the contribution of immigrant workers. In the NHS for example, one-third of all doctors in the 1970s were born overseas.
- *The economy*: Most immigrants came to Britain to work, and make a better life for themselves and their families. In this way, they have made an enormous contribution to the British economy by paying taxes. Many immigrants have specialised in particular businesses such as retail, food and textiles. Many have also become successful business people, even billionaires.
- *Culture*: Immigrants have enriched British culture in many ways. Greek, Indian and Chinese food, in particular, have become firm British favourites. By 1975, there were thousands of ethnic restaurants and takeaways across the country.
- *Music, dance and cinema*: These were heavily influenced by immigrant culture. Reggae, soul, Motown, steel bands and Bollywood are well-established features of British life as is the Notting Hill Carnival in London, which first took place in 1958.
- *Religion*: Religion played a key role in the development of multicultural Britain. By the mid-1970s, the Hindu, Muslim and Sikh faiths were well established in many parts of Britain.

Comment

Britain has become a truly multicultural society, despite the warnings of Enoch Powell in 1968. Whilst tensions often remain between certain communities and extreme political parties attempt to undermine social cohesiveness, for the most part relations between cultures remain positive and co-operative. Despite the upheavals and problems of earlier years, immigration has had a significant positive impact on the economic and cultural development of Britain since 1945.

13.4 The changing role of women, 1950–75

Between 1945 and 1975, there were significant changes to the lives of most women in Britain. Opportunities, expectations, income and even the legal status of women changed.

Women in the early 1950s

Work

As you saw on page 149 the Second World War removed the taboo on women doing a paid job outside the home. However in 1951:

- Only 36% of women had paid employment and only 26% of married women.
- There was still an assumption that if a woman got married she would leave her job; and almost certainly if she had a baby she would do so.
- Some jobs (e.g. heavy industry or farming) were almost entirely done by men. A woman would not even think of trying to get such a job. Women were much more likely to work as typists, secretaries or cleaners.
- Women found it hard to get promoted to top jobs and many did not want top jobs or ever applied for them.
- Women got paid less than men even if they did the same job.

Personal life

Women's lives were much more focused around the home and childcare.

- On average women spent nearly 8 hours a day on housework.
- Women had very little leisure time – but when they were able the favourite pastime was going to the cinema.
- Contraception was unreliable so unplanned pregnancies were common. Abortion was illegal.
- Unmarried women were not expected to have sex and there was a deep taboo against unmarried mothers.
- Divorce law was biased towards men so women found it hard to get out of failed or violent marriages.

But…

Lists like that make life sound bleak! Who would want to be a woman in 1951? But you know that is not the whole story. It's hard to measure happiness but many women would say they were happy with their working life, their social life, their family life. Britain had been through a traumatic period of depression then war and many people, women and men alike were just very glad to be trying to get back to normal. However deep change was already underway.

Changes in the 1950s and 1960s

Over the next two decades a combination of developments brought major change for women.

- **The Welfare State** – The dramatic changes introduced by the Welfare State (see page 160) were already having a real impact on the lives of women by the 1950s. For example:
  - mothers had always born the anxiety and responsibility for family health care, now ill-health was no longer such a fear because of the National Health Service;
  - unemployment was less feared because of National Insurance;
  - new houses were being built to replace those damaged by wartime bombing;
  - the Education Act had improved schools for all children
- **Prosperity** – After the war Britain's economy grew again and many families had more money.

- **Technology** – mechanisation was affecting every aspect of life and affordable washing machines, vacuum cleaners, electric fires etc all lightened the load of housework.
- **Work** – women could easily find work if they wanted to. It tended to be low-paid and low-skilled but the jobs were there, which gave women more money of their own to spend.
- **Choice** – all these changes gave women more choice over how to spend their time.
- **Media** – women's magazines boomed in the 1950s then in the 1960s television took over. Magazines and TVs provided women with honest and practical advice on almost aspects of life and also supplied different role-models to aspire to.
- **Family planning** – in the 1960s the first oral contraceptive – the Pill – gave women for the first time in history reliable control over how many children to have and when to the have them.
- **Expectations** – many women found that these changes increased their expectations of what they could achieve.

The women's movement

The campaign for equal rights for women had been active since the nineteenth century (see pages 145–146 for the suffrage campaign for example). These groups had not gone away. The Fawcett Society and the Six Point Group were still active after the Second World War campaigning for equal pay for women and equal treatment under the law. Meanwhile changes taking place elsewhere, particularly in the USA civil rights movements and feminist movements (see pages 138–139), were also deeply affecting women in Britain. The feminists specialised in consciousness-raising – making women more aware of discrimination affected them personally and helping them seize opportunities to change their own lives or campaign for change for other women. In the 1960s women's groups were very active in the Campaign for Nuclear Disarmament (CND).

Encouraged by feminist writers such as Germaine Greer, who in 1969 published the influential book *The Female Eunuch*, the women's movement gathered momentum. In 1970, the women's liberation movement was launched at a national conference and made four demands:

- equal pay
- equal education and opportunities
- 24-hour nurseries
- free contraception and abortion on demand.

The main campaigns

Equal pay

In 1955 the Conservative Government had agreed to give equal pay to men and women doing jobs in **the public sector** such as teachers or civil servants. But it was the political campaigns of the women's movement that finally achieved an Equal Pay Act in 1970. This extended 'equal pay for equal work' throughout the private sector although the Act was not enforced until 1975. It was a major achievement but despite the act women continued to earn less than men on average because they did different jobs. It also did little to help women gain promotion.

Comment

There is no doubt that the period 1945–75 saw a transformation in the rights women had under the law. Changes to the law on equal pay, employment, divorce and abortion all helped to give women greater rights and freedoms. Equally, developments in medicine helped women control the size of their families. Whilst these changes helped women, the attitude of society in general still imposed significant restrictions on how free women were to pursue careers at the expense of their role in family life.

Revision task

These developments are related to each other. Write each bold heading on a sheet of paper then draw lines between them to show the connections. Label each connection to explain it (using the knowledge you have gained from the rest of the course as well as what is in this revision guide).

Key term

Public sector: Any part of the economy that is paid for by the local or national government. The 'private sector' is everything else!

Contraception

Family planning had been available since the 1920s, but in reality women had very little control over the number of children they had. Family planning was very much a taboo subject, even between husband and wife.

In 1957, medical researchers produced the first oral contraceptive pill and this was made available free on the NHS, in 1961. 'The Pill' transformed the lives of women because they could control how many children they had. After 1965, the birth rate fell dramatically – the average number of children per family fell to two or three from the six, eight or ten of previous generations.

Abortion

The women's movement also campaigned for legal abortions. In the early 1960s, there were about 200,000 illegal abortions per year in Britain. Many of these took place in unhygienic and unregistered premises, but many women were prepared to take this risk rather than bear the social stigma of being an unmarried mother. However, in 1967 the Labour Government passed the Abortion Act. Abortion was now legal if a woman gained the agreement of two doctors.

Divorce

In 1969, Parliament passed the Divorce Act, which allowed a divorce on the grounds that a relationship had broken down, in contrast to the previous requirement to show some type of offence by either the husband or wife. In 1970, the Matrimonial Property Act was passed giving women a share of the assets built up during a marriage. Before this Act, many women were left in poverty after a divorce.

Source evaluation: women's attitudes

Social history is one of the hardest topics to research and write about. Everyone has different views and different experiences so it is hard to generalise. What's more when researchers try to examine attitudes they face the problem that not everyone is honest. This has been particularly true in studying women's history: in the 1950s and 60s historians examining changing attitudes found that women wanted to 'say the right thing' rather than being honest. There was a taboo against speaking out.

However sociologists such as Hannah Green or Nancy Sears carefully interviewed women in confidence, alone, away from the pressures of home and family and believe they came up with more honest findings. Sources 9 and 10 are based on such research findings. If you read these sources without knowing this you might think to yourself that these are simply two opinions – only as a valuable as the next person's – but you can tell from the way they are written and what you know about the methods of the researchers that they are carefully considered and a fair reflection of attitudes of the time. However that does not mean they both say the same thing!

Revision tasks

Draw a graph with the dates 1945-1975 along the bottom and the status of women up the side.

1 Plot a line to show how women's status changed during this period. If you think women were second class citizens, facing discrimination the line would start low, if you thought their status was equal with men it would be high. There is no right answer! This is your judgement based on what you have found out in your course.

2 Label on your graph any developments mentioned on these last two pages which significantly affected the status of women and write a sentence to explain how it affected the status or role of women.

3 Write one paragraph to explain your view on 'How much change had taken place for women by 1975?'

Exam practice

1 Read Sources 8 and 9. How far does Source 9 challenge the views in Source 8? Use the sources and your knowledge to explain your answer. (8 marks)

SOURCE 8

An extract from a survey of women's attitudes by the sociologist Nancy Sears in 1962.

The biggest obstacle to women is that in subtle and not so subtle ways an atmosphere is created which still makes it appear peculiar or comical for women to be both feminine and use their abilities to the full.

SOURCE 9

An extract from a 1963 report by a researcher in Sheffield.

There are signs that some girls are tending towards more independence in their dealings with men, and that they will not be content to sign over their lives to their husbands on marriage ... They are determined to remain smart and in control of events after they have married; they are not prepared to be bowed down with lots of children, and they will expect their husbands to take a fuller share than their fathers in the running of the home.

13.5 Growing up in the 1950s, 1960s and 1970s

In the years 1945–55, young people were growing up in a country still recovering from six years of war. Rationing was not lifted until 1954.
Young people:
- often dressed in a similar way to their parents
- mostly had the same set of pre-war values as their parents and grandparents
- only had access to one TV channel (if their family had a TV which was still quite rare)
- listened to the same type of music as their parents.

Changes in the 1950s

From the mid-1950s onwards changes began. Many people in Britain benefited from an improving standard of living. Unemployment was very low and wages were increasing faster than prices. This increasing prosperity meant that many young people had more money and more leisure time. They were able to buy fashionable goods and a new teenage culture began to develop. Teenagers began to:
- wear different clothes to their parents
- spend more time with their friends, meeting in coffee bars and listening to music, particularly 'rock and roll' from American stars such as Elvis Presley or Bill Haley
- go to the cinema to watch new Hollywood films
- as a result, record sales and cinema attendance boomed.

Some young men became known as teddy boys because of their distinctive way of dressing. Some teddy boys joined gangs and gained a reputation for trouble and violence. These groups, however, did not represent the majority of young men in 1950s Britain.

Changes in the lives of teenagers in the 1960s

The 1960s was a controversial decade for teenagers. Change became more rapid, involved millions more young people, and was affected by the key factors below.

Teenage consumers

By the 1960s teenagers had more money and were able to spend more than their predecessors in the 1950s. Teenagers became consumers, and record labels, fashion houses and technology companies responded to the new teenage market with new products and advertising.

Teenage products

- Radios became portable because of developments such as the transistor and better, more lightweight batteries. This meant that teenagers could listen to their favourite music with their friends rather than the rest of the family.
- Similarly, record players became much cheaper in the 1960s meaning many teenagers could have one of their own. Consequently, the number of 'singles' sold by record companies jumped from 5 million in 1955 to 50 million in 1960.

TV and radio programmes

TV and radio producers began to produce programmes specifically for teenagers. Probably the most significant of these was launched on Friday 9 August 1963 at 7p.m. It was called *Ready, Steady Go!* and in many ways it summed up the new 'swinging sixties'.

- The audience was made up of fashionable, good-looking teenagers.
- The main presenter, Cathy McGowan, was an attractive teenager.
- Popular bands played on the show, including The Beatles and The Rolling Stones.
- The studio sets were changed each week and cameras were placed at unusual angles, unlike traditional programmes.

Transport

In the early 1960s, teenagers were able to take advantage of improvements in public transport, particularly in cities, and scooters and bikes became much more affordable. As a consequence, many teenagers were able to travel more widely and meet up with their friends at fashionable places.

Music

The most significant development was the explosion of the music industry. In the 1940s and 1950s, music was dominated by big bands of musicians and geared around family listening. The 1960s changed all that.

- Small bands of young men wrote songs for people their own age.
- Groups such as The Beatles and The Rolling Stones became instant superstars with millions of fans worldwide.
- The lyrics and music were often rebellious and challenged traditional values – for example, The Rolling Stones sang about sex and drugs.
- Huge concerts became fashionable and millions of teenagers watched their favourite groups on shows such as *Juke Box Jury* and *Top of the Pops*.
- Pirate radio stations began broadcasting popular music in contrast to the traditional music still played by the BBC. The hugely popular Radio Caroline, for example, broadcast the latest records from a ship in the North Sea. When it was eventually closed down, the BBC revised their entire radio programming and, in 1967, launched Radio 1 to appeal to teenagers.

Fashion

As with music, the fashion industry of the 1960s broke with the past.

- New young designers, such as Mary Quant, made informal, stylish and lightweight clothes for young people. Quant used young models such as Twiggy to show off her designs, and most notably introduced the 'mini' skirt.
- The Kings Road and Carnaby Street became the capital of youth fashion for London and the rest of the world.
- Photographers, such as David Bailey, and hairdressers, such as Vidal Sassoon, became celebrities who appealed to 1960s youth culture.

The teenage rebel

The 1960s break with the past brought new attitudes to sex and traditional figures of authority.

- TV shows such as *That Was The Week That Was* challenged traditional institutions, such as government and church, with satirical comedy in a way never seen before.
- New publications, such as *Private Eye* which was launched in 1962, poked fun at authority figures.
- The 1961 stage production of *West Side Story* seemed to challenge traditional views about what was good behaviour, despite the fact that it was based on Shakespeare's *Romeo and Juliet*.
- Pop stars were regularly criticised for challenging traditional values. In 1966, John Lennon unintentionally upset many people in the USA when he was quoted in an interview as saying that The Beatles were now 'more popular than Jesus'. However upsetting for some, his point was that 1960s popular music was more influential than a declining Church.
- The 1960s is widely seen as a period of sexual revolution. However, evidence from researchers of the period, such as Michael Schofield, shows that teenagers were not as sexually active as is suggested.
- Rebellion for most teenagers in the 1960s was little more than staying out a little longer than they should or listening to music their parents didn't like.
- Occasionally rebellion turned into violence, as in 1964 when teenage groups of 'Mods' and 'Rockers' clashed in some British seaside resorts. The press printed hysterical headlines at the time, but recent evidence suggests that there was very little actual violence and generally a lot of chasing around on scooters!

Changes in education: comprehensive schools

In the 1960s secondary schools were either grammar schools or secondary modern schools. To get a place in a grammar school, children had to pass a test called the 11-plus. Once at grammar school, most pupils went on to university and well paid jobs. Those who failed the 11-plus went to a secondary modern school, left school at fourteen or fifteen, and entered a lower paid job.

Supporters of grammar schools claimed that they helped open up opportunities for the brightest children, whatever their social background. Critics of the system claimed that virtually all children at grammar schools were from the middle classes since their parents could afford coaching to help their children pass the 11-plus. They argued that the system increased the class divide rather than narrowed it.

In 1965, the Labour Government published a document called 10/65 that forced local authorities to produce plans to abolish grammar and secondary modern schools and create new comprehensive schools that would admit all children from the local area, whatever their ability or background. Although there was plenty of resistance to the plans, particularly from Conservative-controlled local authorities, 1,145 comprehensive schools had been opened by 1970.

There is still much debate about the success of comprehensive schools, but by the end of the 1960s more children were staying on longer in education.

Universities and polytechnics

In 1939, only 50,000 young people studied beyond school. By 1970 there were nearly 400,000 young people in higher education. Both Labour and Conservative governments saw the need to create a better educated workforce and therefore created new universities and colleges.

- Thirteen new universities were built during the 1950s and 1960s.
- 32 new polytechnics were built for students wishing to study more vocational courses in science and technology.

> ## Revision task
> Put these factors in order of importance in bringing about changes in the lives of teenagers in the 1960s.
> - Money
> - TV & Radio
> - Music
> - School
>
> Then write some notes to explain why your top factor is most important.

- Art colleges were established to attract students from poorer middle-class and working-class backgrounds.
- Grants (loans that did not need paying back) were introduced to pay living expenses for students from poor backgrounds. The Government also paid tuition fees.

Teenage and student protest

In the 1960s there was a wave of protest in many countries, fuelled by the civil rights and anti-war movements in the USA. Young people challenged traditional values and in different ways.

Some simply opted out of society and became 'hippies'. Their culture centred on peace, love, communes and usually drugs. Others joined political campaigns, protest, marches, or took direct action.

However, student protest in Britain was much less radical than that seen in France or the USA. Many teenagers also supported the peace movement, which dated back to the late 1950s, and the Campaign for Nuclear Disarmament (CND). Some students began to demonstrate against their own university.

- In 1967, students at the London School of Economics (LSE) demonstrated about the appointment of a new director because he had worked in Rhodesia (now Zimbabwe) and therefore was judged to be a supporter of white-only rule there.
- There were sit-ins at Leicester and Essex universities and students at Hull occupied the university administrative centre in protest at the 'crude qualification that led to money and materialism and poverty'.
- There were anti-Vietnam War demonstrations outside the American Embassy in London in 1968.
- However the majority of British students were not committed revolutionaries. According to a Leeds University poll, 86 per cent of students found student politics boring. A nationwide poll found that 80 per cent of students were happy with their conditions and treatment.

Comment

The expansion of higher education not only gave many more young people the opportunity to study beyond school, but increased the range and variety of subjects available (such as sociology, psychology and vocational courses). By the 1970s, Britain was producing a new generation of well-qualified, well-travelled young people with much higher aspirations and greater expectations than their parents.

Revision tasks

1 Copy and complete the table below to show how life changed for teenagers and students in the 1960s and early 70s.

Topic	Changes in the 1960s	Extent of change (1–5)	Explanation of score
Fashion			
Music			
Television and radio programmes			
Education			
Attitudes towards • authority • sex			

For column 3 you will have to consider whether all, most, some or only a few young people were affected by that change.

2 For column 4 write a sentence for each topic to explain your score.

Summary/revision plan

You need to have a good working knowledge of the following areas. **Tick off each item** once you are confident in your knowledge.

- ❑ **1 The impact of the Second World War**
  - Presence of foreign troops
  - Women's experience of war work
  - Young people's experience of evacuation
- ❑ **2 The Welfare State**
  - The Beveridge Report
  - The National Health Service (NHS)
- ❑ **3 Immigration into Britain, 1945–75**
  - Immigration from the Caribbean
  - Immigration from East Africa
  - Immigration from India and Pakistan
  - Experiences of immigrants in Britain
  - Reactions to immigration
  - The political response
  - The contribution of immigrants to British Society
- ❑ **4 The changing role of women, 1950–75**
  - Women in the early 1950s
  - Changes in the 1950s and 1960s
  - The main campaigns
- ❑ **5 Growing up in the 1950s, 1960s and 1970s**
  - Changes in the 1950s
  - Changes in the lives of teenagers in the 1960s
    - The teenage consumer
    - The teenage rebel
  - Changes in education
    - Comprehensive schools
    - Universities and polytechnics
  - Teenage and student protest

Check your knowledge online with our Quick quizzes at www.hodderplus.co.uk/modernworldhistory.